A picture is only the start of the story ...

Richard Wintle
Calyx Picture Agency

The Hobnob Press

First published in the United Kingdom in 2020
by The Hobnob Press, 8 Lock Warehouse, Severn Road, Gloucester GL1 2GA
www.hobnobpress.co.uk
© Richard Wintle 2020
Calyx Picture Agency   www.calyxpix.com
The Author hereby asserts his moral rights to be identified as the Author of the Work.
All rights reserved. No part of this publication may be reproduced, stored in a retrieval system, or transmitted in any form or by any means, electronic, mechanical, photocopying, recording or otherwise, without the prior permission of the publisher and copyright holder.
British Library Cataloguing in Publication Data
A catalogue record for this book is available from the British Library
ISBN 978-1-906978-82-2

A picture is only the start.....

As a press photographer I take pictures of life; and, as an archivist of pictures, I store life's stories. Stories that quite often have a theme; stories, some happy some sad. Some stories amaze people and some deflate egos.

Most stories have a begining, middle and end, and with many picture stories the start is a long way from the end in time; sometimes years.

In wading through my archive, I have found links between stories that never existed at the time.

Here are a few timelines that my research has thrown up, along with images from the forty-plus years of Swindon history that I and my colleagues have recorded.

Many of the pictures have been published nationally and even internationally, so these stories are about Swindon's national image, as well as of local interest.

Some of the images have succumbed to the rigours of the press industry, where a quick turnround sometimes damages the negatives, so please excuse some of the marks on the pictures. I have tried to remove most of them in that infamous photo managemant software, but some damage is irreparable.

To add to the headache of technological advances that forty years of photography have seen come and go; in 2000 there was a massive revolution in media photography, when we went from film to the digital capture of images. This change gave us a problem, in as much as storage of film is easy and very cheap, digital archiving however requires a lot of digital storage and work on the metadata, and this costs quite a lot in both time and money.

We opted for storage on writable CD and DVD discs, as hard drives were in their infancy and very expensive. CDs and DVDs, we were told, were indistructible and would last for ever, you could eat your dinner off them and they would still work. This turned out to be a slight exaggeration on behalf of the CD production companies: they don't!!

From 2000 until about 2007, many of the discs I used for storage have degraded and in some cases are totally unreadable, hence there are some gaps in the archive.

Some of the missing images I have managed to retreive from the agencies that syndicate my work, but others I just have to write off.

I hope you enjoy the meanderings of a crazy press photographer as much as that photographer has enjoyed the journey of compiling this missive.

Richard Wintle was born in 1951 in Gloucester, England. Richard moved from the Worcestershire village of Bredon (made famous by John Moore in the Brensham trilogy) to the Gloucestershire town of Dursley in 1959, where he became interested in the art of photography when he was given a Kodak Brownie 127 camera as a birthday present on his 9th birthday.

While attending the local secondary modern school, he had his first experience of having a picture published, when the local weekly paper, the *Dursley Gazette*, used and paid for two images of the school's CSE science project; to build a hot air balloon and fly it. The two images of the balloon in flight set the destination for the budding photographer with a determination to have more published, at national and international level.

While in Dursley, he helped a local freelance photographer, supplying the *Gloucester Citizen* and *Western Daily Press* newspapers with local picture stories, while honing his media photographic skills.

A move from Dursley to a job in the Science department at Brunel Technical College (now the City of Bristol College) followed. After marrying Pat in 1973, he moved to the CF Mott College of Education in Liverpool as Education Technician.

In Liverpool, one of the technicians was a former *Daily Express* photographer who mentored Richard, resulting in a chance photograph of youths crossing the M57 at Knowsley appearing in the Manchester edition of the *Daily Mail*. The first national picture gave a turbo boost to getting more and better pictures published.

He then moved to Swindon in 1974 to take up a position at Raychem in Dorcan, six years of which were spent in the Marketing Department, travelling the world setting up exhibitions and doing the marketing department's pictures.

On leaving Raychem, Calyx was set up as an adventurous step into the world of freelance photography.

Richard and his team have supplied images of local and national news events to the world's media, and between 1999 and 2012 he was the only video cameraman to follow the Royal Family in a freelance capacity, with his footage being used on television news and in TV documentaries throughout the world.

Now in semi-retirement, he has a chance to reflect on the 2 million film images, plus the 2 million images stored in digital files. This has been gathered into an archive, which tells the story of local news over the 40 years of taking pictures in Swindon and the surrounding area.

My journey has taken a twist, well more of a jolt I'd say.

In 2017 I was diganosed with a rare cancer: they call it the secret cancer as it creeps up on you and hides itself as another ailment. Mine was as asthma. That cancer is Neuroendocrine Cancer and I hope to raise awareness of the cancer through this book and any talks I give as a result of this tome.

The prognosis of my particular type of Neuroendocrine Cancer is good, well as good as it can be, as it's the typical type, the lesser and least aggressive of the four types, on my lungs. Recently some famous names have made headlines, having succumbed to the more virulent form in the Pancreas; they are Steve Jobs and Aretha Franklin. BBC political Editor Nick Robinson had a Neuroendocrine tumour removed from his throat; yes, they can appear almost anywhere in the body.

Rare yes; about 4000 people in the UK are diagnosed with some form of Neuroendocrine Cancer each year, that's about 40 people in a million.

Neuroendocrine cancer is a term used to cover a group of cancers that start in neuroendocrine cells. These cancers may also be referred to as NETs, NECs, NENs or even Carcinoids.

I will be donating £1 of every book sold to the Neuroendocrine Cancer UK charity.

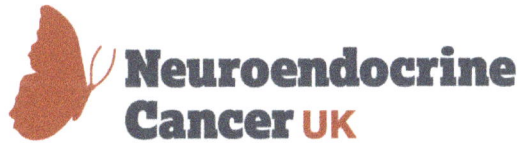

(Formerly NET Patient Foundation)

Before you start to meander through this archive the Health and Safety Executive needs me to cover what has become known as House Keeping:
    There should be no fire alarms...

But, in all seriousness, a few notes on the archive; especially the technical aspects of the images, and how they came into being.

When I first held a camera, at the age of nine, I fell in love with the art of photography, particularly the candid action shots.

Starting with a Kodak Brownie 127, a bakelite camera which used cut-down 120 roll film, I annoyed friends and family alike recording their games and battles etc.

I progressed to a German bellows camera, a 120 version of the infamous press camera the Speed Graphic, which I still possess.

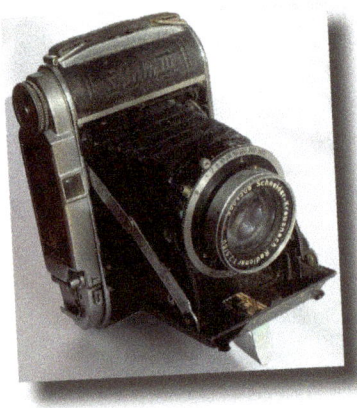

From that to a Yashica Mat, and then Rolleiflex twin lens cameras and on to the Nikon range of SLR cameras.

In December 1999 Nikon revolutionised the press photography industry with the launch of the D1 digital camera, which came with a 32 megabyte CF card. and used a chip producing approximately 2.7 megapixels.

Development began on the D1 in 1996, when digital imaging was in its infancy. At that time the major market leader for DSLR cameras was Kodak, who produced their own image sensors and assembled digital cameras under the brand Kodak DCS. The DCS cameras were based upon Nikon F90 film camera, replacing the film back with one incorporating a CCD sensor. This in turn was connected to a power supply, and an image processing and storage unit that was either carried separately or attached to the base of the camera body.

While these cameras offered the convenience of digital imaging to normal photographers, their appeal was limited by huge price-tags and issues with sensor size, resolution, and performance in comparison with film for the press photographer.

Nikon sought to design and produce a professional-grade camera from a blank sheet of paper, using large high-resolution sensors, for only a few thousand pounds at a time when the Kodak DCS 460 was retailing for something in the region of £20,000.

The Nikon D1 was a mass-produced high-resolution and high-sensitivity sensor camera that could be powered by batteries and sustain a continuous frame-rate, suitable for photojournalistic use.

But there had been revolutions to our industry before then. In the 20 years previous to the digital revolution, the means of sending images had become de-unionised through the Rupert Murdoch's Wapping dispute and the transformation of the telephone system to a digital system. The *Today* newspaper published by Eddie Shah (who built and developed the Wilts Hotel and golf complex outside Royal Wootton Bassett) used colour news images, and in consequence we had to change our thinking, as a picture in black and white doesn't always work in colour.

Film quality had advanced too. The grainy high-speed films processed in concentrated developer had developed into fine grain films that were more flexible in film speed, and processed in the same chemicals as colour negative films.

Transparency film (slides) no longer needed to be sent away to be processed, as small labs could handle the new, more flexible, chemistry.

Swindon had one of the first digital exchanges in the country and Calyx Picture Agency was at the forefront of the new way to transmit images.

Using an AppleMac 2CI, a HP desktop scanner, and a rather expensive piece of Hasselblad equipment called a DIT box, we converted the digital TIF image into an analogue signal which was then sent down the dedicated wire line.

One morning Ken Brown, who was helping us with our technology, burst into the office waving a floppy disc. 'Look what came this morning, it's photoshop 2.5.5.'

To the uninitiated, that may seem like a 'so what' moment, but that piece of software changed our industry.

Within that disc was a Jpeg software plugin, which meant that computers without a special circuit board could compress images for sending via the standard telephone network using a dial-up modem.

My photographer came back from Cheltenham, where he had taken a picture of Cheltenham High Street for the *Sun*.

He wandered off and processed the film. In the meantime, Ken loaded the software and contacted the News International Tech team. They agreed to do a test run, as it was their first transmission with the new software.

When the print arrived, it was scanned, compressed and the resulting fully digital Jpeg image was sent down the telephone line.

On checking if it was OK, they cleared it as usable; so we asked if they could get it to the *Sun* picture desk, to which they agreed. So our picture became the first image of software compressed Jpeg to go into News International, beating one of the major sports agences by 5 minuites.

The era of digital photography had arrived.

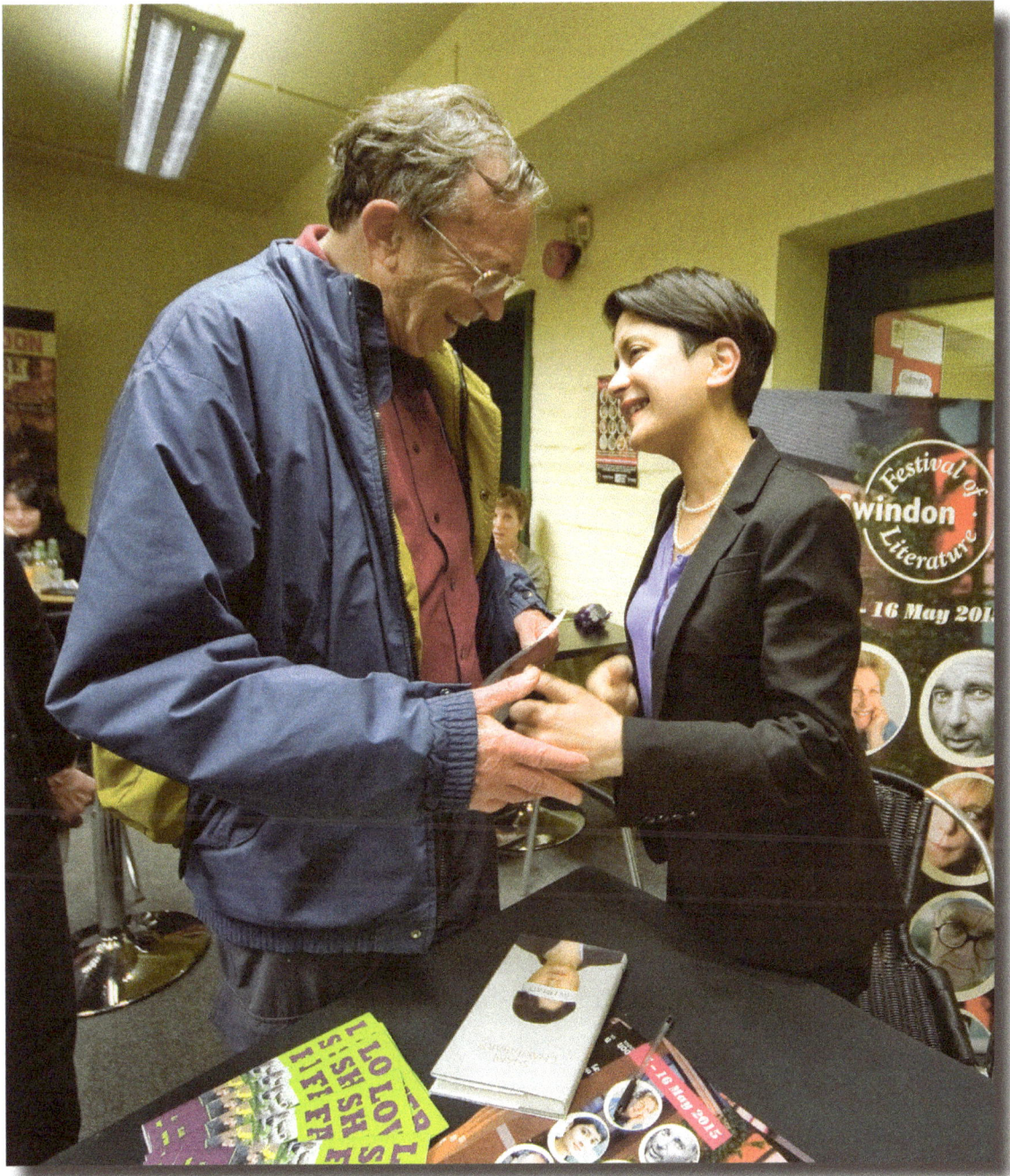

The late **Lord Joel Joffe of Liddington met Baroness Shami (Sharmishta) Chakrabarti** at the 2016 Swindon Festival of Literature in the Swindon Arts Centre. The human rights lawyer was signing her book, while Lord Joffe waited patiently at the end of the queue to meet her, and get his book signed. I managed to capture the look of amazement as the two generations of human rights advocates met for the first time. The picture was in Lord Joffe's *Times* obituary.

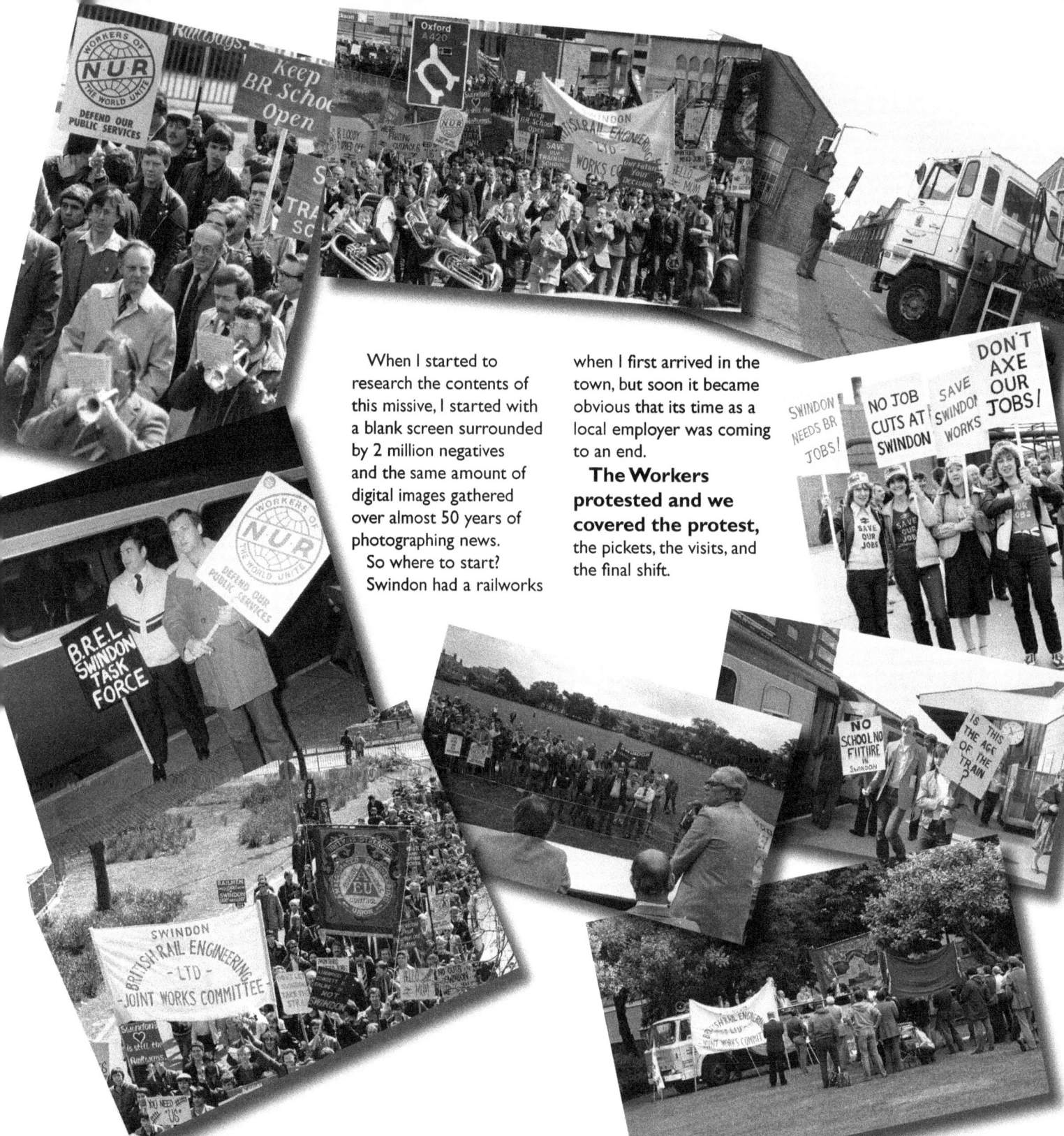

When I started to research the contents of this missive, I started with a blank screen surrounded by 2 million negatives and the same amount of digital images gathered over almost 50 years of photographing news.

So where to start?

Swindon had a railworks when I first arrived in the town, but soon it became obvious that its time as a local employer was coming to an end.

The Workers protested and we covered the protest, the pickets, the visits, and the final shift.

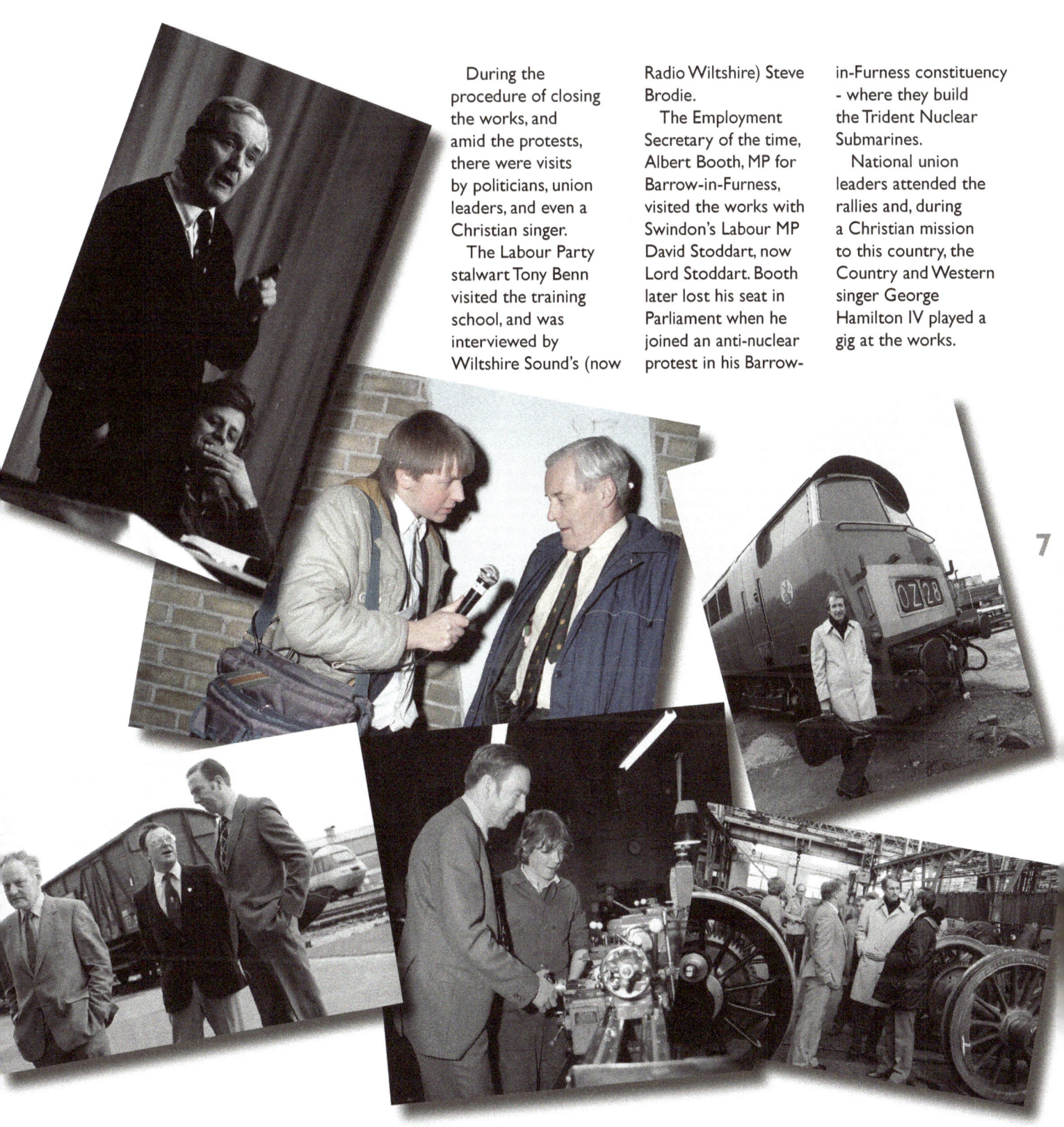

During the procedure of closing the works, and amid the protests, there were visits by politicians, union leaders, and even a Christian singer.

The Labour Party stalwart Tony Benn visited the training school, and was interviewed by Wiltshire Sound's (now Radio Wiltshire) Steve Brodie.

The Employment Secretary of the time, Albert Booth, MP for Barrow-in-Furness, visited the works with Swindon's Labour MP David Stoddart, now Lord Stoddart. Booth later lost his seat in Parliament when he joined an anti-nuclear protest in his Barrow-in-Furness constituency - where they build the Trident Nuclear Submarines.

National union leaders attended the rallies and, during a Christian mission to this country, the Country and Western singer George Hamilton IV played a gig at the works.

On 15 May 1985 there was a protest about the works' closure outside the Railworks Manager's Office, alongside the main line, where hundreds of workers gathered.

As Press we were not allowed to join them, so we went to the Railway Industrial Estate opposite the works, from where we had a good view of the gathering and the dog handler who was walking along the tracks. In those days you didn't need a high visibility jacket; what a fit Health and Safety would throw today!

Fortuitously, in the preceding days I had purchased a 300mm lens and was using it when some of the workers raised a noose on the end of a stick over the protest for a few seconds.

My colleague from the Swindon paper only had a standard lens on at the time, so I finished up with the only picture of the episode from our side of the protest..

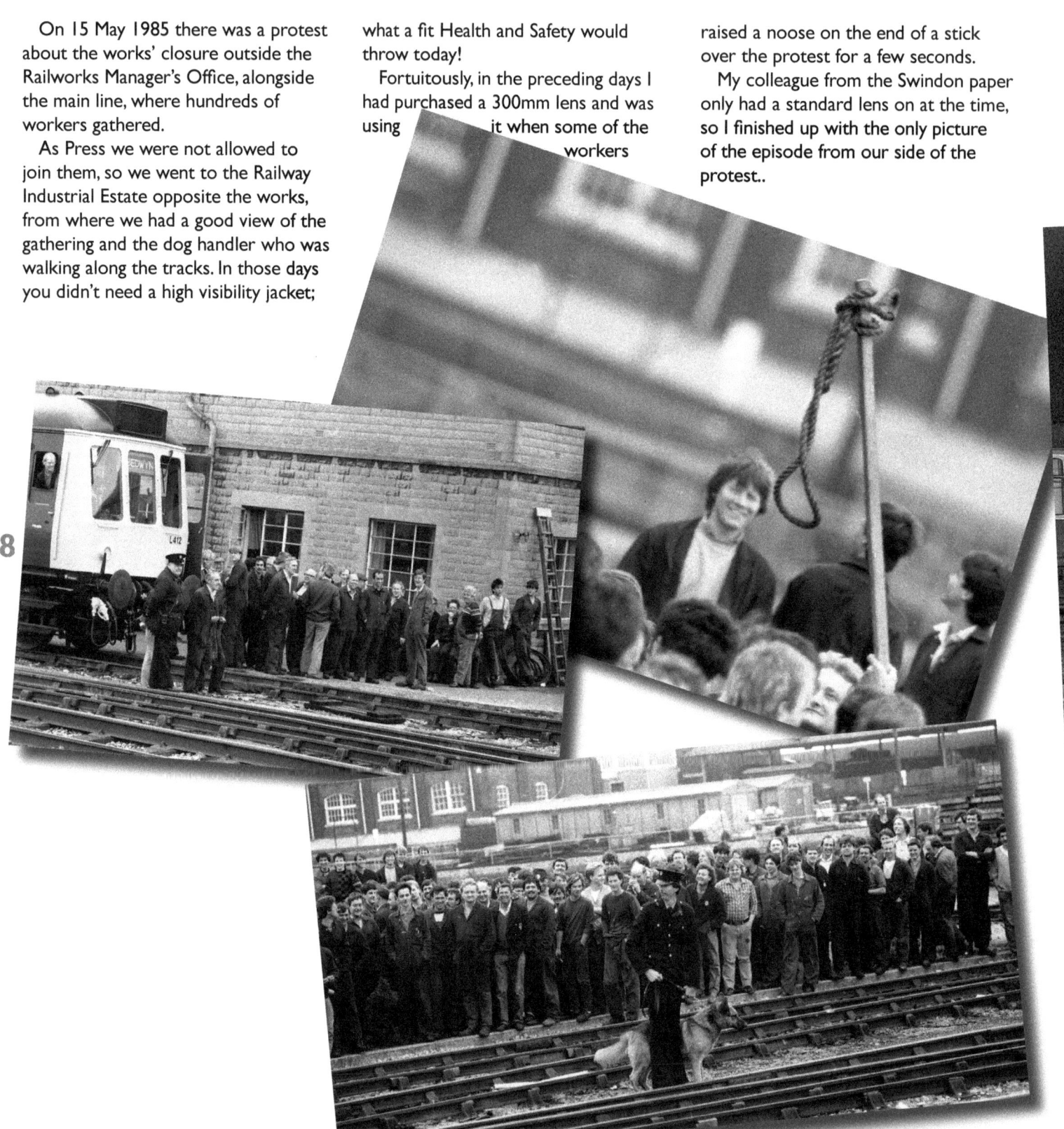

No feature about the Swindon Rail Works would be complete without a mention of the famous locomotives that came out of the plant, most notably **King George V.**

I photographed the iconic masterpiece of Swindon engineering when it returned to the works from Bulmers in Hereford for a boiler refit. As a security measure, they had removed the famous bell from the front of the King, which makes this picture somewhat rare.

The King was on the Gloucester line, having been pulled by a diesel loco under partial steam, which allowed the brakes to work.

The night shot was taken using multiple flashes, which enabled me to get the Railwaymen's Church in the background.

I returned later in the day to record the King's return in daylight.

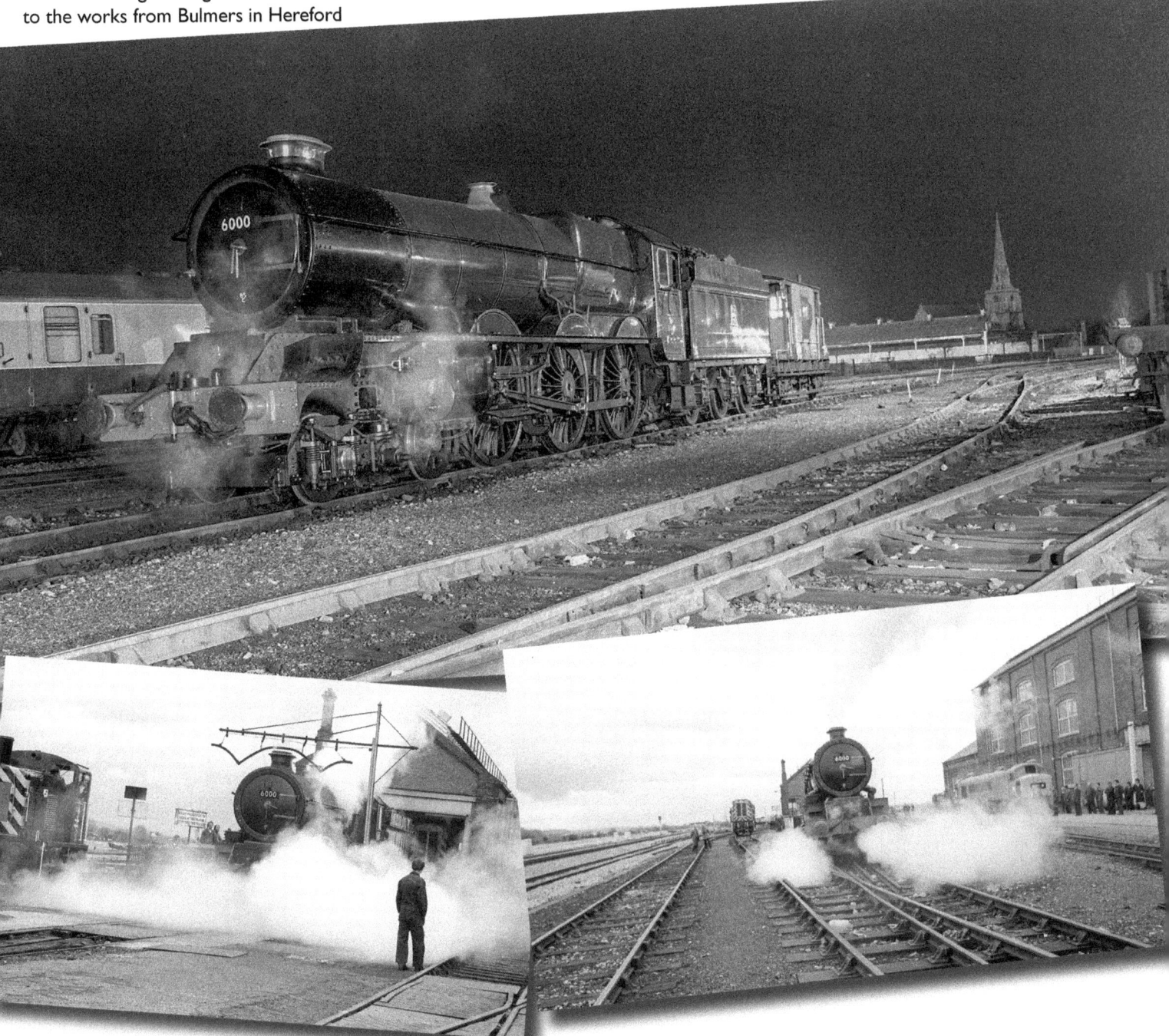

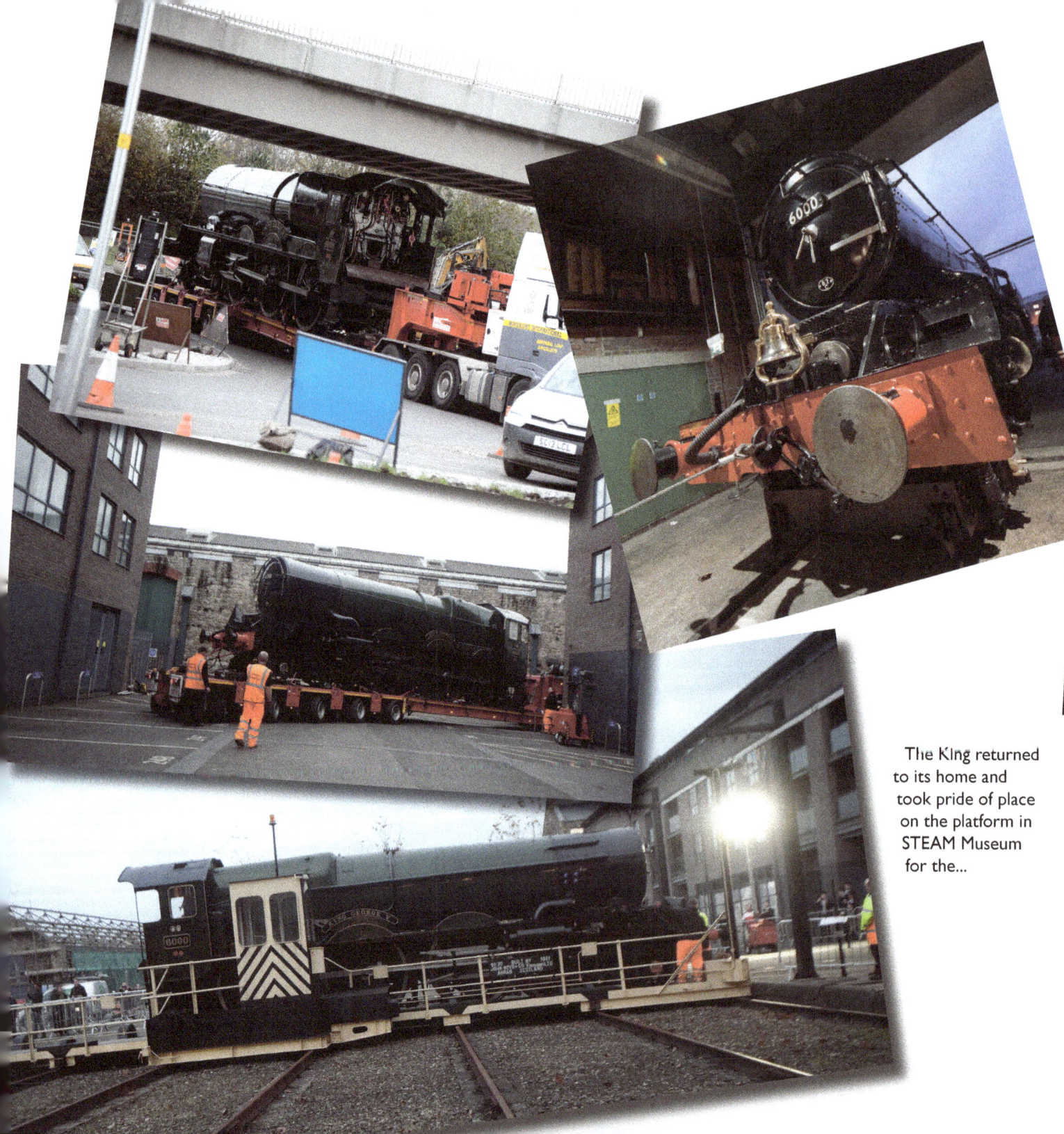

The King returned to its home and took pride of place on the platform in STEAM Museum for the...

...**Swindon 175 celebrations,** which saw a year long celebration, in which the town remembered its founders, Isambard Kingdom Brunel and most notably Sir Daniel Gooch, who was the brains behind developing the Rail Works at Swindon...

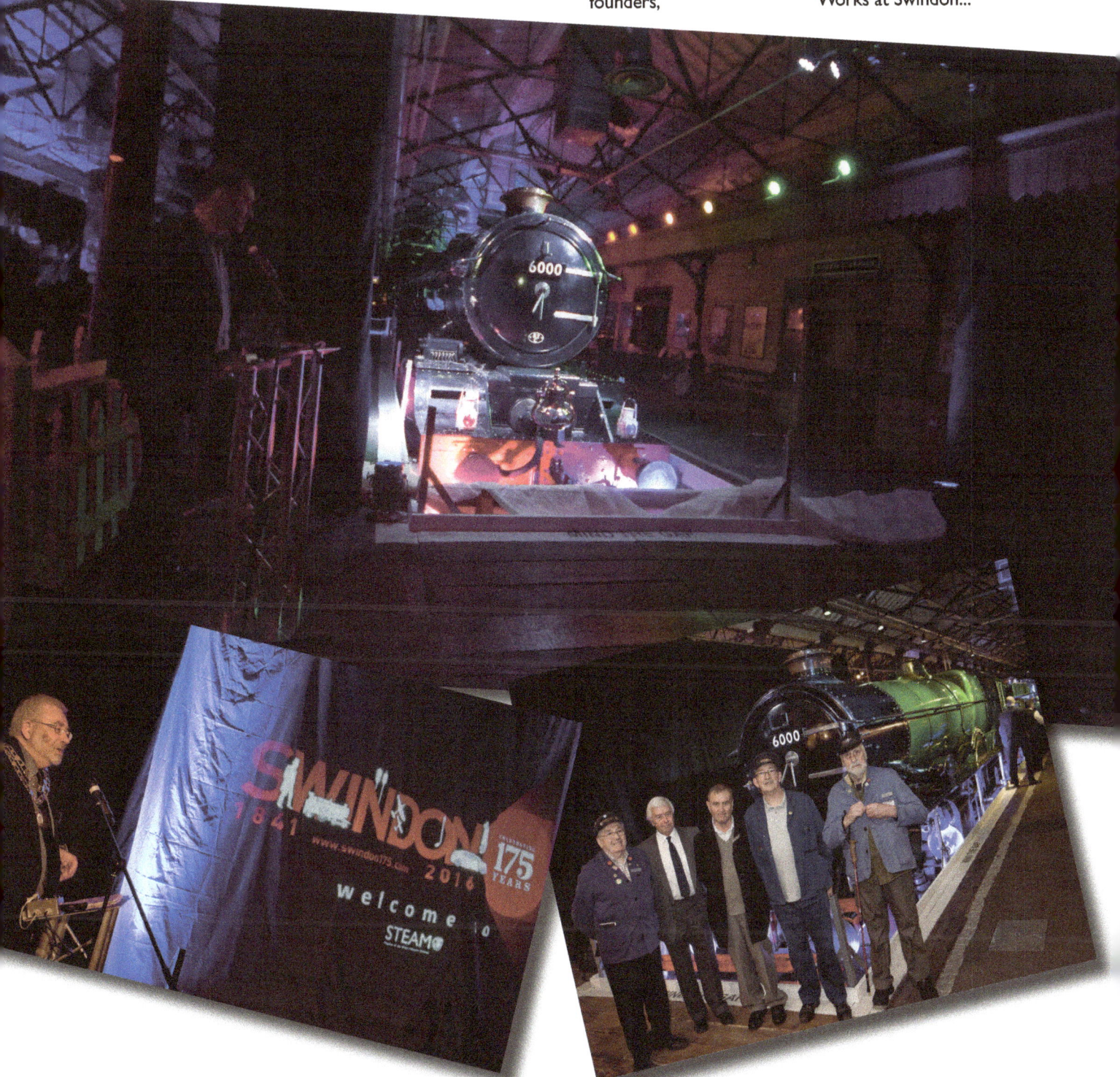

...Swindon is on the main line from London to the West of England, so we see a progression of new traction units coming through the station.

From steam locomotion to the new electric units, we seem to have photographed them all head to head, in either Swindon or Paddington; or even at the STEAM... Museum.

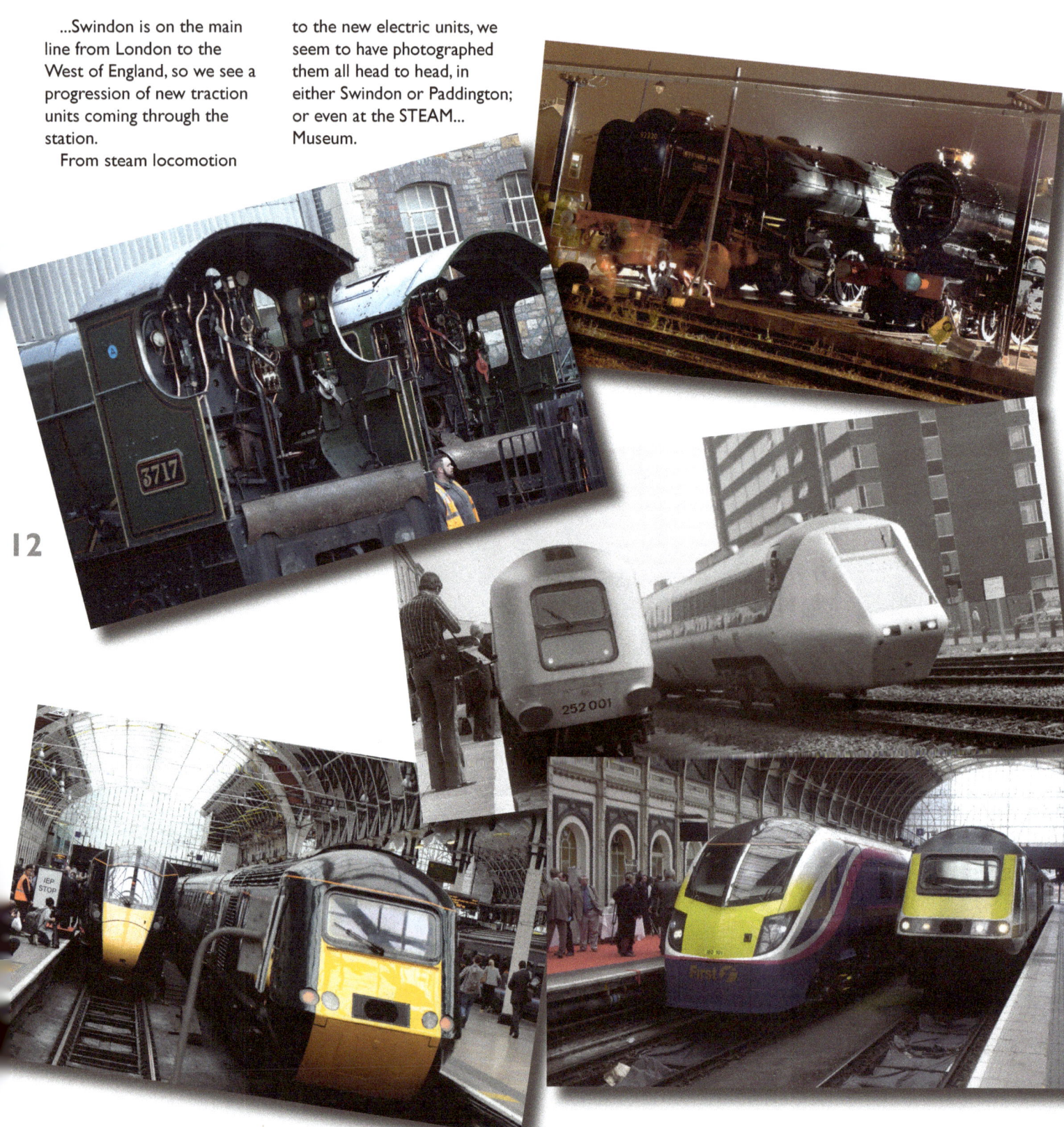

...But I digress!

When looking through the archive for memories to put in these pages, I remembered incidents, or events that I was involved with. I can quite often remember the images; and even some of the images that were never printed.

I am sharing with you a set of images that took even me by surprise, even though it was a turning point in Swindon's history. It's a time capsule of a pivotal moment in the town's recent history.

In 2016 we celebrated the 175 years of new Swindon's existence; which, thanks to Daniel Gooch's foresight, enabled Swindon to become a town rather than a village on the hill.

The sounding of the hooter, which so regulated Swindon life for well over a century, dominated both the closing of the works and the celebrations of the same event thirty years on...

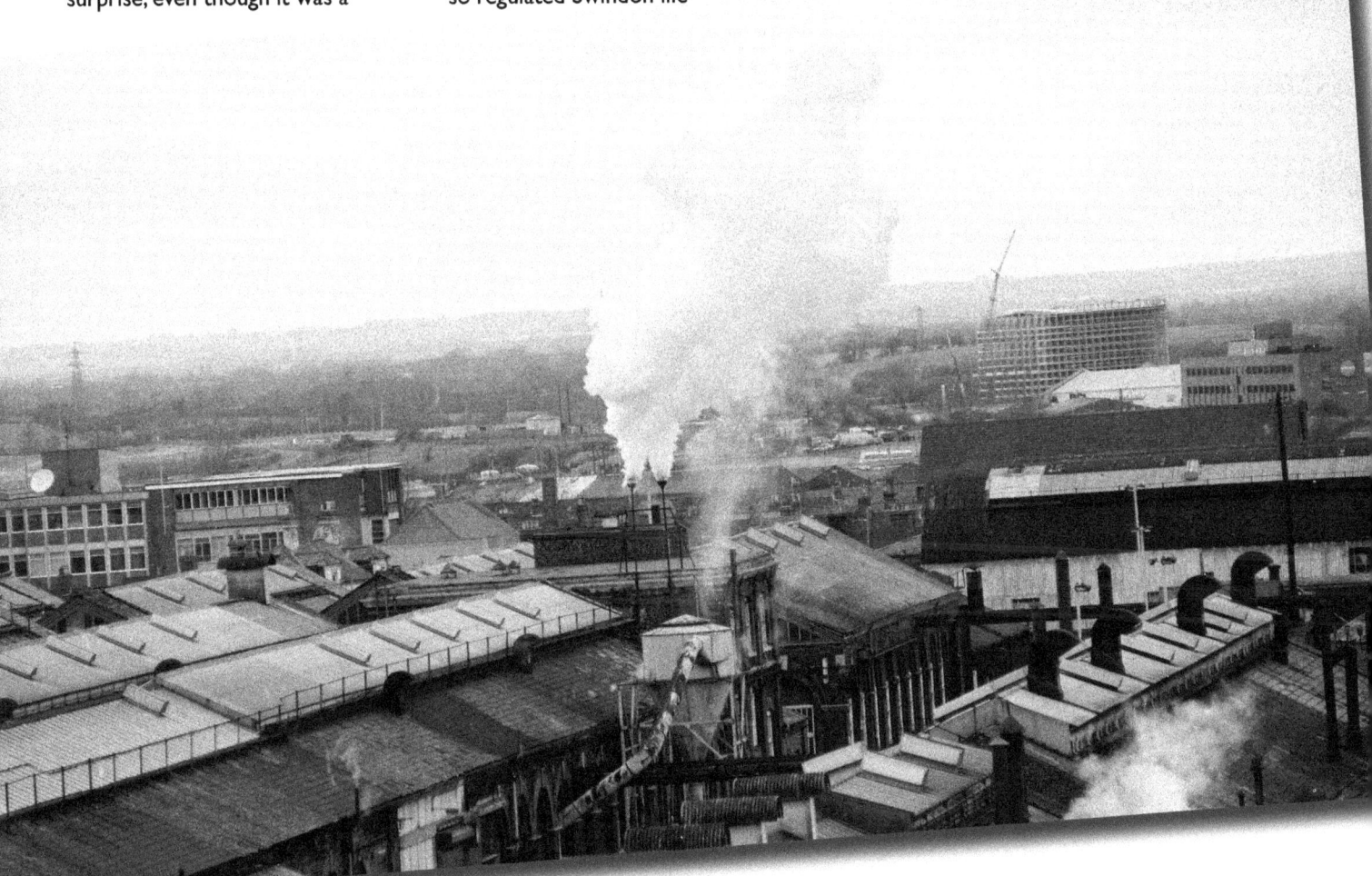

The final blast of the Swindon Rail Works hooter was recorded, but the picture has more significance now than when it was taken, as the whole scene has changed; even the building with scaffolding which was the Shorko Films plant has gone to be replaced by the town's recycling centre; so have the works and the fields in the middle distance.

Of course the foreground has changed dramatically too; the Outlet Village has utilised most of the buildings, and The National Trust Heelis Headquarters has appeared there as well.

I knew I had some images of the last sounding, but I only remember them in terms of being distant, and not very representative of the event. So, on the day that Swindon 175 were re-creating the final hooter blast, I dug out the file thinking that I may be able to do something with a scanned image.

I had the advantage, for a change, of knowing the exact date; so, finding the sheet of negatives was no problem, but what I found changed my day.

Instead of one or two sheets of negatives, there were eight sheets and the job sheet said we had sent many more to papers in London, including *The Times*, who had commissioned us to do a feature on the day.

I think I need to briefly explain the workings of a picture agency in the mid nineteen-eighties for you to understand how our precious negatives found their way to picture desks in London.

In this digital age, we use data files to send images round the world in seconds. A picture taken on a phone can make its way on to social media almost as soon it is taken, but in 1986 you had to take the picture on a film camera, then take the film back to the darkroom and process it.

The processing of a black and white film took about ten minutes, and a colour negative film about twenty. You then had to make a print from your selected negative. This took another five minutes or so to do.

Today, with the press of a button or a drag and drop on a computer, the picture vanishes down the internet, and seconds later it is being opened on the picture desk. Back then, when the Rail Works closed, things took a little longer.

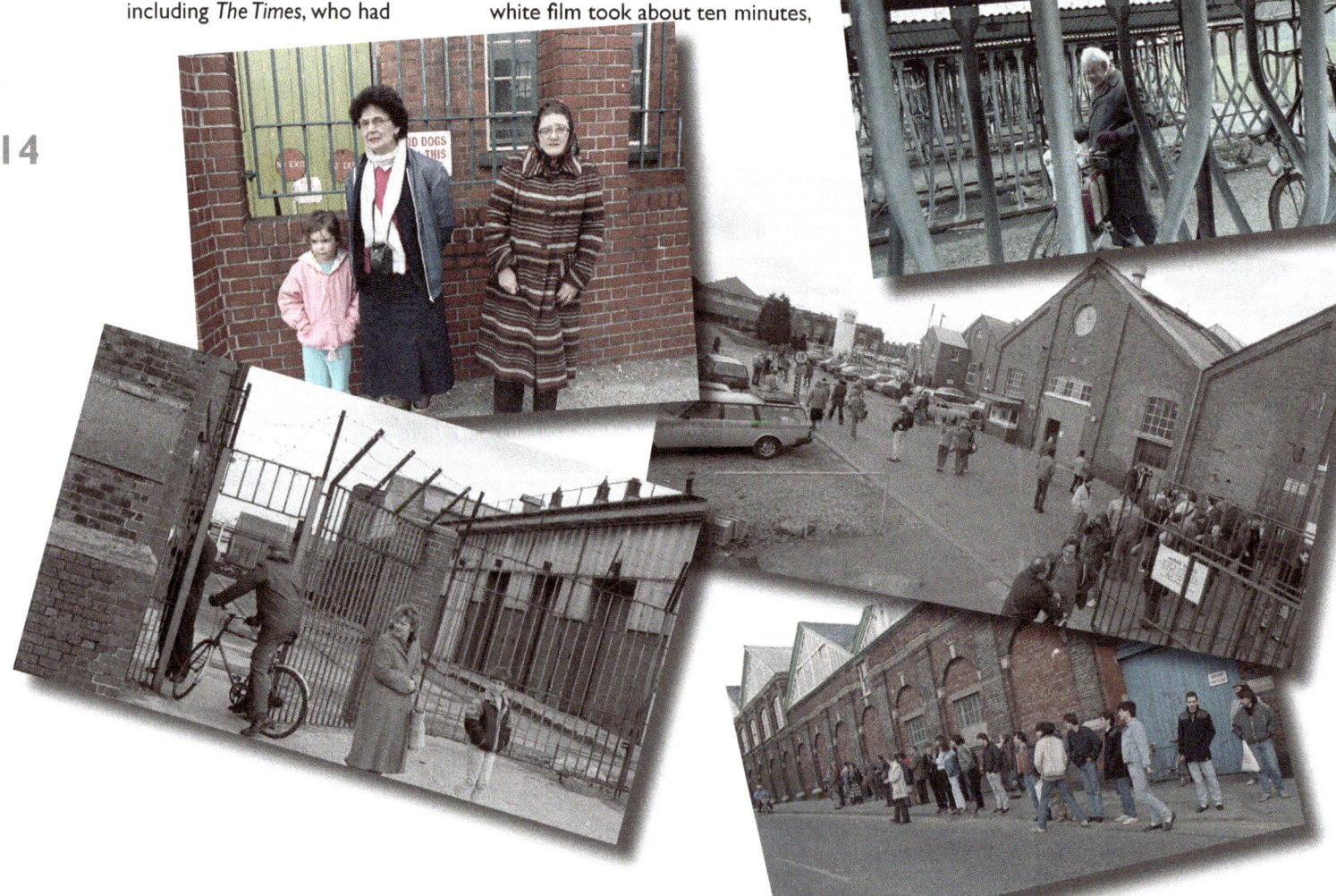

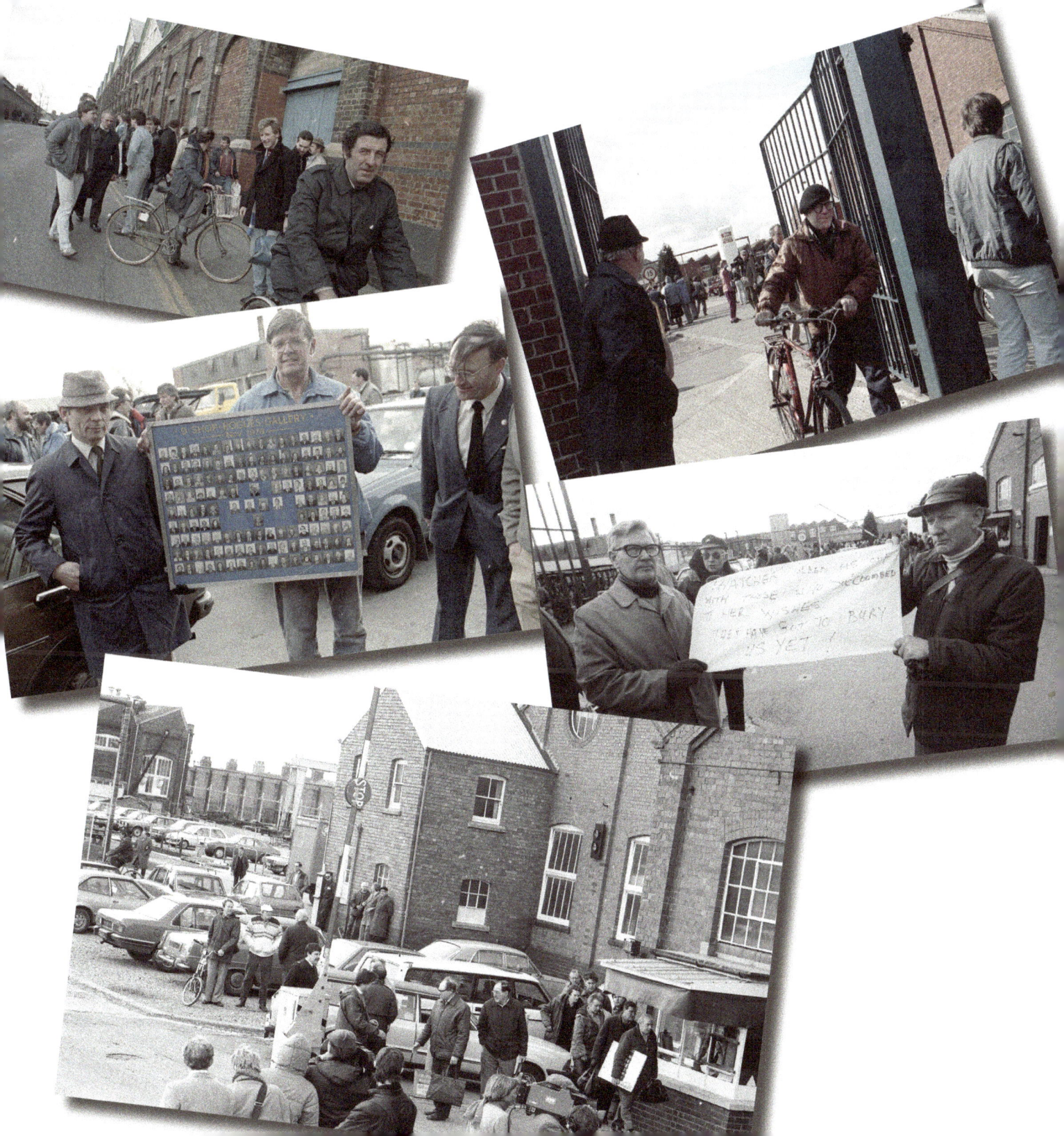

Anyway, back to the day they closed the works down.

Actually, I don't recall much about the day. I had several photographers covering the events on that day, indeed looking through the negatives I seem to recall photographing at the gates when the last shift finished. I certainly remember my snapper returning with the hooter pictures and thinking those won't make the papers, because they didn't have enough impact...

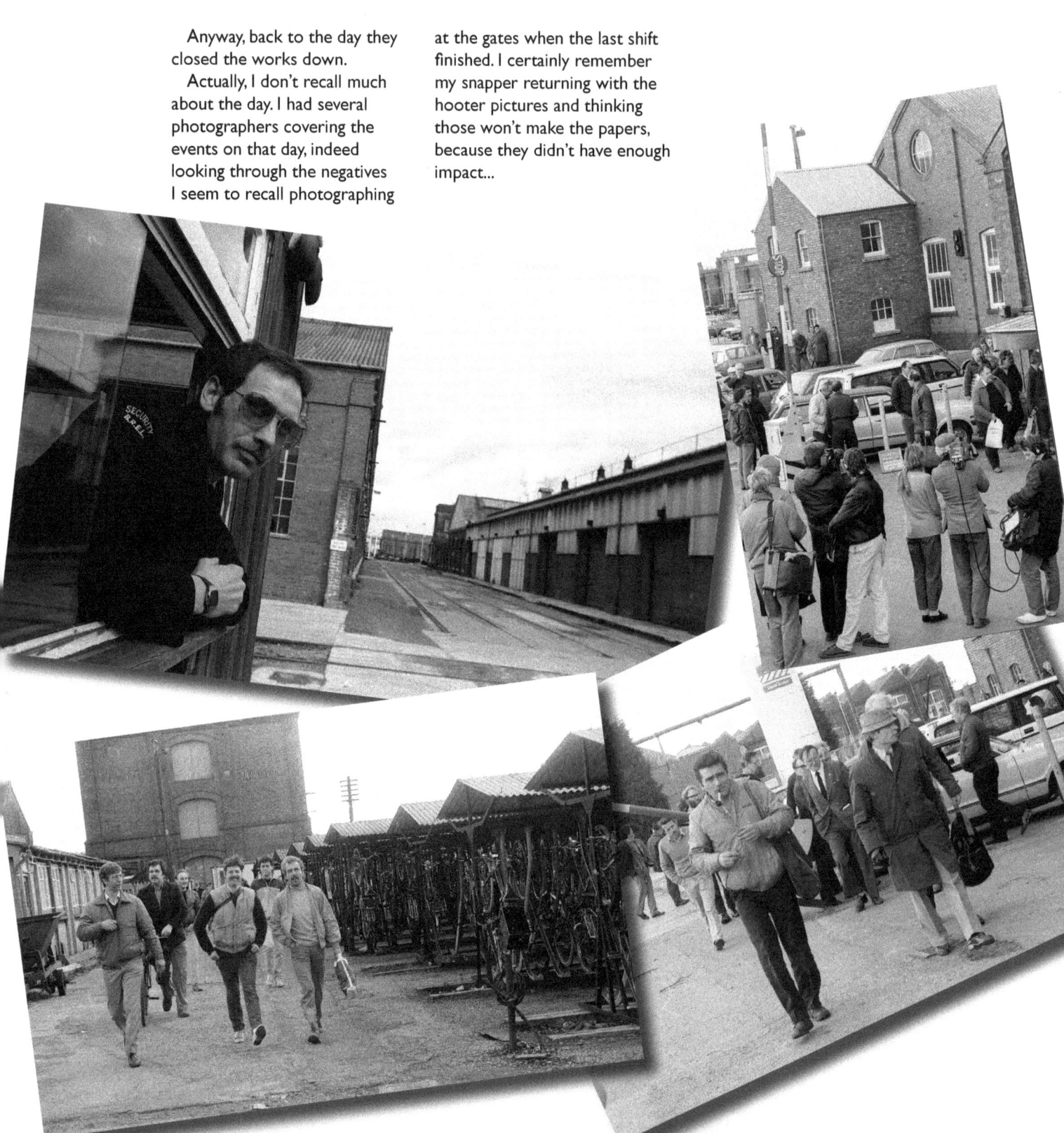

...But time changes our concept of images, and when I found the black and white film with just three frames of the hooter blowing, I realised that historically these were more interesting than the pictures that were used at the time.

Close-up images of the hooters belching out their last emissions of steam made the papers. At the time it was a graphic description of the end of an era, but little else, and anyway we have re-created the same pictures with the replica hooters.

Our pictures show the hooters emitting their final call over a run-down works within a landscape that, in the thirty years since, has changed quite a bit. In the background the Shorko Films plant is being built. That has gone, and the closure of that plant removed one of the features of Swindon of the eighties and nineties; the plastic smell that their production of cellophane made.

Where my photographer of the hooter blast took the image from remains a mystery, and maybe I don't want to know, but to find that gem in with a mass of pictures telling of the last throes of a once mighty institution made my day, and gave me the job of finally putting this time capsule into the public domain...

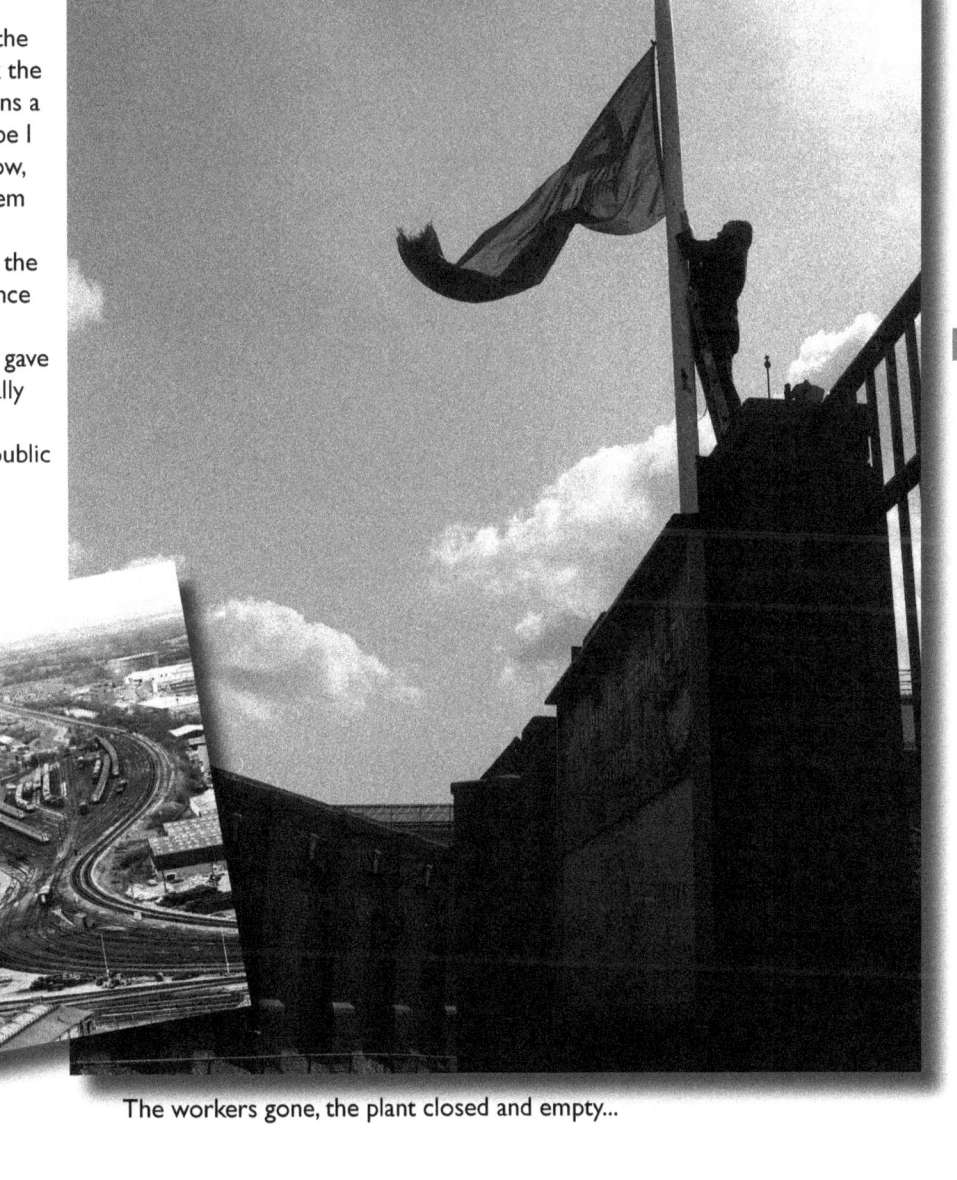

The workers gone, the plant closed and empty...

...So, when they sold the works they cut up **A Shop** with a welder and angle grinder.

The ground shook as they pushed over the cranes and the sparks flew as they dismantled one of the biggest covered areas in the world at 11.25 acres (4.55 hectares).

I was allowed access to the final throes of this edifice for the *Guardian*, and used colour film even though the final images were in black and white, as we could transmit monochrome images from colour prints.

About this time we were flying on a frequent basis, taking aerial pictures of the Wiltshire crop circles; and, on one of these flights we included the town centre on our flight plan.

During that sortie we took images of the former Rail Works, including the site of the demolished A Shop.

The area has now been developed with, among other units, the Churchward Estate, Iceland and Sainsbury's,

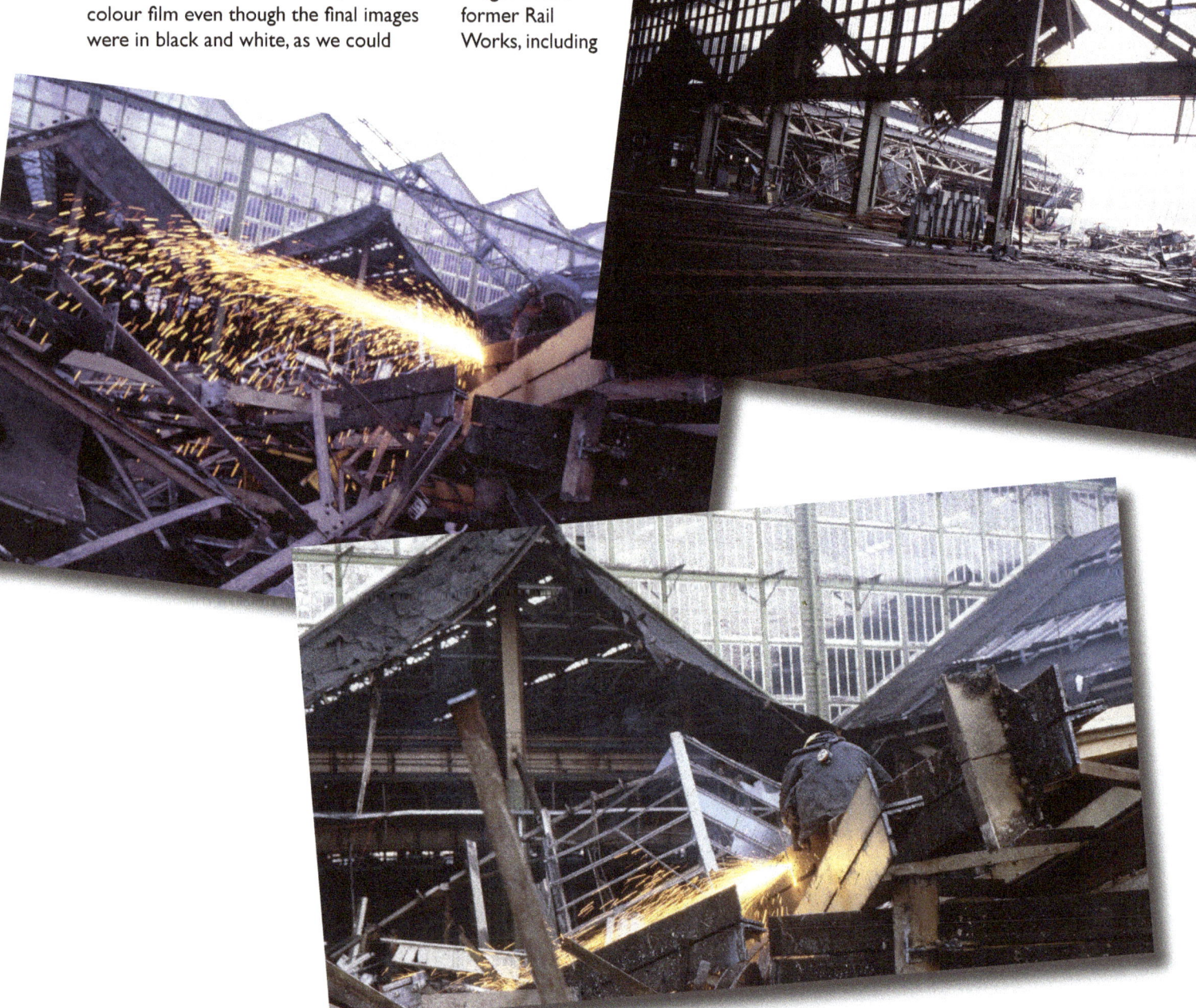

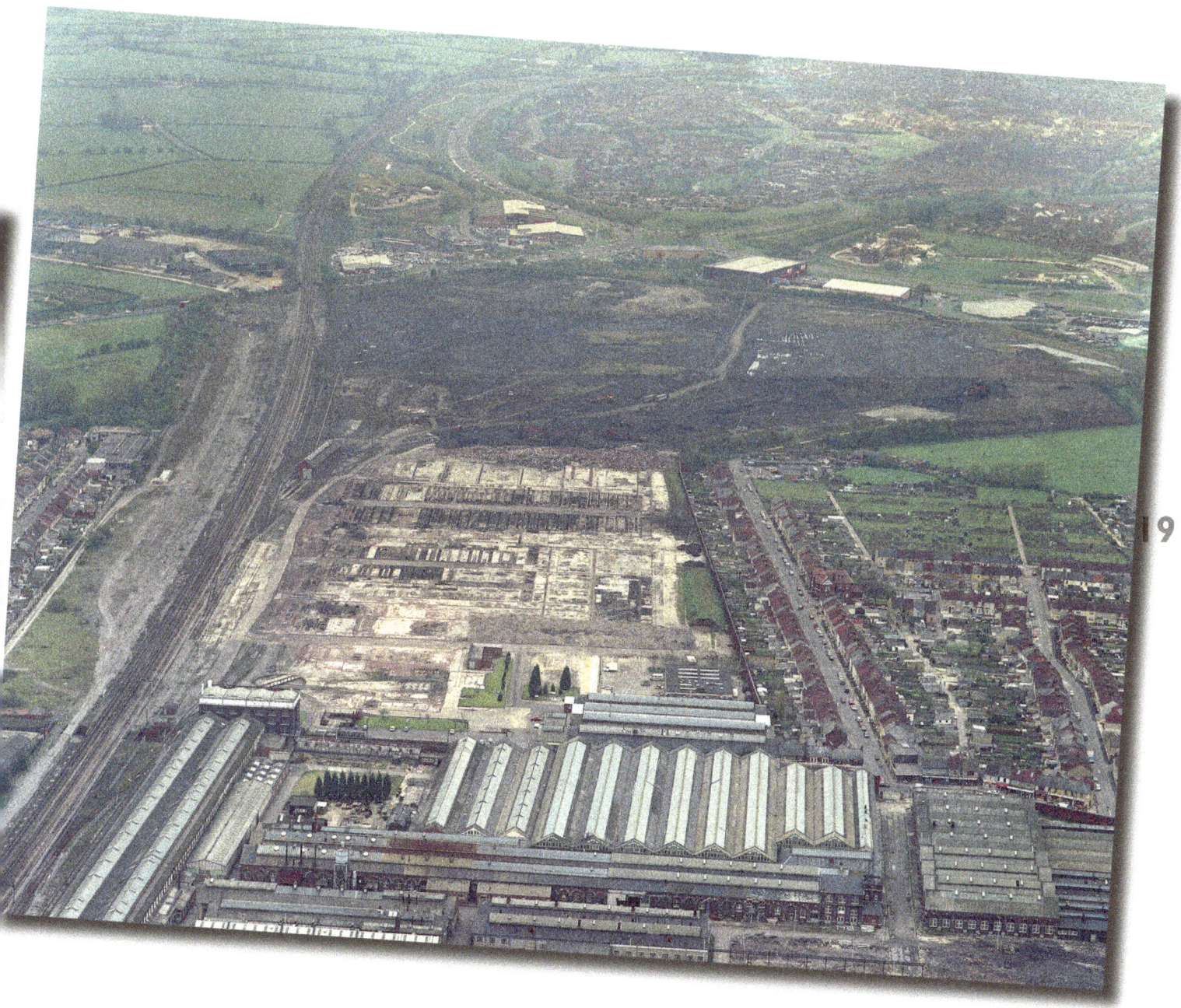

But what else did they make in the Rail Works?

During the First World War, the Rail Works were responsible for the production of some of the **Howitzer guns** used on the front line and, to celebrate the centenary of the end of the First World War, local steam enthusiast Colin Hatch, whom I worked with before taking up the camera full time, towed a replica gun over the other Swindon icon; the Magic Roundabout. The transit of the roundabout took place as the gun was on its way to the Rail Works for a press call.

The procession of the gun, being towed by a steam driven traction engine, took in the Magic Roundabout and finished up in the same place that the original guns were photographed during the conflict. (*WW1 Picture: Steam Museum issued for press release*)

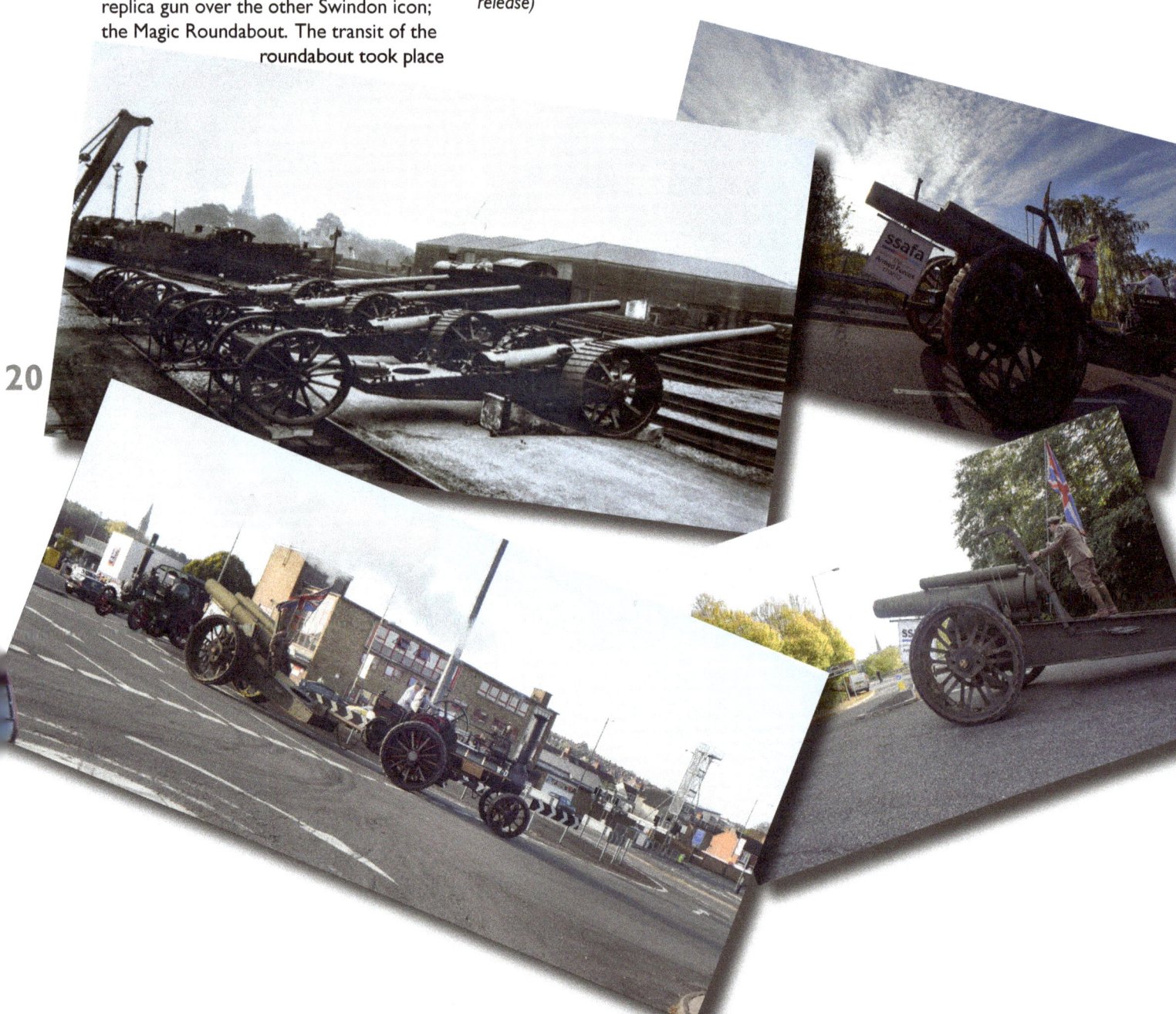

To celebrate the 175th year of Swindon, **The Magic Roundabout** featured in a bizarre event.

The council shut the roads for a weekend of maintainance and, before they re-opened it, they allowed a carnival of Swindon-built cars to parade around the iconic landmark.

The cavalcade included an incredible collection of seventy-plus classic and modern cars including Minis, MGs, Jaguars, Rileys, Triumphs Rolls Royces and more - all of which had steel body parts made in Swindon.

And what better place to celebrate than our very own, world- famous, Magic Roundabout!

However, if you look closely at the images, you may see one or two non-Swindon cars that crept in; including an American Corvette.

Thinking of the Americans and the Magic Roundabout; I once had an e-mail from a small town newspaper in Arizona USA, asking if they could use one of my Magic Roundabout images in their paper.

I asked what they were going to use it for and was amused by the reply.

'We are about to install our first roundabout in the town, and a lot of people have complained saying it's complicated, and objecting to it.

We thought we should show them your roundabout and say; If ours is complicated try this!'

I let them publish the picture!

So what did happen to Swindon's carnivals?...

...**The Carnival** is not quite over.

I know it's sad when you recall the first LP you bought, but I just have. I think it must be an age thing!

I saw the folk group The Seekers in pantomime in Bristol, and as a consequence went out and bought the 'Best of the Seekers' album.

Just as a point of interest, the Seekers hit song 'Georgie Girl', was, I believe the first pop group video to be shown on Top of the Pops.

The group were, as I have mentioned, appearing in pantomime at the Bristol Hippodrome, and couldn't get to the studio in London to do the usual TOTP live broadcast. To overcome this problem, the BBC sent a Bristol-based cameraman to film Judith Durham and the boys window shopping in Park Street.

This was then edited and inserted into the show, where the live number should have been.

As it happens, I met and photographed Judith, on 18th November 1989. I had a long chat with her after a solo show at the Wyvern and she remembered the film well.

So what significance has this to my archive? The third number on the album is 'The Carnival is Over', and buried in the archive are many, many carnivals and most are in the older files. Local estate carnivals seem to have gone out of fashion, whether because of cost, health and safety, or the fact there is just a lack of community spirit, who knows? But they don't seem to happen as much as they used to.

There was Penhill Carnival and Stratton Carnival. Cricklade's carnival has transformed into the Cricklade Festival. Freshbrook even managed some carnivals too.

There are still carnivals organised by a dedicated band of volunteers. In Swindon, Old Town now has a procession at the start of the Old Town Festival, and includes the Gay Pride Parade, which is part of an event in the Old Town Gardens. Purton, Royal Wootton Bassett, Aldbourne, and Wroughton all have carnivals as well.

I suppose the St George's Day Parade through Swindon Town Centre counts as a carnival procession, with the carnival atmosphere of the Swindon's Got Talent competition counting as the carnival fete.

Recently I was talking to a local councillor, who hinted that one area was thinking of reviving its carnival, and this conversation started me thinking about carnivals of the past, and is the reason I went on what turned out to be a rather fruitful search.

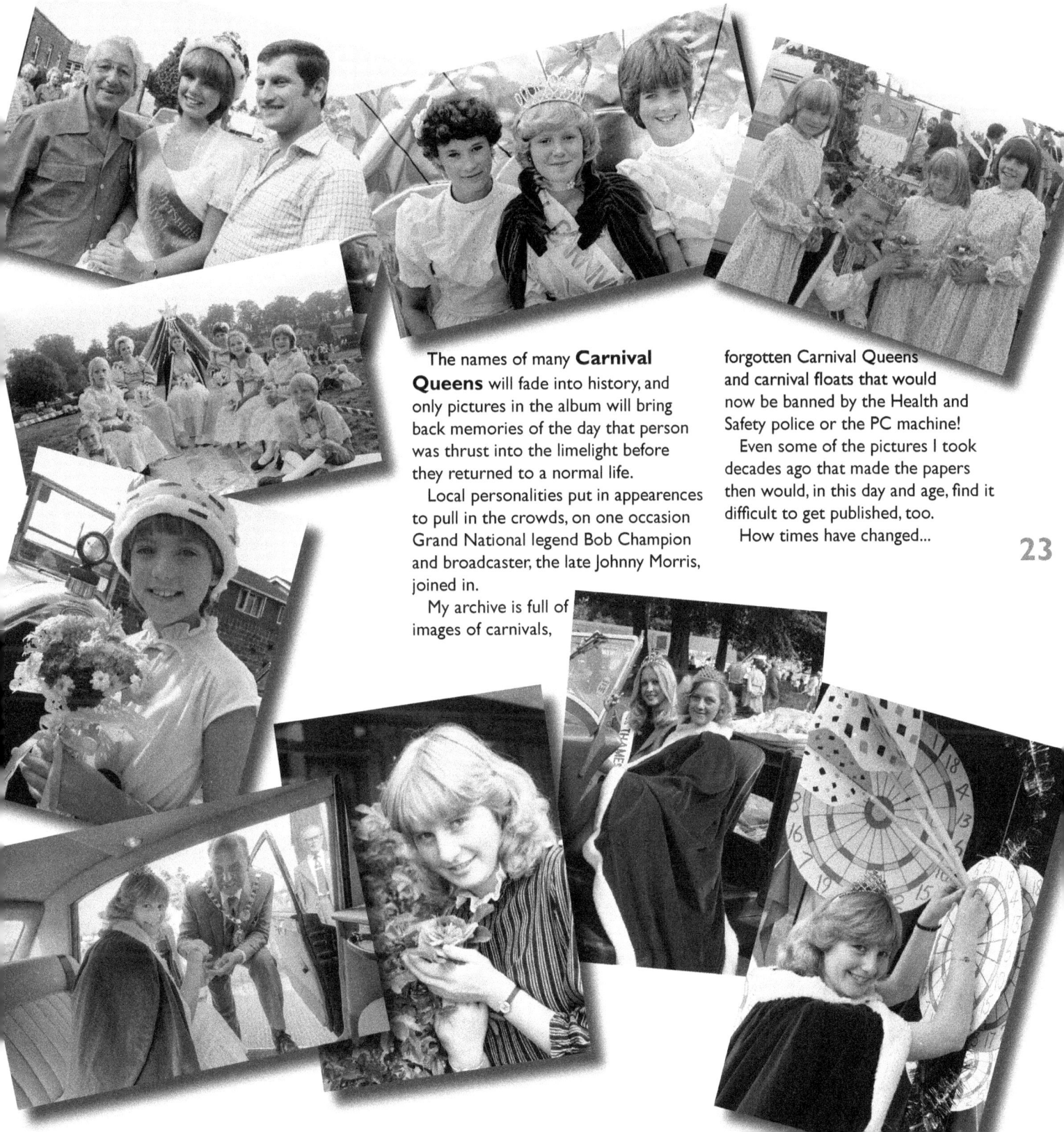

The names of many **Carnival Queens** will fade into history, and only pictures in the album will bring back memories of the day that person was thrust into the limelight before they returned to a normal life.

Local personalities put in appearances to pull in the crowds, on one occasion Grand National legend Bob Champion and broadcaster, the late Johnny Morris, joined in.

My archive is full of images of carnivals, forgotten Carnival Queens and carnival floats that would now be banned by the Health and Safety police or the PC machine!

Even some of the pictures I took decades ago that made the papers then would, in this day and age, find it difficult to get published, too.

How times have changed...

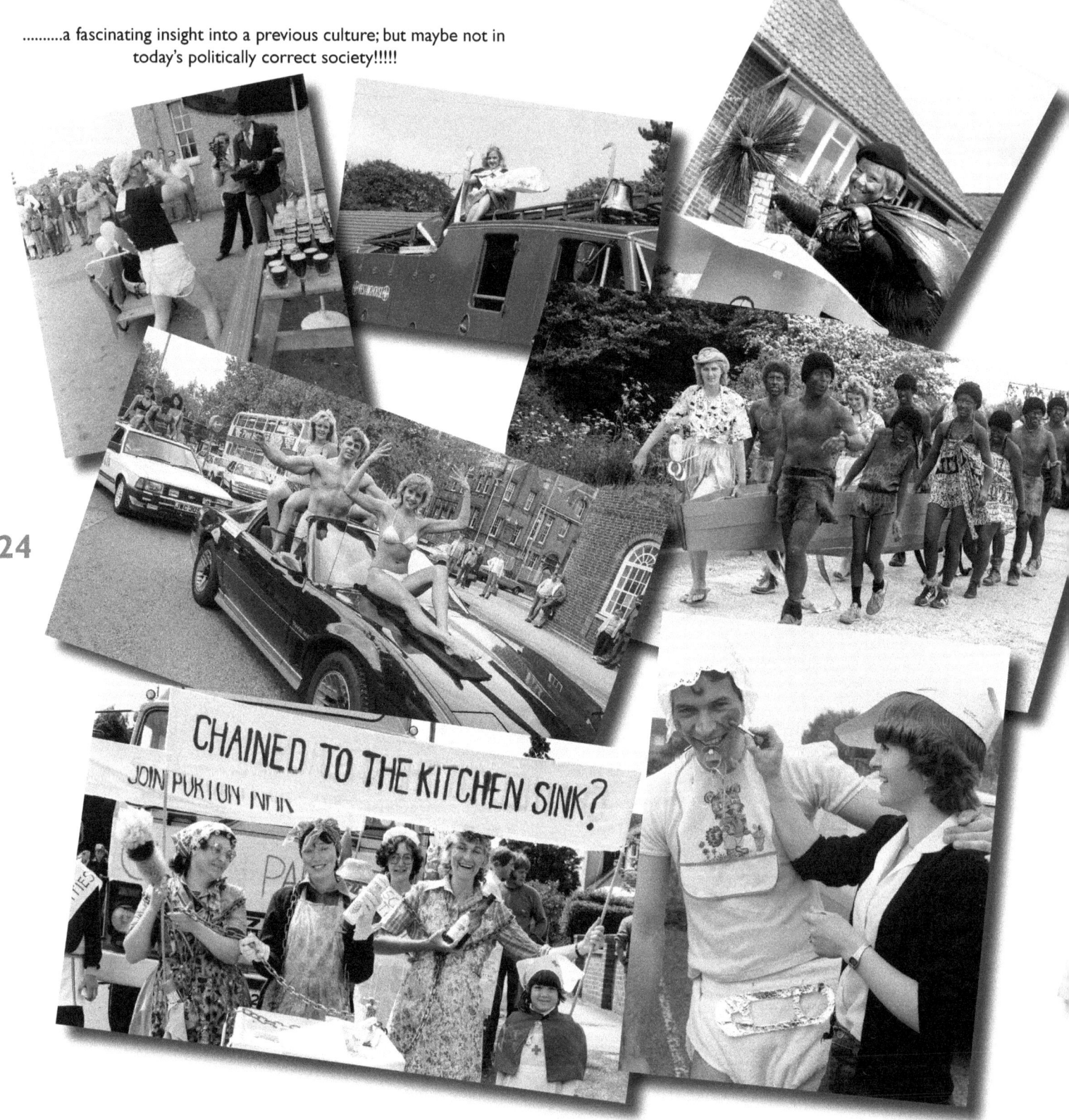

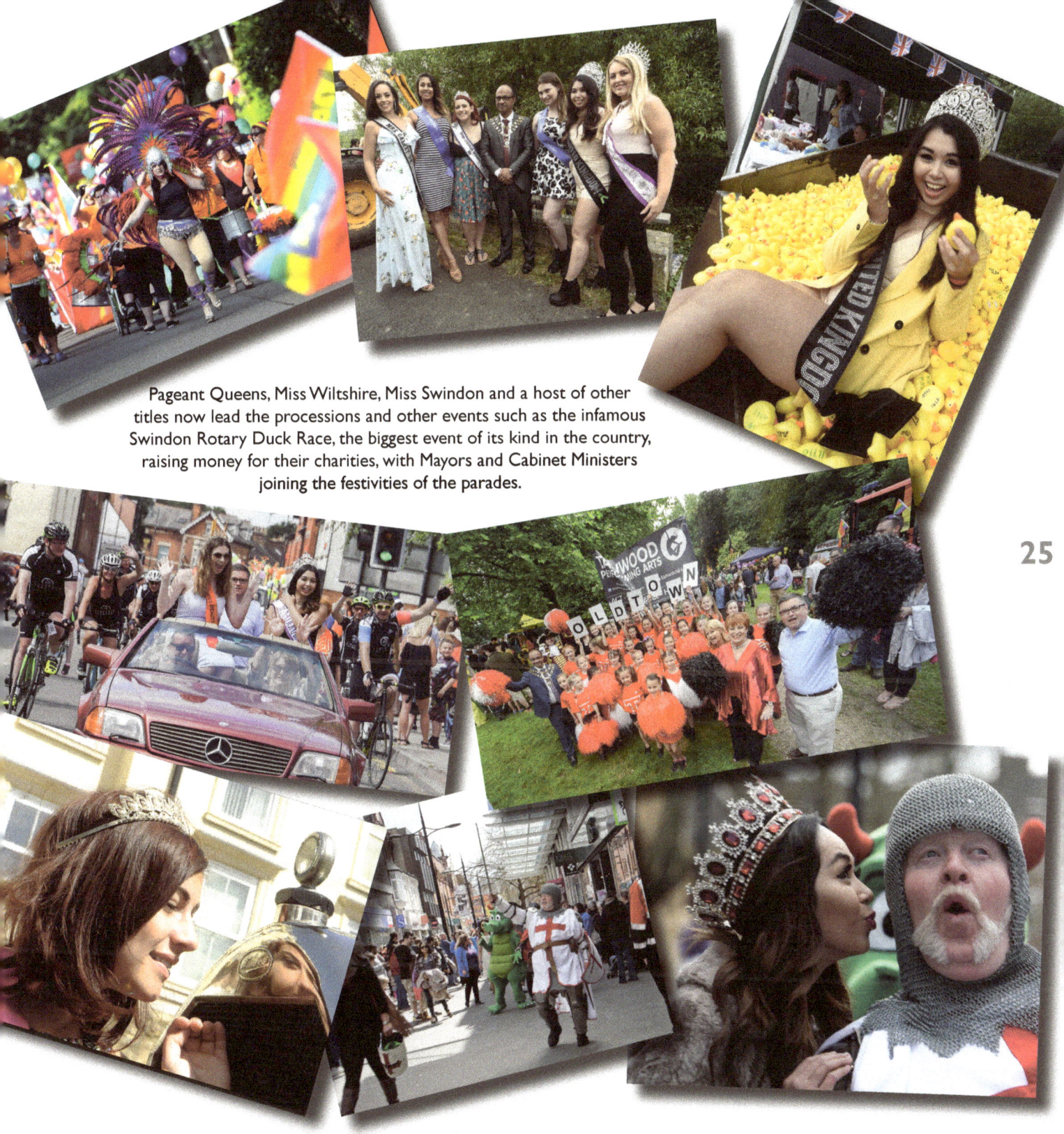

Pageant Queens, Miss Wiltshire, Miss Swindon and a host of other titles now lead the processions and other events such as the infamous Swindon Rotary Duck Race, the biggest event of its kind in the country, raising money for their charities, with Mayors and Cabinet Ministers joining the festivities of the parades.

The incumbent Miss Thamesdown usually led the Swindon carnivals. The most famous of these was Anna Dinning, who went on to national fame as Miss Lovely Legs of Great Britain.

This was a competition organised by The Pretty Polly Hosiery Company with Butlins Holiday Centres in 1984.

Anna was also involved with many charities, including collecting sweets for children in Africa and riding around in a sponsored Sinclair C5.

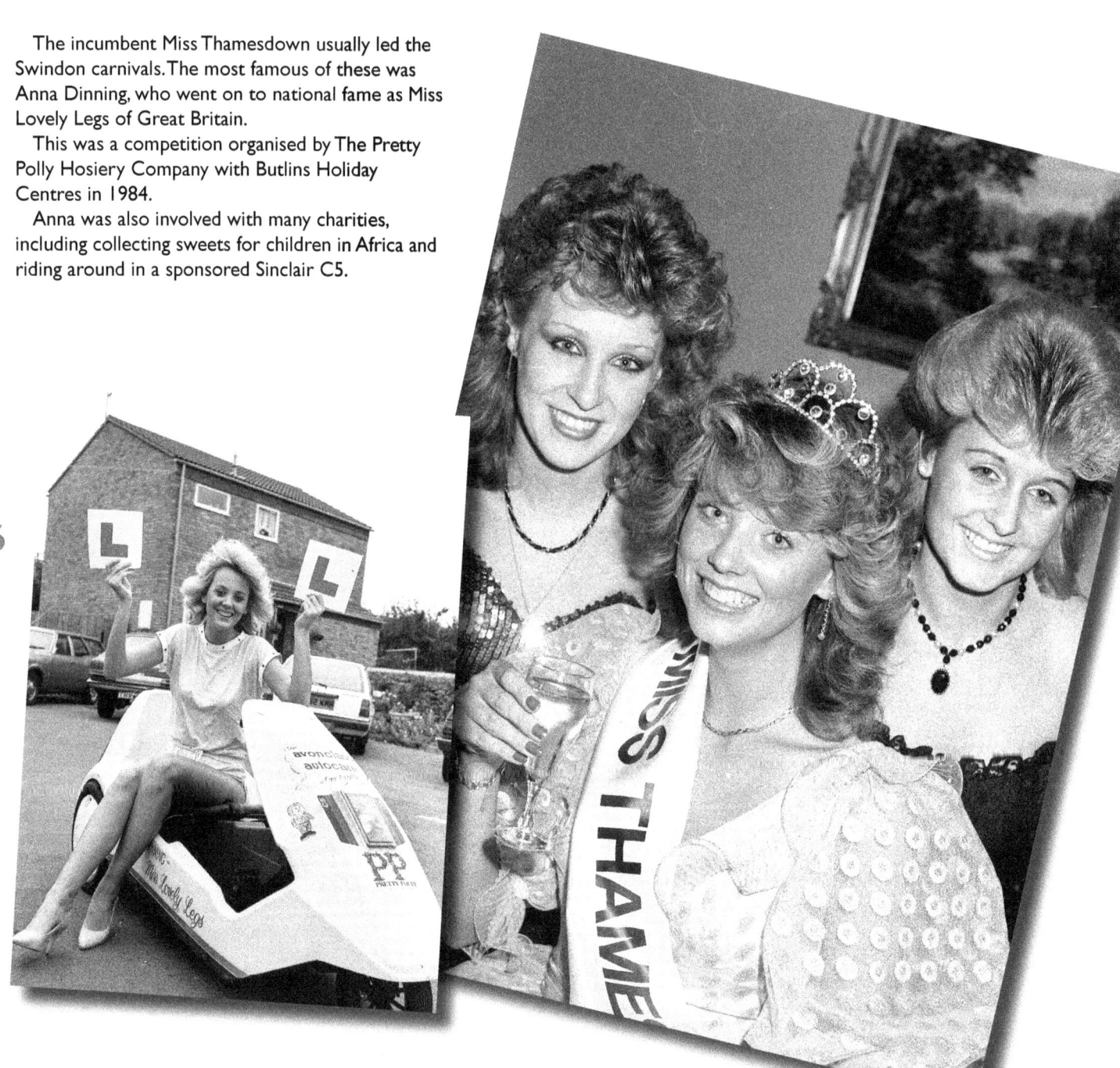

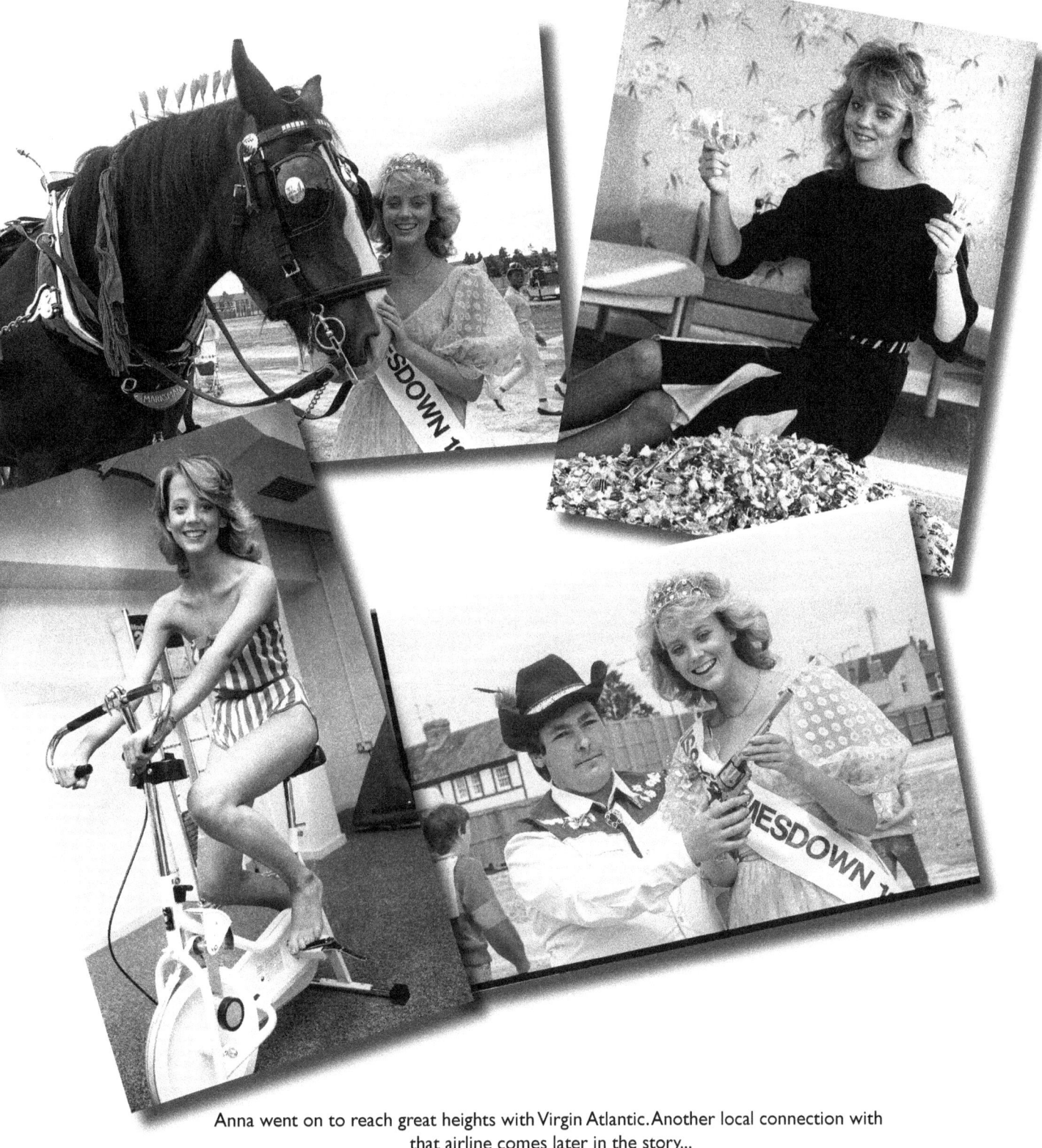

Anna went on to reach great heights with Virgin Atlantic. Another local connection with that airline comes later in the story...

...One of our Carnival Queens that found international fame through her roles in many high profile advertising campaigns was Amber Bezer, who headed the 1985 Purton Carnival. Later that year she starred in the famous Levi Jeans advertisement starring pop idol Nick Kamen. The advert was produced in 1985, and has been voted fourth in a poll for the 100 top adverts of all time. For the music buffs among you, the advert's success also caused the re-release of Marvin Gay's 'Grapevine' which subsequently became a big hit all over again. The ad was 'Launderette' and was shown for the first time on Boxing Day 1985.

Amber first found fame when she was 11 years old, and won a part as an orphan in the West End musical Annie.

By the age of 16, she had appeared as a cover girl in *Girl* magazine, modelled on the cover of Black Lace's Christmas album, and appeared with Rita Tushingham in a stage tour of the play 'Children, Children.'

She has also starred in the TV series Second Thoiughts, War of the Worlds, and the Childrens series Mission: Top Secret.

Over the years, Amber did a number of commercials for products as diverse as Maltesers, Lloyds Bank, Ford Cars, an American bubble gum advertisement, as well as becoming the face of Oil of Ulay (now known as Olay).

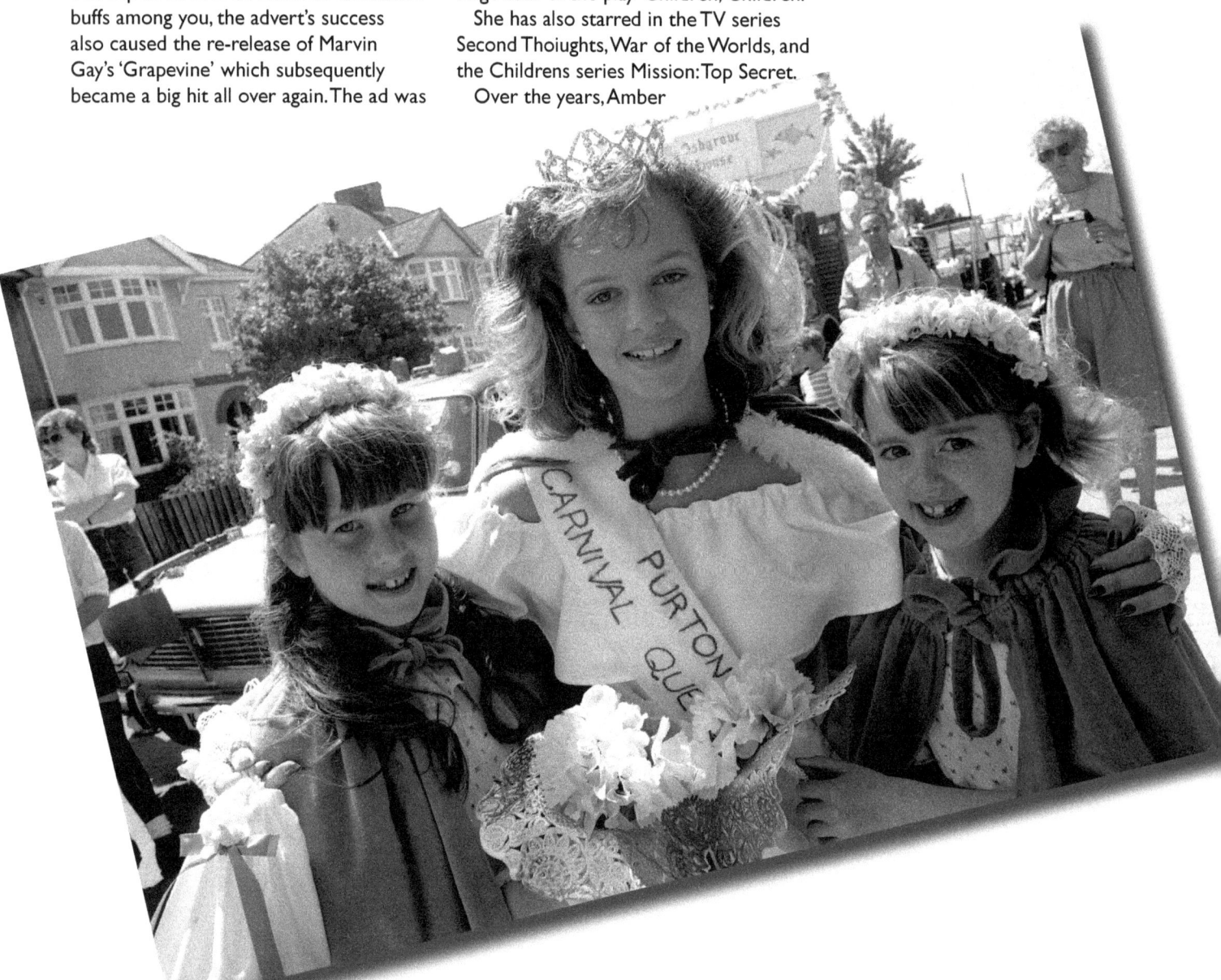

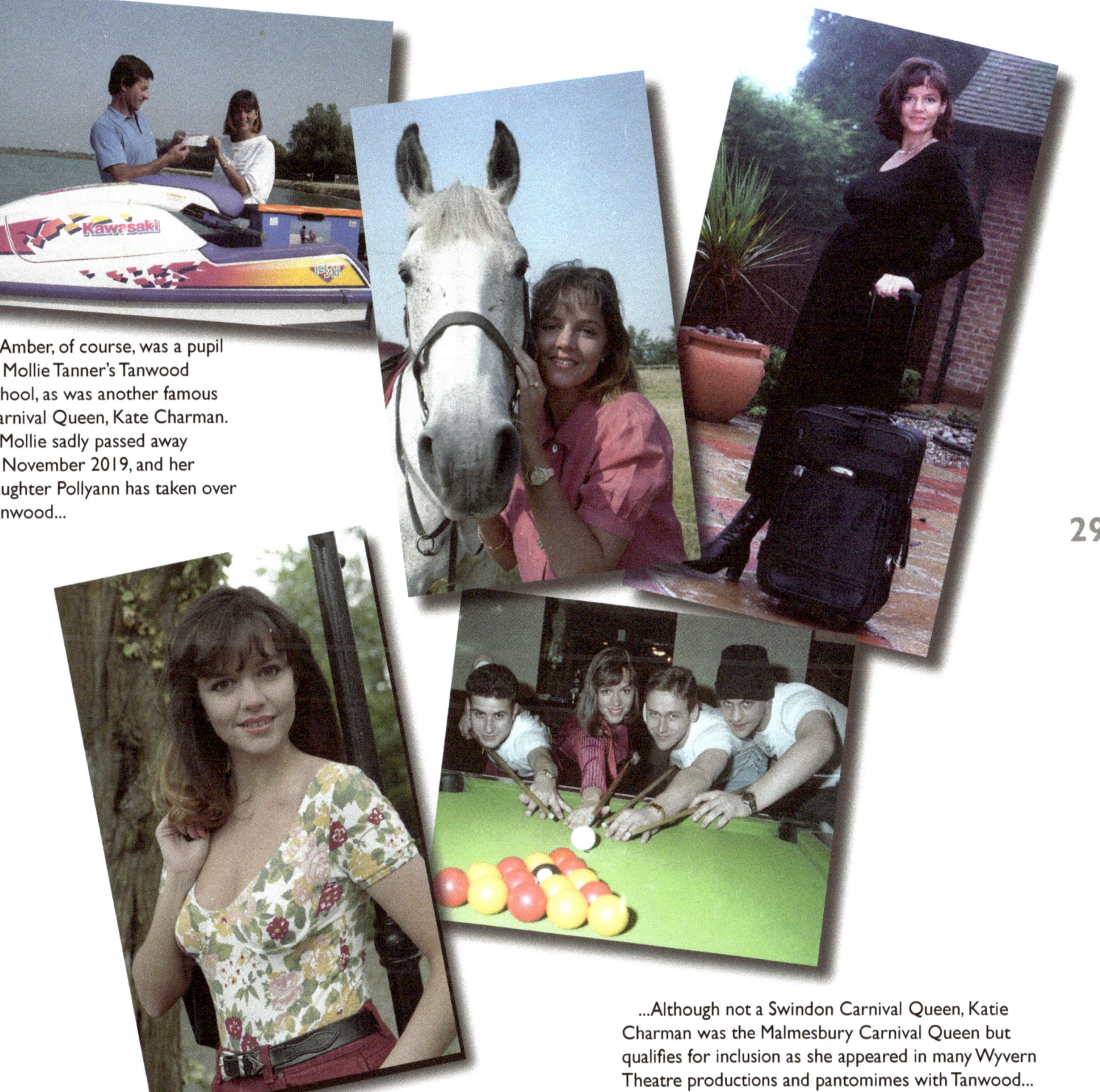

Amber, of course, was a pupil at Mollie Tanner's Tanwood School, as was another famous Carnival Queen, Kate Charman. Mollie sadly passed away in November 2019, and her daughter Pollyann has taken over Tanwood...

...Although not a Swindon Carnival Queen, Katie Charman was the Malmesbury Carnival Queen but qualifies for inclusion as she appeared in many Wyvern Theatre productions and pantomimes with Tanwood...

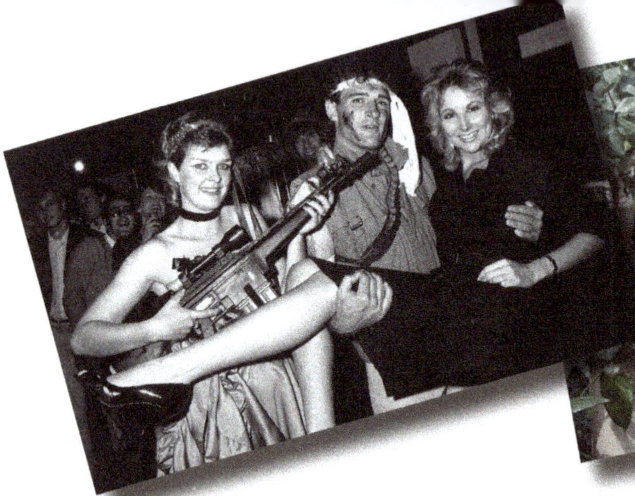

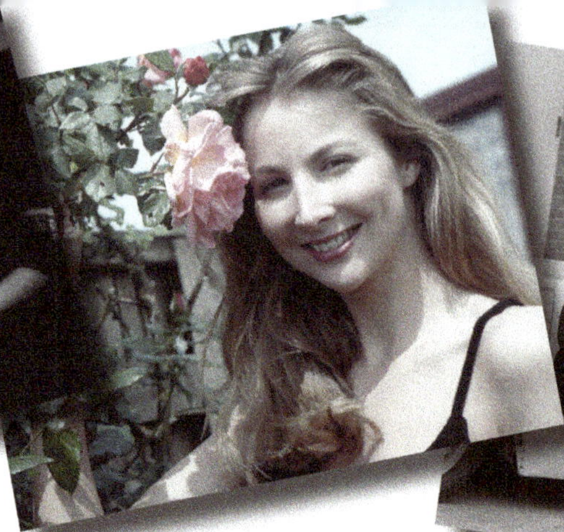

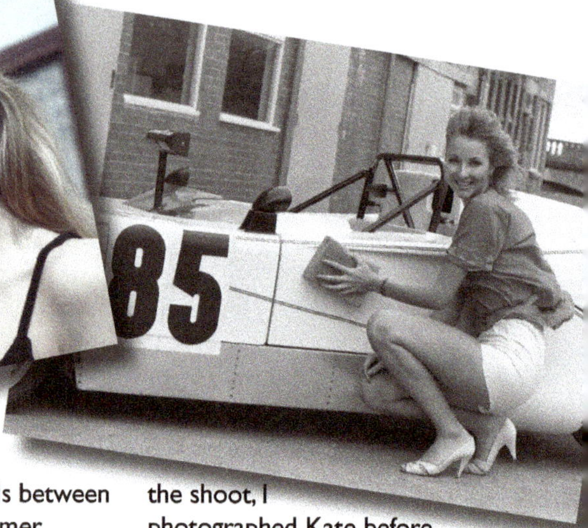

...Kate Charman (Durr) who is now married to Heartbeat and Casualty star Jason Durr, is a renowned garden designer who works with the Prince of Wales at Highgrove. As an actress, Kate starred in Eyes Wide Shut (1999), Scandal (1989) and The 100 Greatest Kids TV Shows (2001). She also presented the TV show Guinness World Records between 1999 and 2001, with former Arsenal footballer Ian Wright who, incidentally, I remember scoring a goal against Swindon Town from the halfway line.

She featured in the Lamb's Navy Rum calendar for 1991, which was shot in Australia. Although, unfortunately, I didn't get to the shoot, I photographed Kate before she left for the assignment.

Kate, like Anna Dinning, also modelled for the Pretty Polly hosiery company...

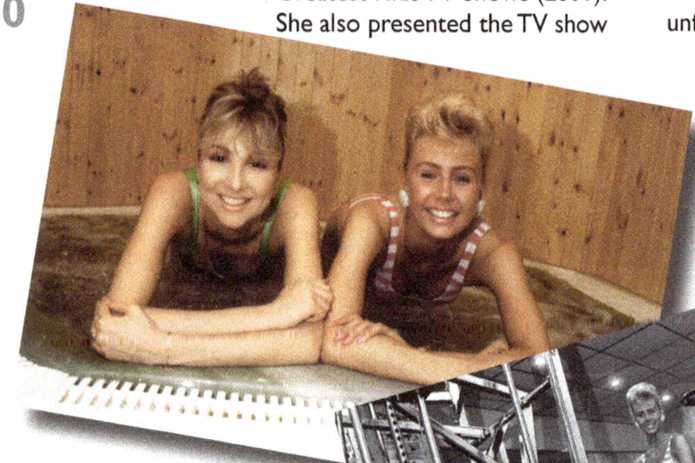

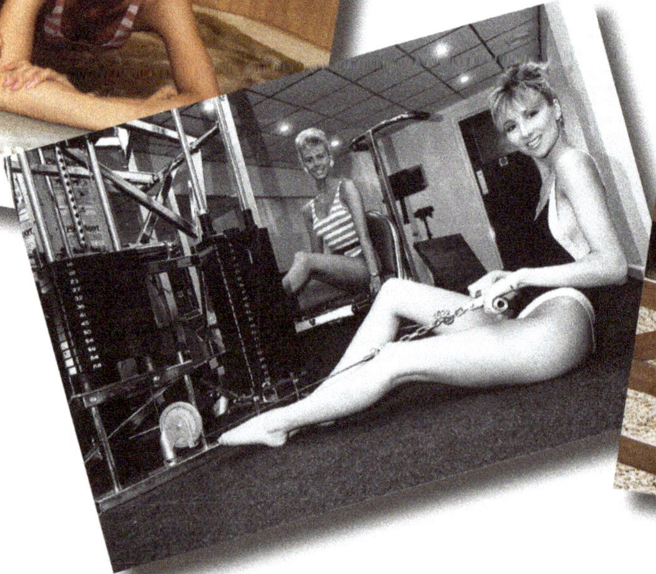

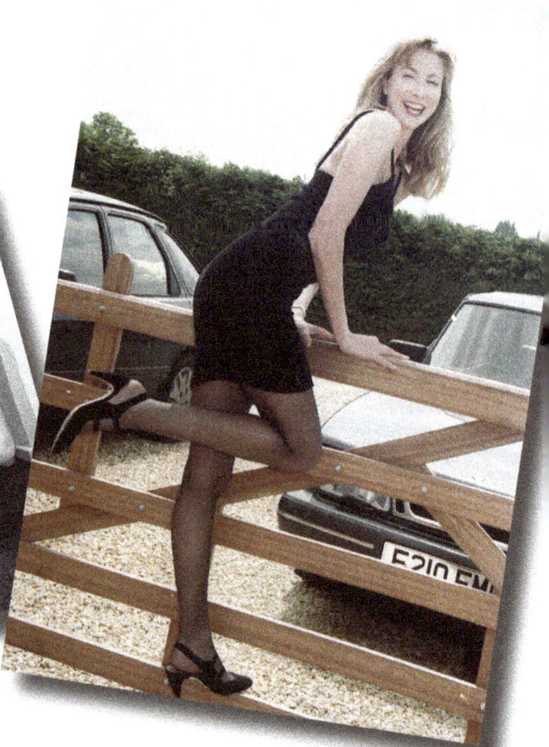

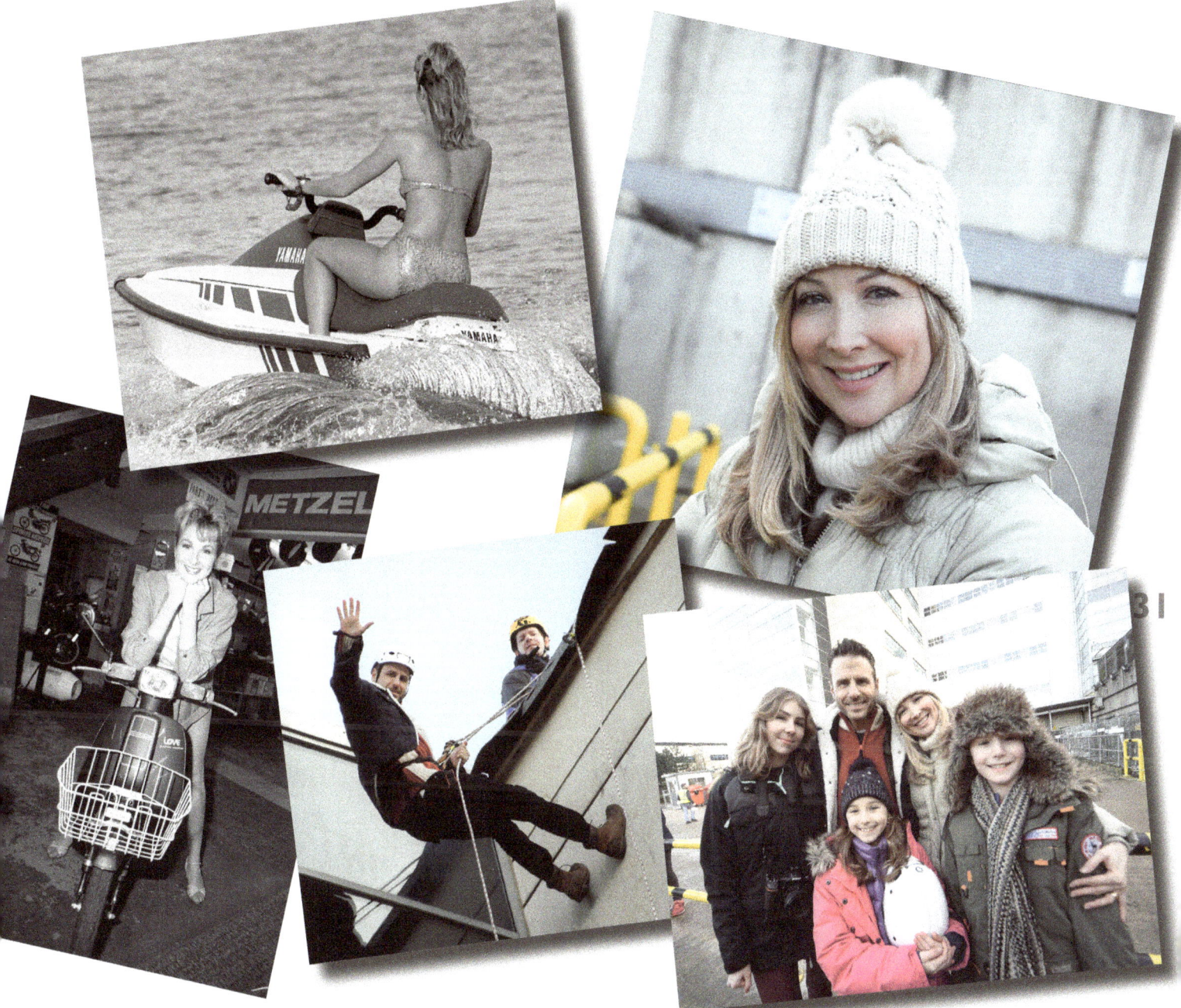

...I met up with Kate recently when husband Jason Durr abseiled down the side of the Great Western Hospital, raising money for the Brighter Futures charity. The Brighter Futures team have done an immense amount of fund raising, including raising the money for a Cancer unit in Swindon; something very close to my heart.

Kate's daugher Blossom has an interest in the arts, and I lent her one of my cameras to capture images of her dad abseiling down the wall.

The picture of Jason was one taken by Blossom.

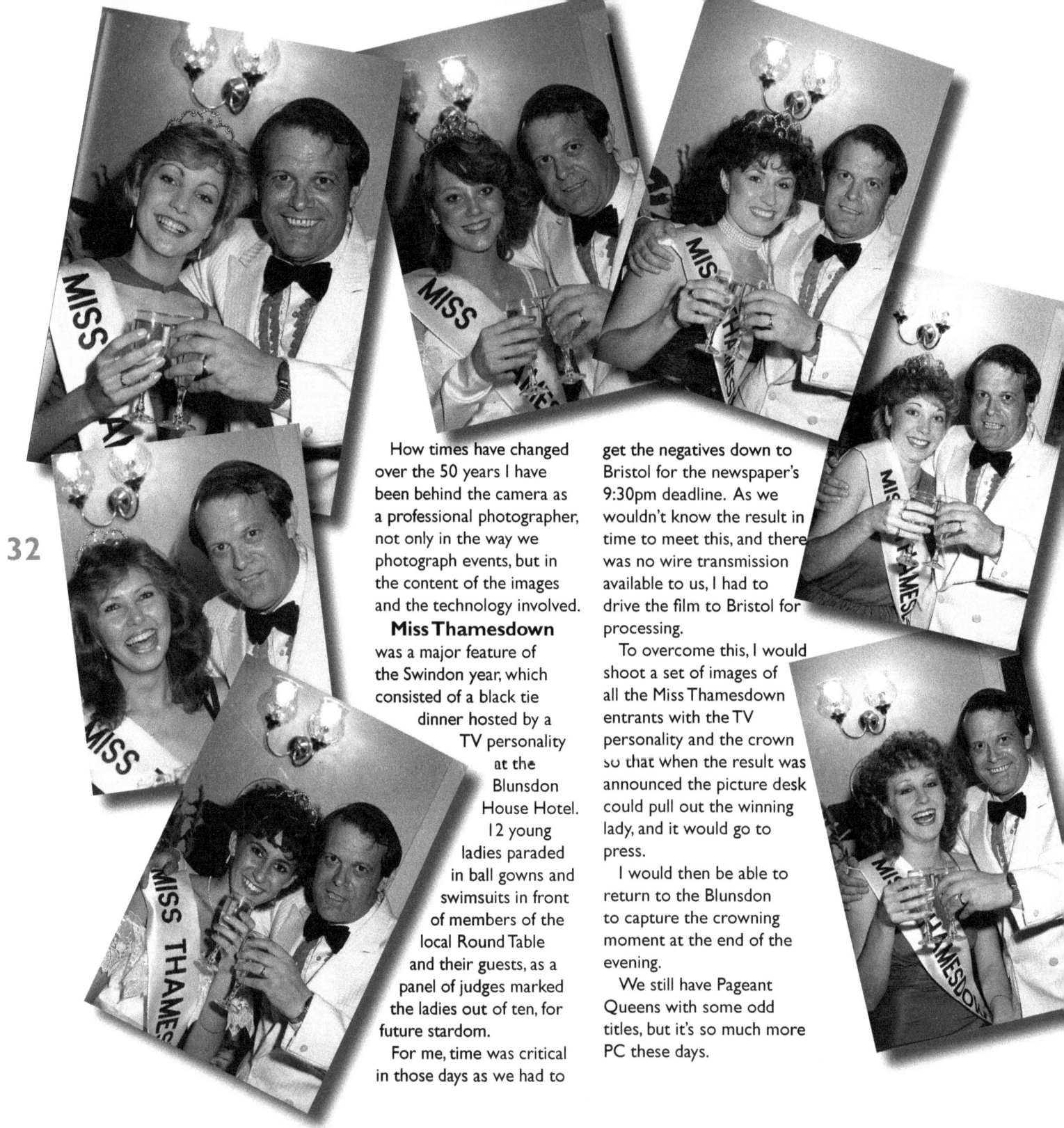

How times have changed over the 50 years I have been behind the camera as a professional photographer, not only in the way we photograph events, but in the content of the images and the technology involved.

Miss Thamesdown was a major feature of the Swindon year, which consisted of a black tie dinner hosted by a TV personality at the Blunsdon House Hotel. 12 young ladies paraded in ball gowns and swimsuits in front of members of the local Round Table and their guests, as a panel of judges marked the ladies out of ten, for future stardom.

For me, time was critical in those days as we had to get the negatives down to Bristol for the newspaper's 9:30pm deadline. As we wouldn't know the result in time to meet this, and there was no wire transmission available to us, I had to drive the film to Bristol for processing.

To overcome this, I would shoot a set of images of all the Miss Thamesdown entrants with the TV personality and the crown so that when the result was announced the picture desk could pull out the winning lady, and it would go to press.

I would then be able to return to the Blunsdon to capture the crowning moment at the end of the evening.

We still have Pageant Queens with some odd titles, but it's so much more PC these days.

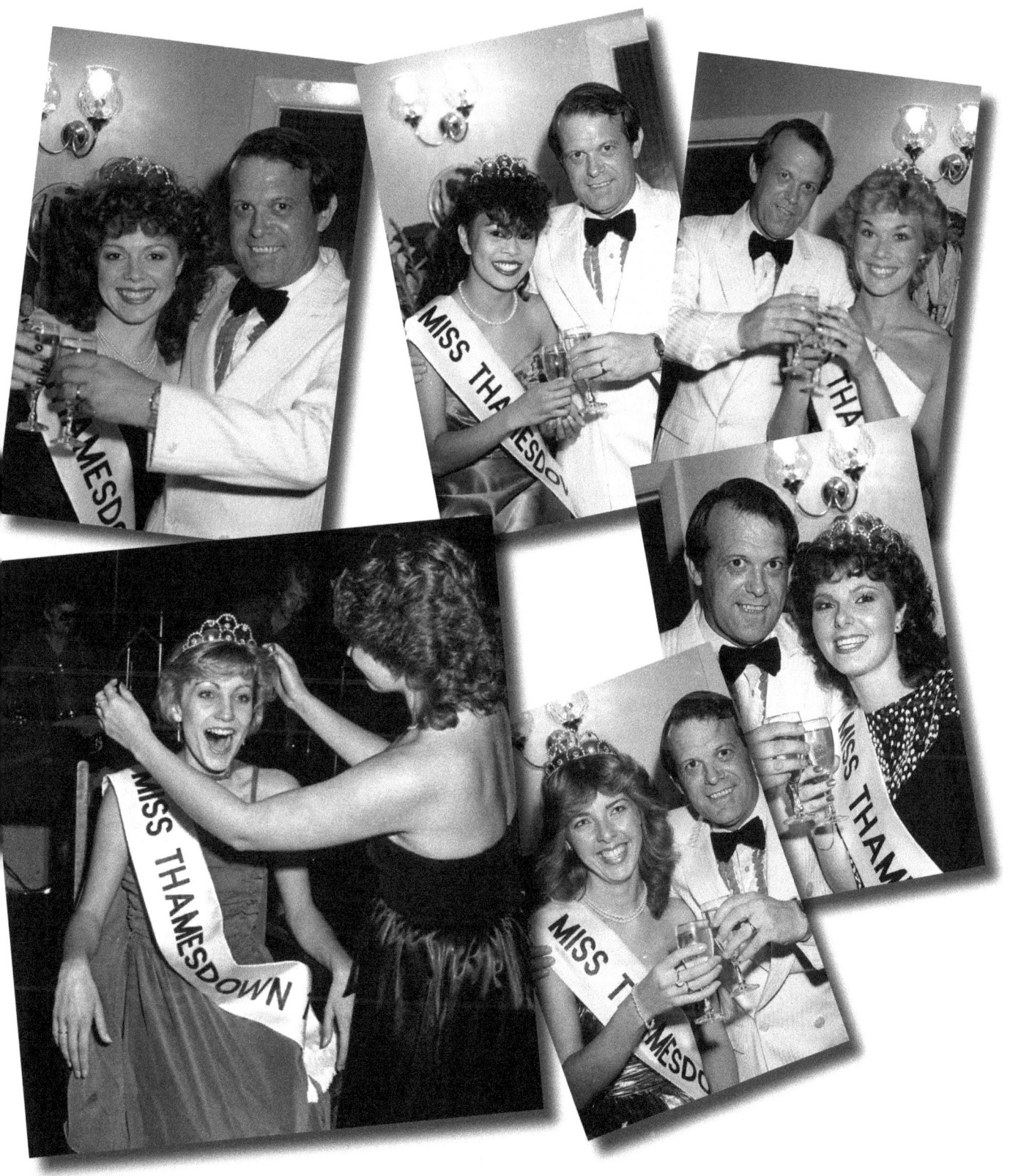

Katherine Thomas AKA The Great Kat.

I mentioned earlier, the trawl through the files for carnival queens was fruitful; not just for the images of the carnivals, but what was hidden beneath one of the sheets of the 1984 carnival negatives.

Over the years I have photographed most of the Swindon-born music and film stars; Diana Dors, Desmond Morris, Andy Partridge, Billie Piper, Jahméne Douglas, and Justin Hayward, to name a few, but the note I found on the set of negatives read 'Catherine Thomas in Tuxedo with violin on top of the David Murray John building', and in a separate annotation 'American musician returns home.'

Fascinated by the relevance of this last note, I made searches on the infamous internet browser and discovered what I had found was a little more than interesting.

I made my way to the Local Studies section of the Central Library, where I quizzed their expert Darryl Moody about the existence of an unknown Swindon-born star Katherine Thomas, who played a concert in 1984. (The search engine came up with Katherine with a K).

The resulting research threw up an article in the Swindon Advertiser, which reported that Katherine Thomas had indeed been born in Swindon's Burderop Hospital in 1966. (This was when her parents were stationed at a local USAF base.)

It also confirmed that she had played the Thamesdown-Hambro Music Festival on the date she was pictured. She had wowed an audience of 60 in the Town Hall Studio with some classical violin pieces. These included Beethoven's Kreutzer Sonata, and as an encore she performed an aggressive and dazzling version of the gypsy piece Cazardas. This was obviously the tone of things to come.

She flew back the next day to New York.

So, who is Swindon's mysterious virtuoso, and what is she doing now?

Katherine went on to become a very big name in the pop world as The Great Kat, effectively playing psychedelic classical music in, amongst other venues, the Carnegie Hall.

As Michael Molenda of Guitar Player Magazine describes her, 'The Great Kat. This Juilliard-trained violinist's turbocharged, speed-metal readings of classical pieces were pretty astounding when she first appeared… They're still impressive, in fact, Kat (born Katherine Thomas) may be one of the fastest guitarists of all time.'

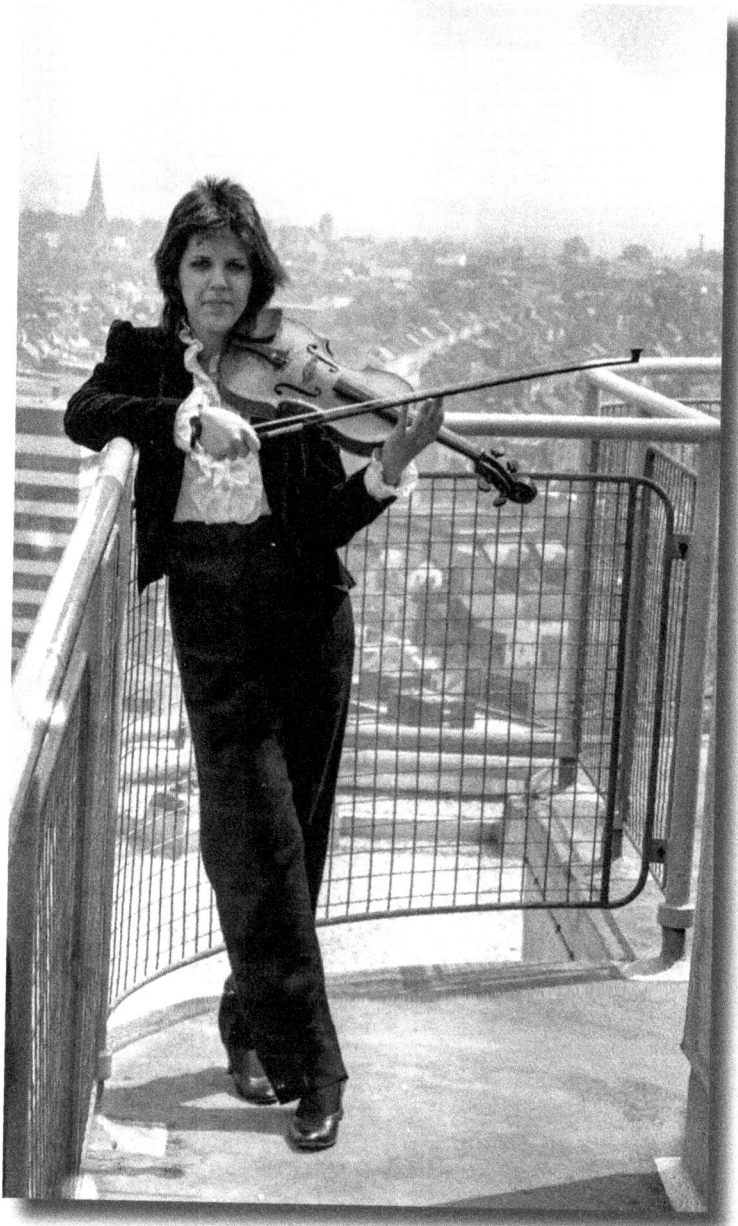

Kat is described on the famous internet encyclopaedia as, 'Her public persona, as portrayed in her publicity photos and videos, is mainly compared to that of a dominatrix, albeit in an over-the-top, abusive tongue-in-cheek manner.'

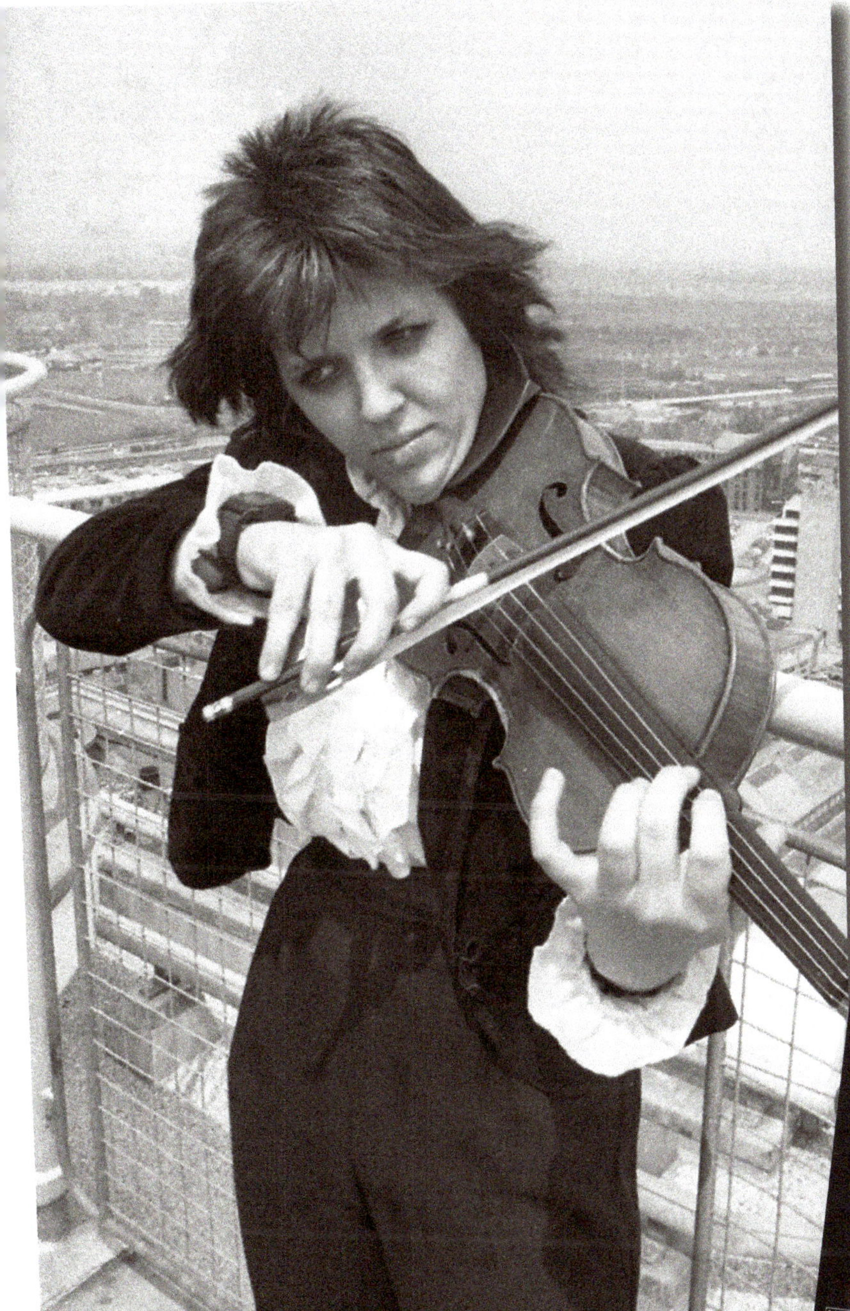

By coincidence, around the time Kat was in Swindon, she was collaborating with the late Timothy Leary, the LSD cultural icon of the sixties and seventies, on a project 'Right Brain Lover'. Timothy Leary wrote the wild psychedelic lyrics and Kat composed the music, reminiscent of Billy Idol and The Ramones. Timothy Leary and Kat recorded 'Right Brain Lover', starring Kat's electric violin virtuosity and rock singing and Timothy Leary rapping the lyrics with his inimitable voice. It is regarded in heavy metal circles as a classic.

The local coincidence however continues; the Moody Blues LP 'In Search of the Lost Chord' included the track 'Legend of a Mind', a song written by the late Ray Thomas in tribute to Leary, and encompassed a flute solo performed by Thomas. This popular number is performed by the Moody Blues, including Swindon's Justin Hayward, when they are on tour.

And Kat's comment on Swindon, 'It's a refreshing change from New York. I enjoyed playing here and I'd love to visit again.'

I look forward to meeting her on her next visit to the UK...

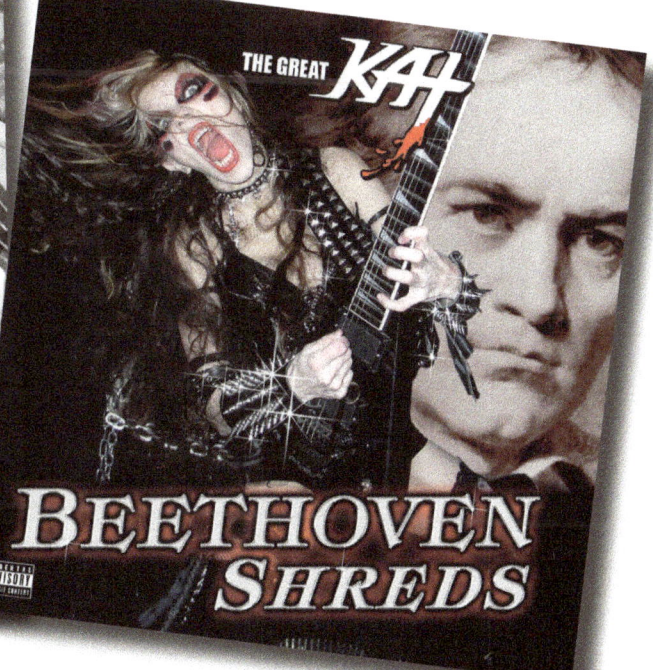

...The Swindon area has produced some very famous pop musicians; **Justin Hayward** of the Moody Blues, Rick Davies of Supertramp, Gilbert O'Sullivan, XTC, Billie Piper, Jamie Cullum and recently Josh Kumar, Jess Hall and Colour the Atlas, Phoebe Maddison and Lilia Slattery, to name but a few.

Justin's links with Swindon continue to this day, as the former Commonweal Schoolboy has done several charity gigs in the town starting in 1991 with a gig at Holiday Inn (now the Marriott) where he jammed with local group Mandrake. The gig, the Moody Blue Bop, raised over £8,000 for the charity.

Hayward had been asked by old school friend Lesley Drewett to raise funds for the Gerry Drewett charity to provide a specialist cancer ward at the now-demolished Princess Margaret Hospital on Okus. Lesley's husband Gerry had terminal cancer and there was a big need for the unit, as Gerry had to travel many miles to Oxford for treatment.

The unit was never completed because of the impending demolition of the hospital, however, the more than £27,000 in the Gerry Drewett Cancer Fund, was eventually donated to the Great Western Hopsital, where it helped build two specialist cancer wards, Sunbeam and Honey.

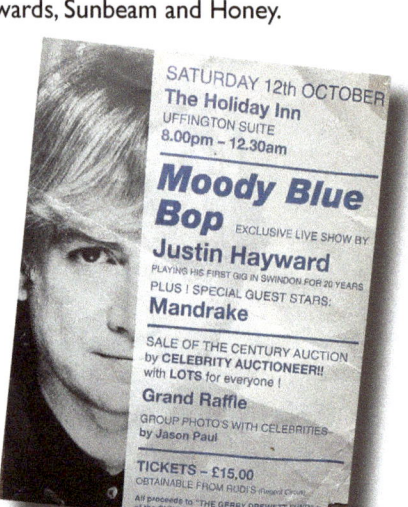

I was privileged to photograph Justin as he toured the ward with Lesley.

I recorded that Moody Blue Bop, and Justin's future ones, including the NSPCC performance at the Allied Dunbar's King George Place at Liddington and, of course, when the Moody Blues did a sell-out show at the Oasis.

Several of these performances were compered by the late Sandy Martin, including a special gig and Question and Answer in the Apartment. During that question and answer session between songs, Hayward remembered cheekily enjoying playing in pubs around the town when he was barely 15; working in an office at Bradley's while furiously answering adverts in *Melody Maker*; and, most notably, learning that he had got the job as the Moody Blues vocalist while looking at guitars in Duck, Son & Pinker in Fleet Street.

He also revealed that he composed the hit 'Tuesday Afternoon' while sat under the Cypress Tree on the lawn of Lydiard House...

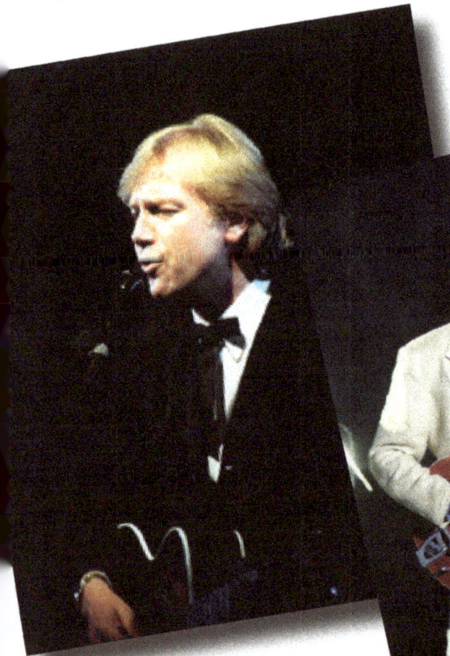

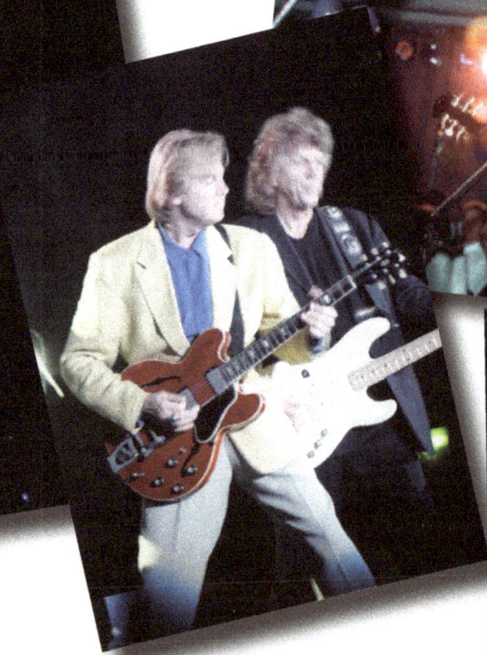

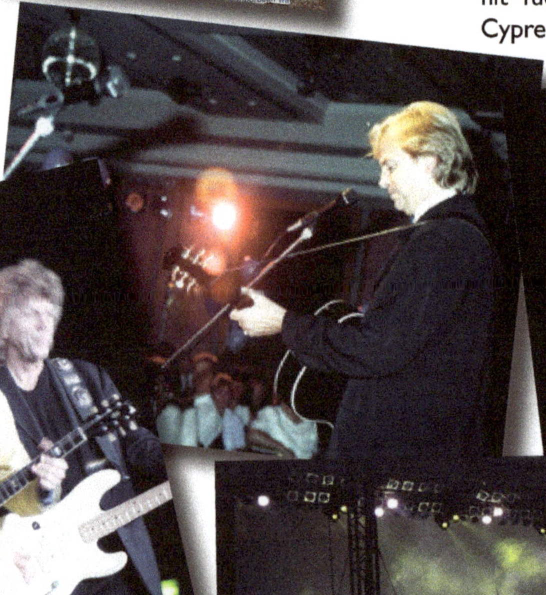

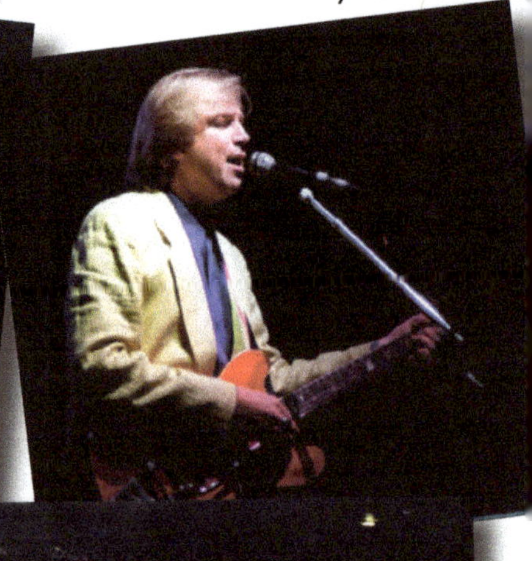

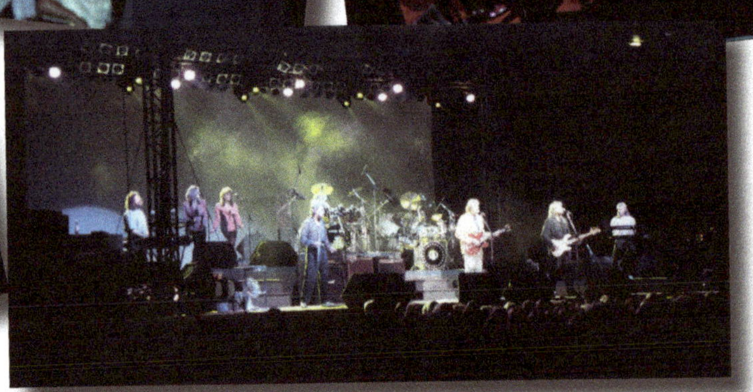

...Recently, Hayward brought a show to Swindon's Wyvern Theatre with his band of Mike Dawes, Julie Ragins and Karmen Gould. So it was that, after many calls, and a lot of persuading, I received a call asking how long it would take me to get to the theatre. Needless to say I dropped everything, grabbed the cameras, and made my way to the stage door of the Wyvern. It was only a quick picture of the group, but as it turned out was an almost exclusive image. As the tour manager put it, 'How did you get that? he hasn't allowed any pictures on the tour.'

So, as I said, almost exclusive as I don't know if any were taken after that...

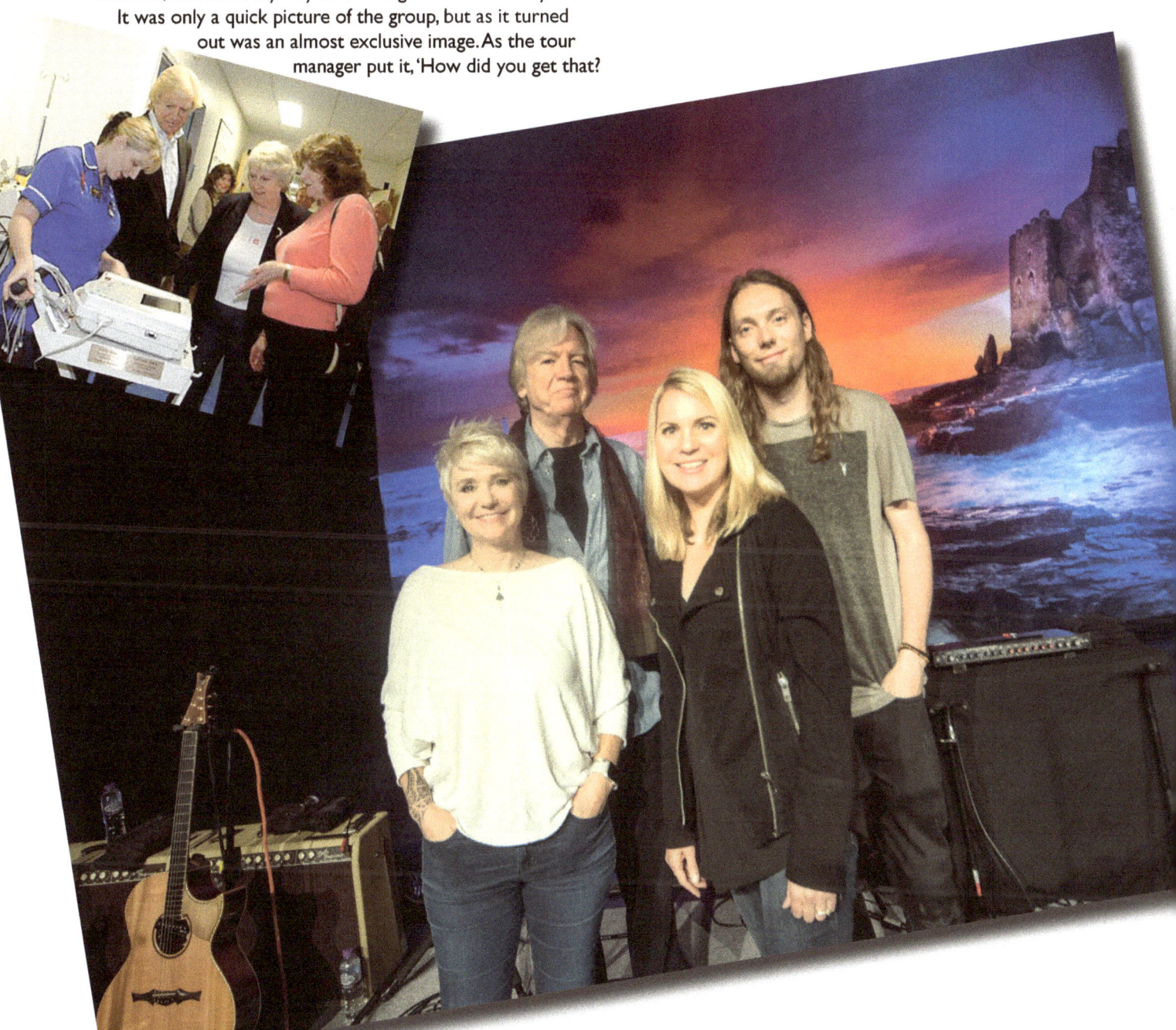

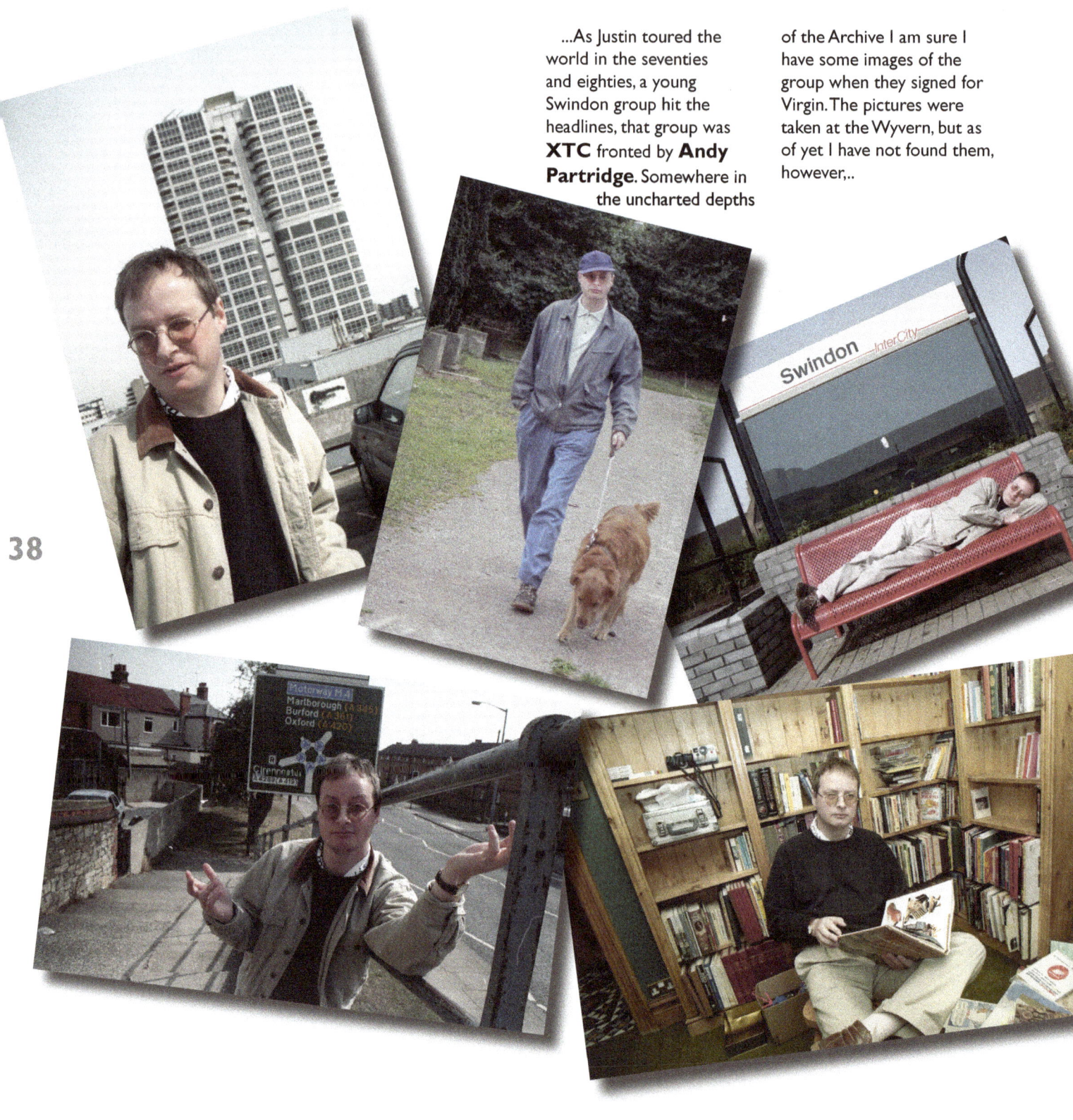

...As Justin toured the world in the seventies and eighties, a young Swindon group hit the headlines, that group was **XTC** fronted by **Andy Partridge**. Somewhere in the uncharted depths of the Archive I am sure I have some images of the group when they signed for Virgin. The pictures were taken at the Wyvern, but as of yet I have not found them, however,..

...I did a series of feature pictures of Andy with Swindon landmarks and, more recently, covered a poetry evening at New College with Former XTC keyboard-player **Barry Andrews;** and the Swindon Viewpoint 40th Birthday gig at Swindon's MECA in Regent Circus, where XTC's **Dave Gregory** played as part of his band Tin Spirits...

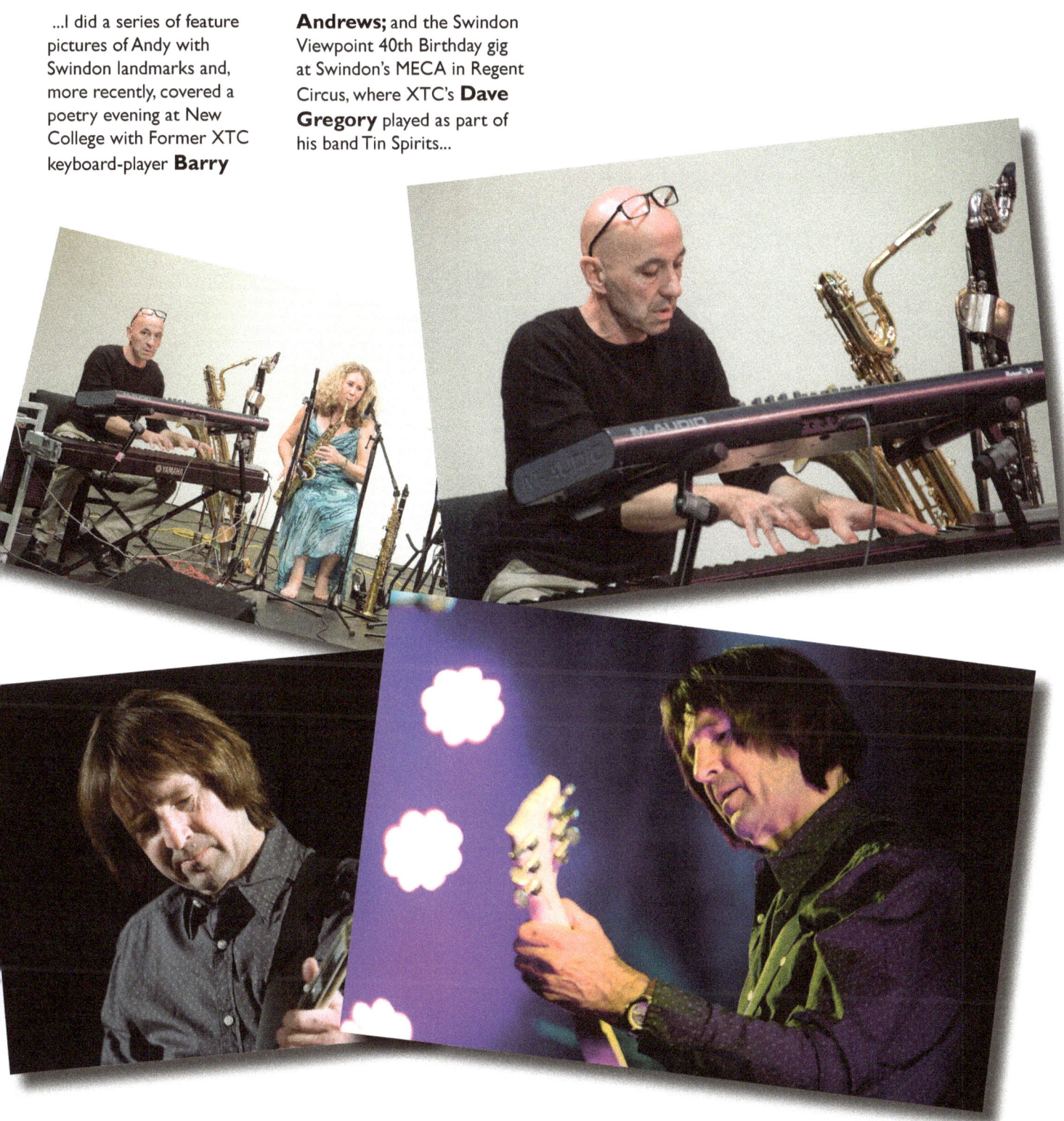

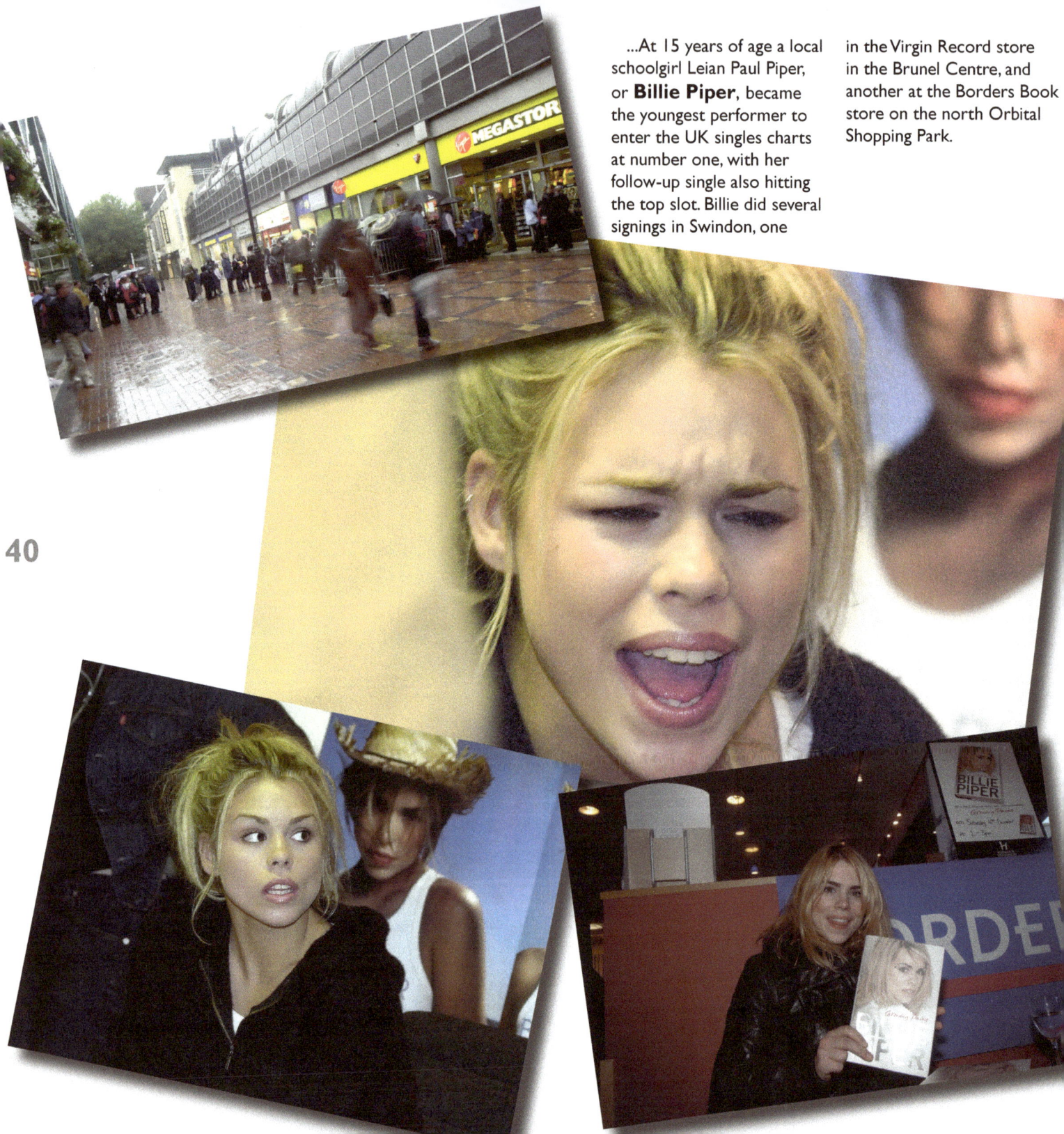

...At 15 years of age a local schoolgirl Leian Paul Piper, or **Billie Piper**, became the youngest performer to enter the UK singles charts at number one, with her follow-up single also hitting the top slot. Billie did several signings in Swindon, one in the Virgin Record store in the Brunel Centre, and another at the Borders Book store on the north Orbital Shopping Park.

She has recently become patron of The Shoebox Theatre, which is now housed in the Health Hydro in Milton Road.

The Shoebox Theatre started out in Artsite in the old Post Office in Theatre Square, where we photographed Billie when she accepted the patronage.

This follows on from her acting career, where she played Rose Tyler in Dr Who, Lily in Penny Dreadful and Belle in Secret Diary of a Call Girl.

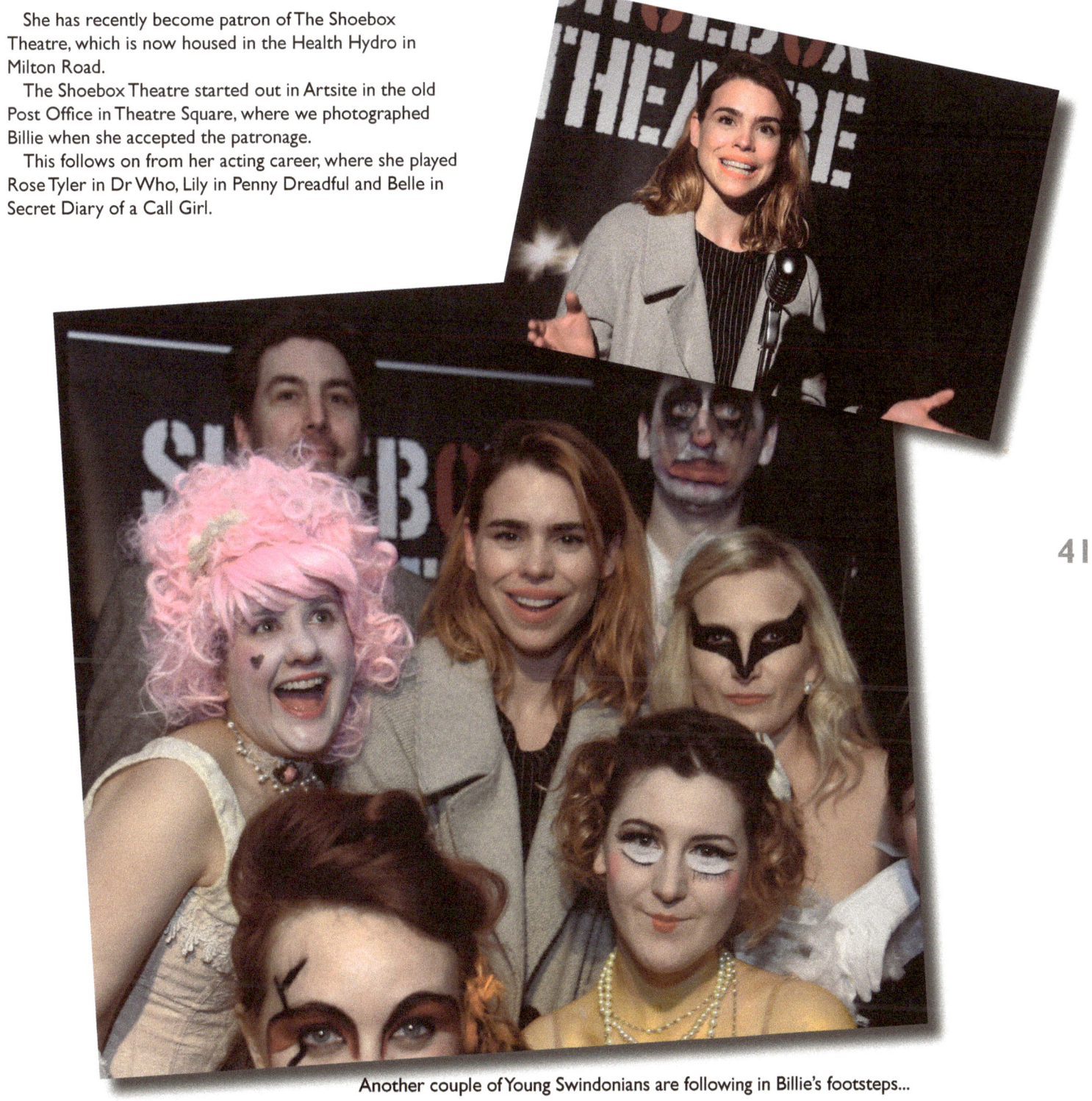

Another couple of Young Swindonians are following in Billie's footsteps...

...As the custodian of an archive, I try to keep up to date with events and personalities; and **Phoebe Maddison** came to my notice when, at nine years old, she made a film about suffering with diabetes and won an Emmy for her part in it. Since then she has gone on to win singing awards, and appeared in the TV show The Voice Kids, winning a chance to perform in front of 80,000 in Trafalgar Square; and of course turned on Swindon Christmas lights with another Swindon star...

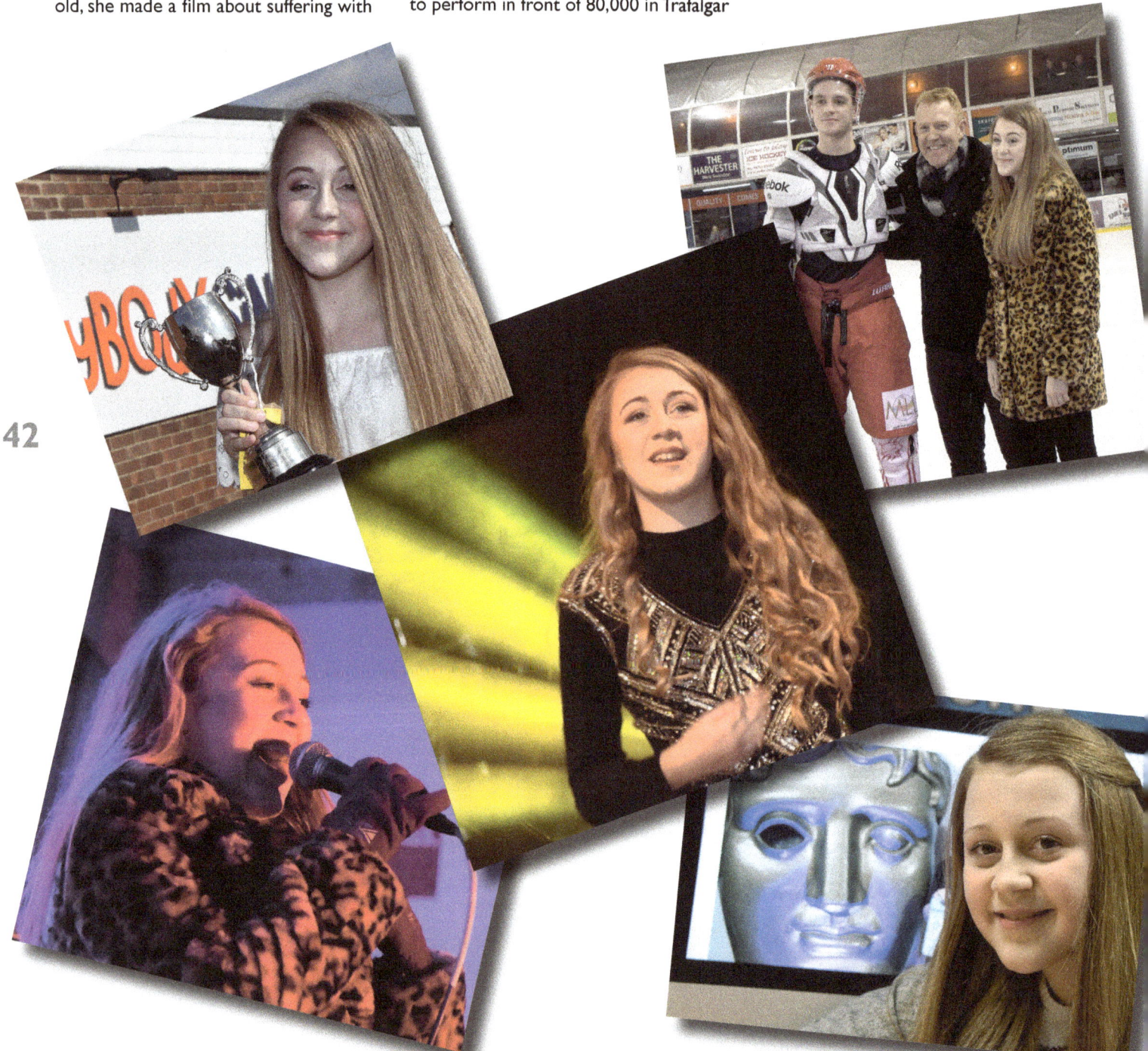

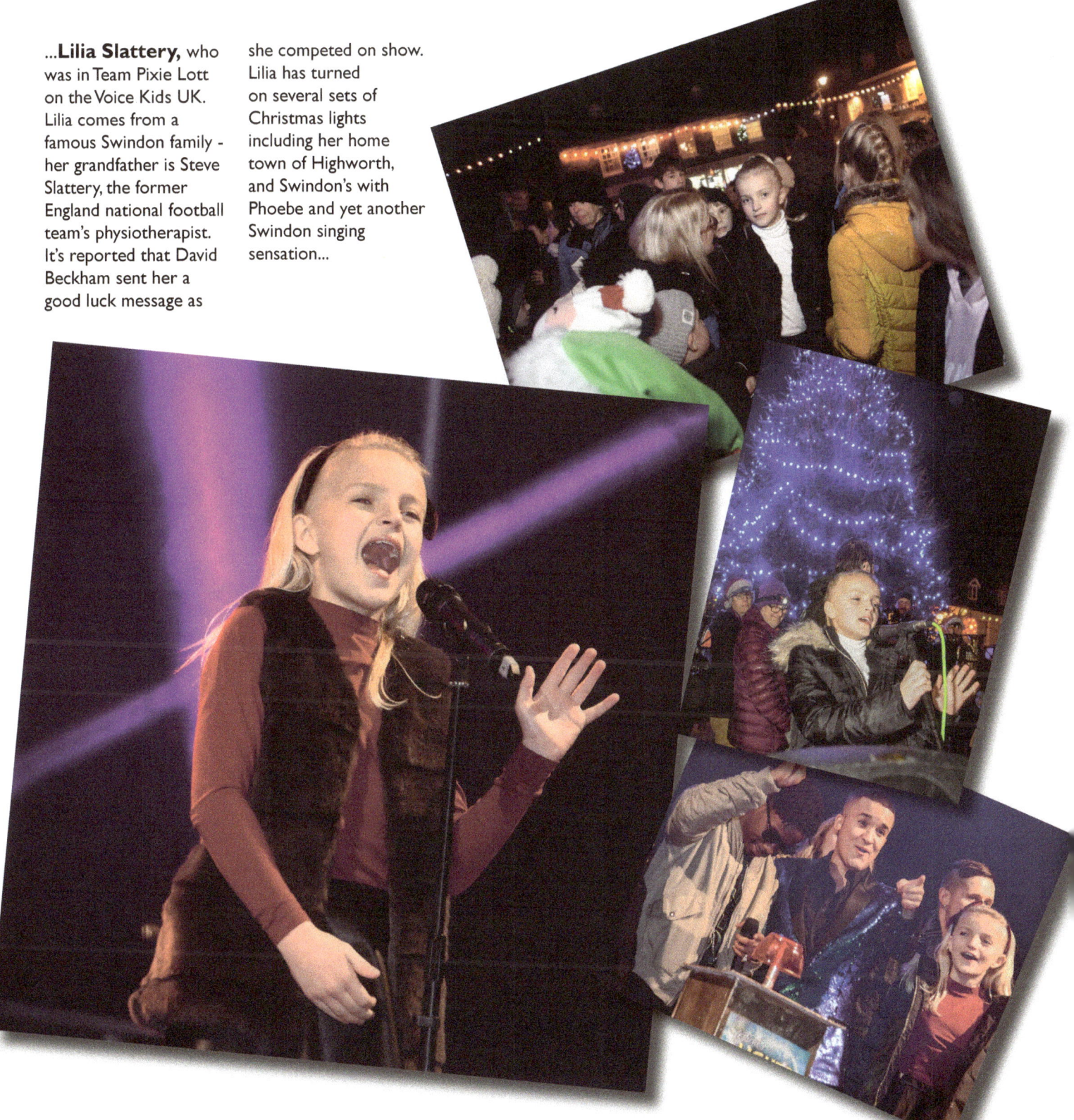

...**Lilia Slattery,** who was in Team Pixie Lott on the Voice Kids UK. Lilia comes from a famous Swindon family - her grandfather is Steve Slattery, the former England national football team's physiotherapist. It's reported that David Beckham sent her a good luck message as she competed on show. Lilia has turned on several sets of Christmas lights including her home town of Highworth, and Swindon's with Phoebe and yet another Swindon singing sensation...

Jahméne Douglas

Jahméne was the runner-up to James Arthur on the ninth series of The X Factor in 2012. He was mentored in the series by Pussycat Dolls lead singer Nicole Scherzinger.

Born in Birmingham, the family moved to the Swindon area where his mother Mandy, who is a women's rights campaigner and author, still lives.

While working at Asda on the North Orbital Shopping Park, where he used to entertain co-workers with his singing, he entered the Simon Cowell X Factor TV show.

As part of that show he appeared at his old store with Nicole Scherzinger and mother Mandy, before turning on Swindon's Christmas lights in Wharf Green.

Jahméne appeared at the Oasis in the Best of Swindon concert in 2013, which also featured some more up and coming musicians...

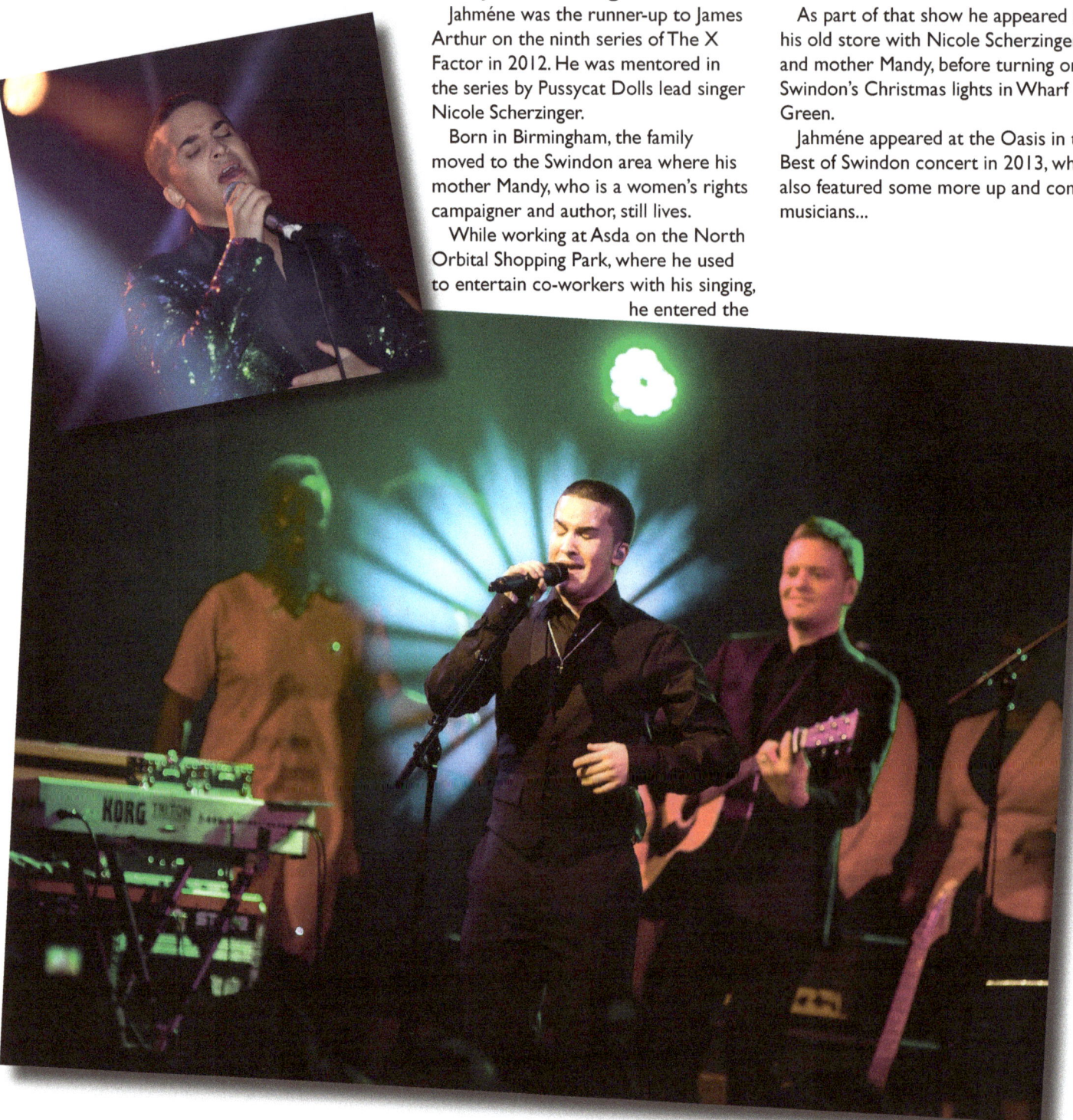

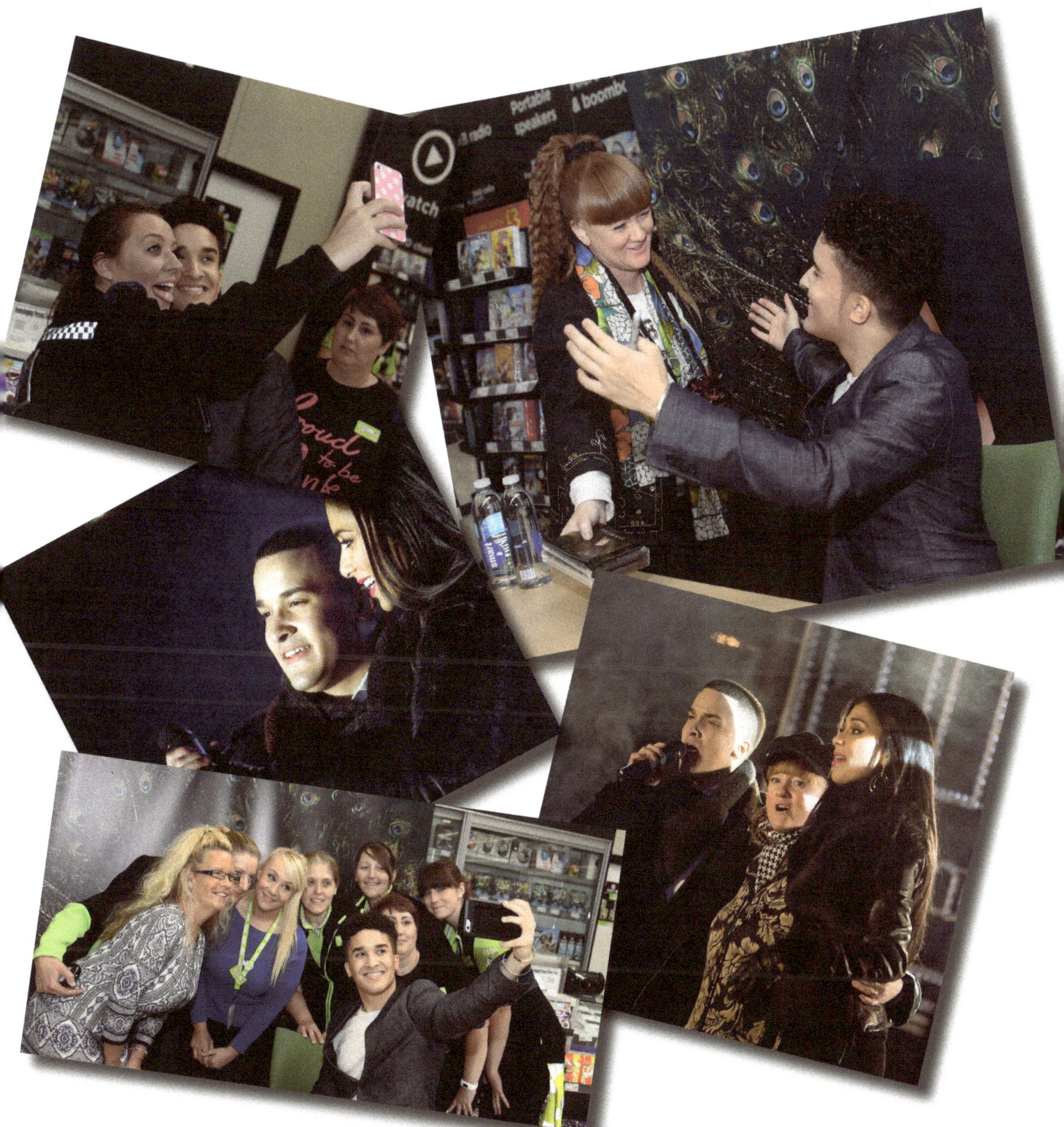

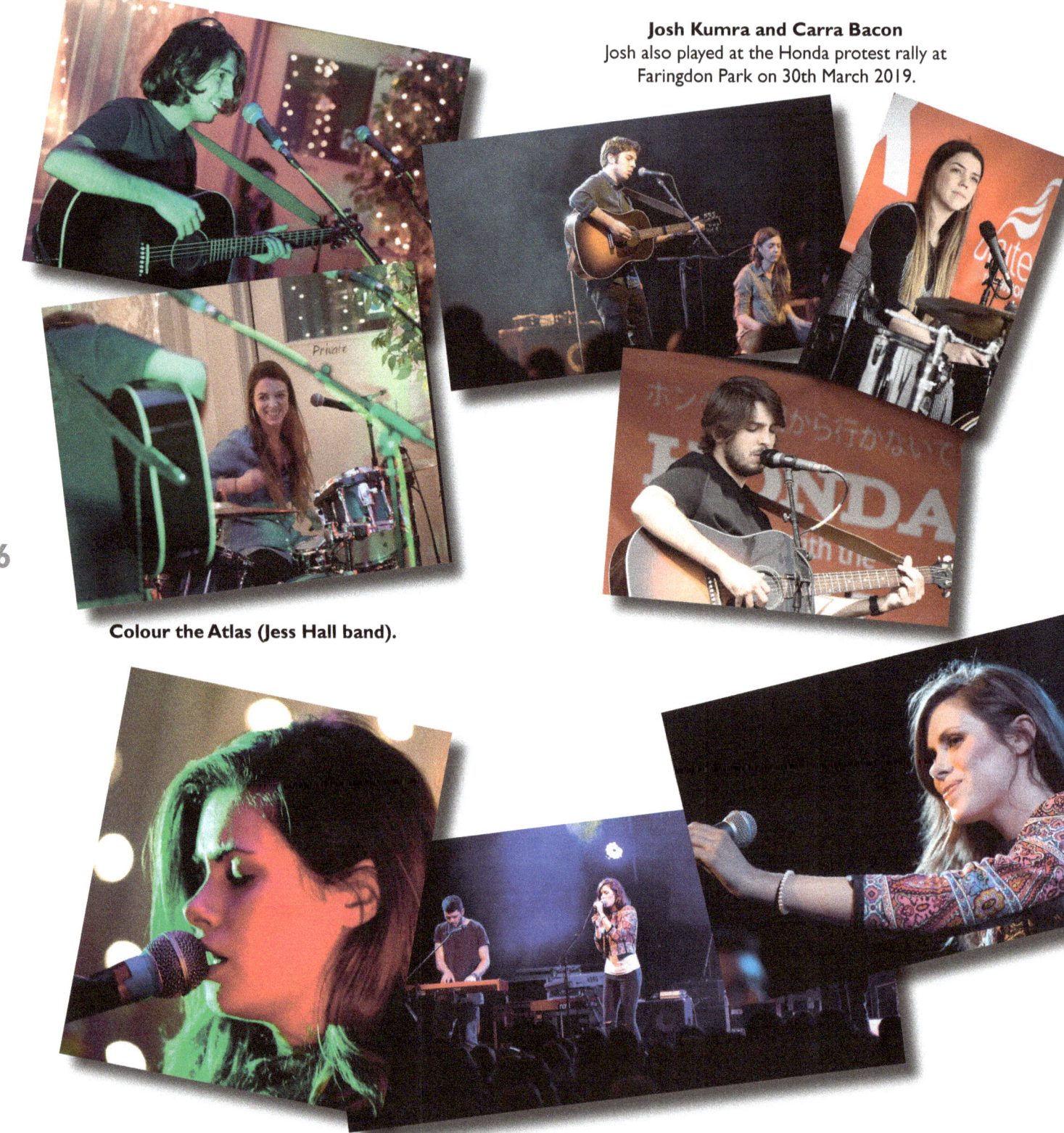

Josh Kumra and Carra Bacon
Josh also played at the Honda protest rally at Faringdon Park on 30th March 2019.

Colour the Atlas (Jess Hall band).

Queen of Hearts (Elizabeth Morphew)

Theo Altieri.

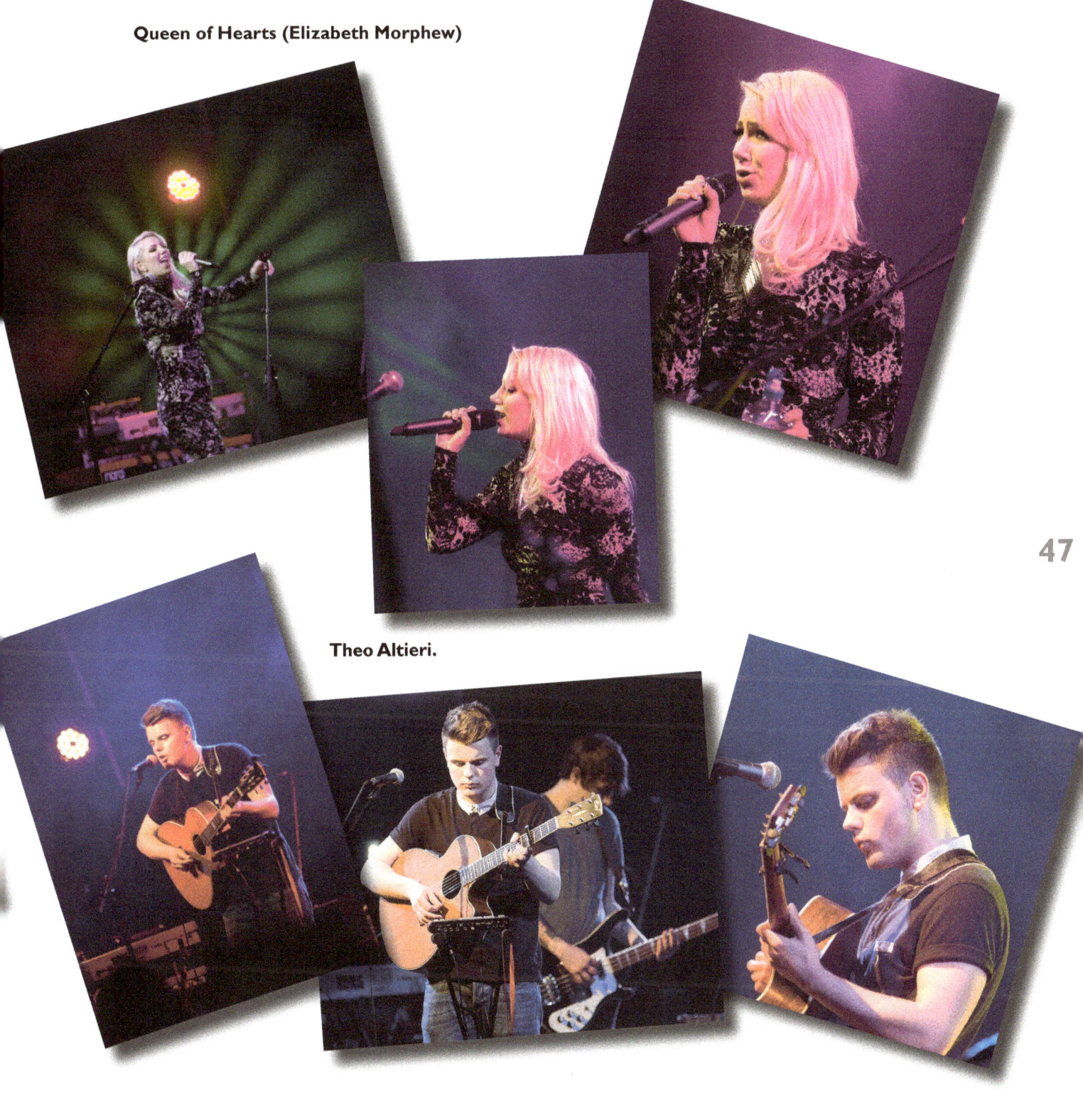

Jamie Cullum

One of my first clients as a Picture Agency was PHH (now Arval) whose HQ is on Windmill Hill, and its MD was John Cullum, so in effect my following of his son Jamie has been for quite a long time.

As I was photographing him at the Jazz Festival in the Designer Outlet village, it was announced that he had signed a record deal with Sony.

Since then our paths have crossed several times. I photographed Jamie when he did a BBC Children in Need charity gig at the Apartment in Havelock Square, but most notably when he and then girlfriend but now wife Sophie Dahl put in an appearance in the Directors' Box at a Swindon Town game at the County Ground.

I think it's the only time I have had a football-related picture hit the diary pages, including a good showing in the Dempster Diary in the *Daily Mail*...

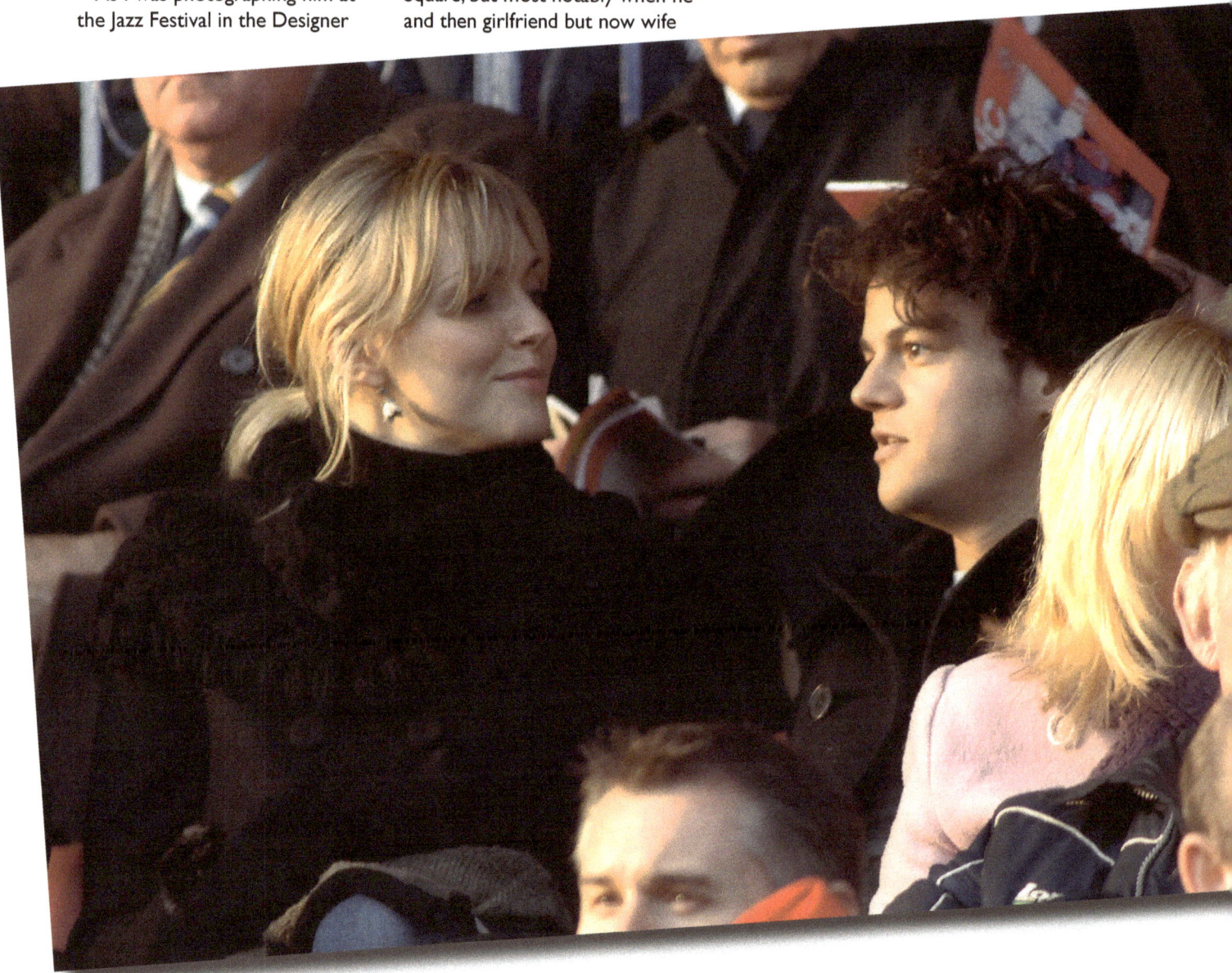

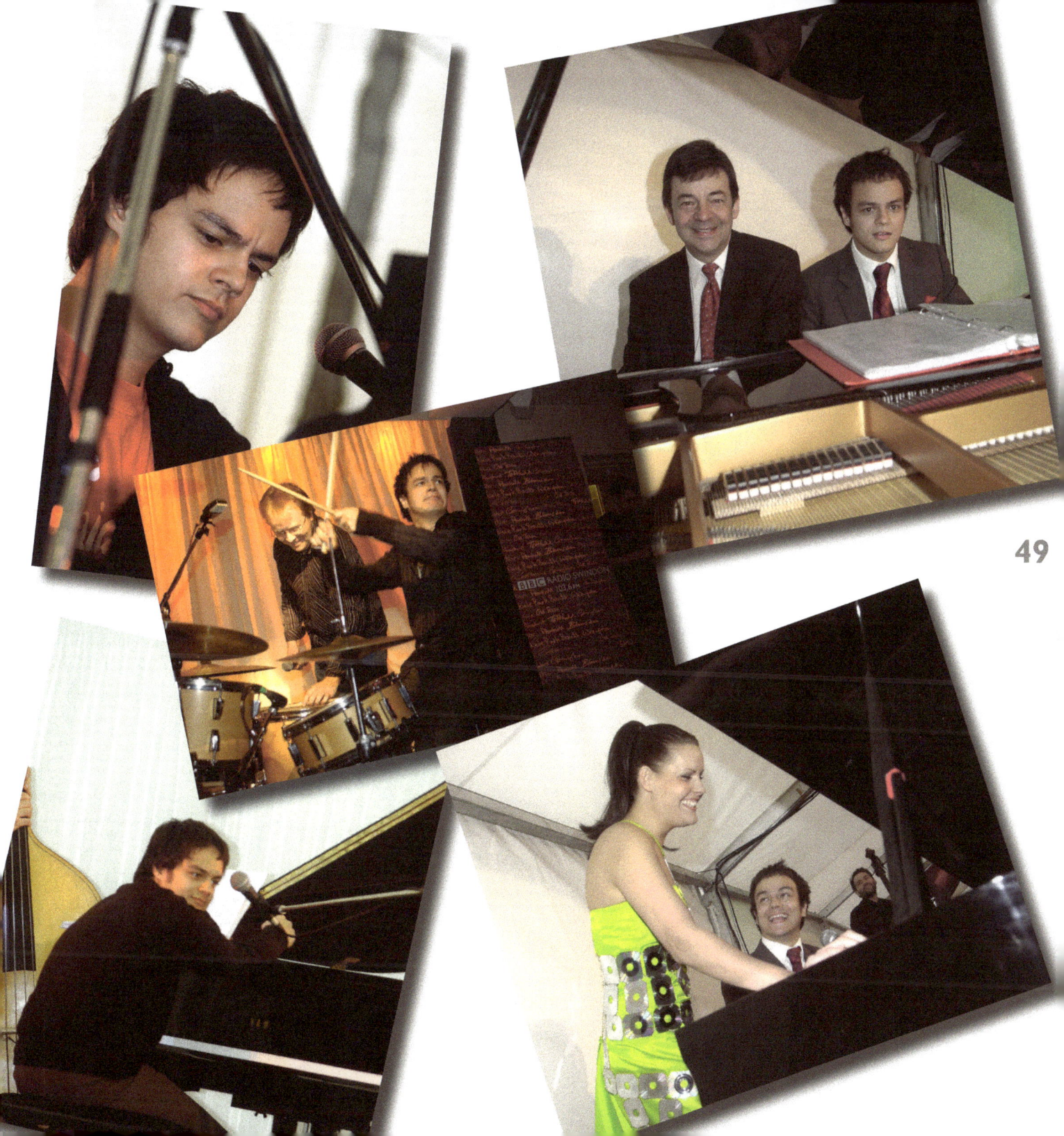

...In 2015, Jamie ran a competition for schools to enter, and the winner received the prize of his autographed old Yamaha grand piano.

As luck would have it, the winning school was Swindon's Commonweal School and, in due course, the piano arrived and was manhandled, with great care, by the moving company into the school's theatre.

After it was settled in, Jamie came to the school and undertook a workshop with some of the pupils.

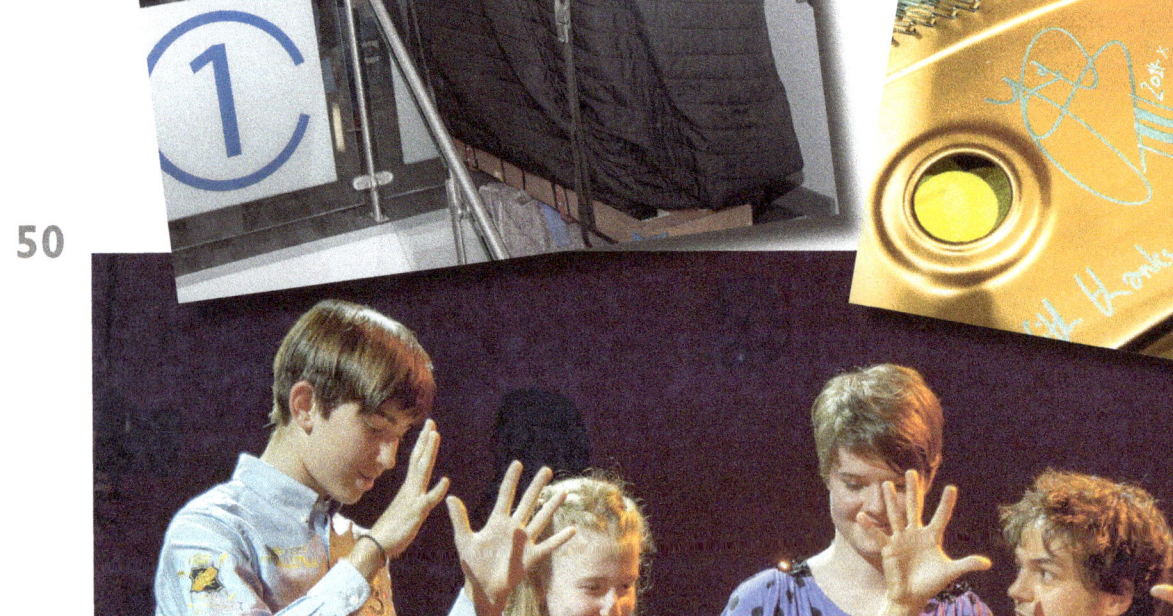

Swindon seems to produce blonde bombshells, with **Melinda Messenger** following in the stilettoed footsteps of Swindon's most famous daughter Diana Dors.

It was a quiet day in January 1997 when the then editor of the Sun picked up a copy of the Daily Star while doing his daily commute to the office in Wapping, London.

In that edition was a story about a Swindon model Melinda Messenger, who was starring in an advertisment for a double glazing company in Gloucester.

I am led to beleive that he phoned the picture desk from the car and said that he wanted that girl on Page 3 the next day.

The rest, as they say, is history.

Melinda went on to a modelling, acting and TV presentation career similar to...

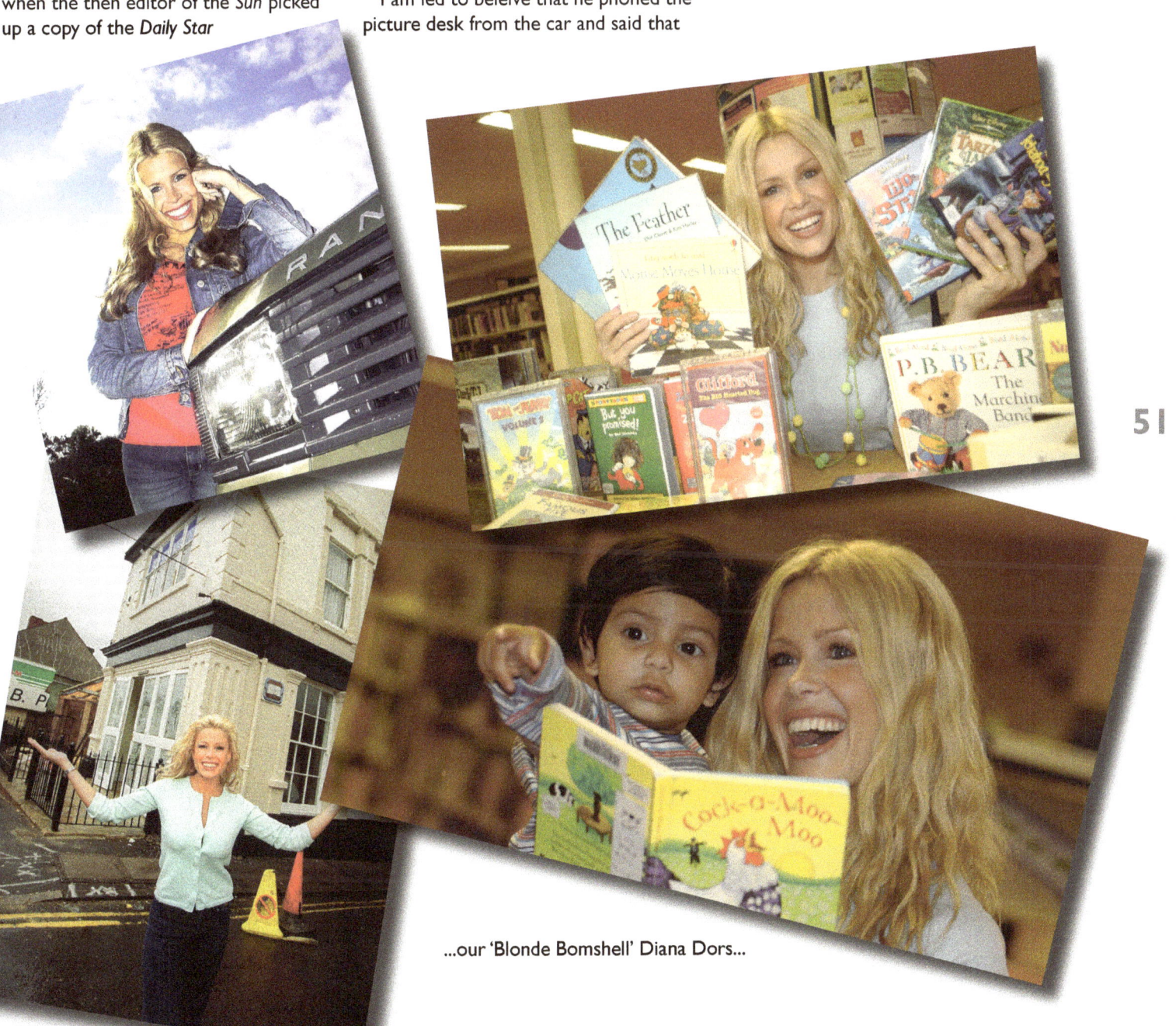

...our 'Blonde Bomshell' Diana Dors...

Of all the stars that Swindon has produced, **Diana Dors** must rate at the top of the list.

Diana Dors was born Diana Mary Fluck on 23rd October 1931 and made her name as a film actress and singer.

Diana's persona was as a blonde bombshell; the British Marilyn Monroe, starting her acting career in the 1947 film The Shop at Sly Corner, where they changed her name to Dors; her grandmothers maiden name.

She is quoted as saying,'They asked me to change my name. I suppose they were afraid that if my real name Diana Fluck was in lights and one of the lights blew ...'

Later in life she appeared on panel shows and even with the Two Ronnies in their comedy series 'The Worm that Turned', which incidently was filmed in my home town of Dursley.

I photographed Diana on one of her last visits to the town where she opened the Princess Margaret Hospital Fete on 21st August 1982.

My colleague Sarah Johnson photographed her in 1983, opening the Swindon Ideal Home Show at the Oasis; where she cut the ribbon to open the event with close friend and Mayor of Swindon at the time Cllr Jim Masters.

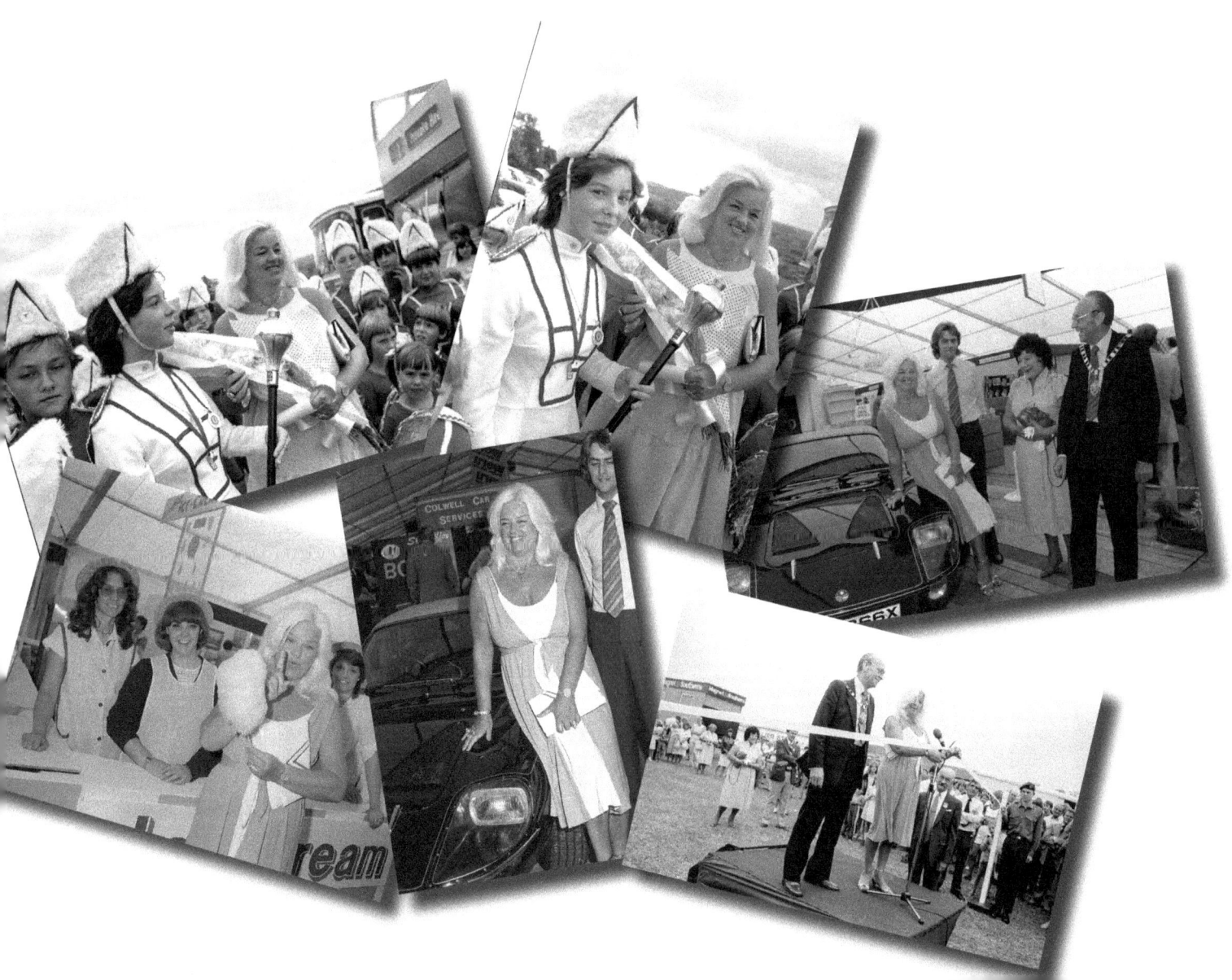

On 14th January 2017, *Swindon Heritage* magazine unveiled a Blue Plaque to Diana on the houses that were the Haven Nursing Home in Kent Road, where Diana was born.

The scene was set with Diana's bright pink American vintage Cadillac parked outside the house. A large crowd gathered, blocking the road and causing traffic to divert.

It was then up to her son Jason and Diana's granddaughter Ruby Dors-Lake to pull the cord and remove the blue cover over the nationally-recognised Blue Plaque to comemorate Diana and her contribution to Swindon.

My picture of the car outside the house made Picture of the Day in the *Telegraph* newspaper.

The family were supposed to go over to Shaw Ridge to see the statue of the superstar, but, due to unforeseen circumstances, that was called off...

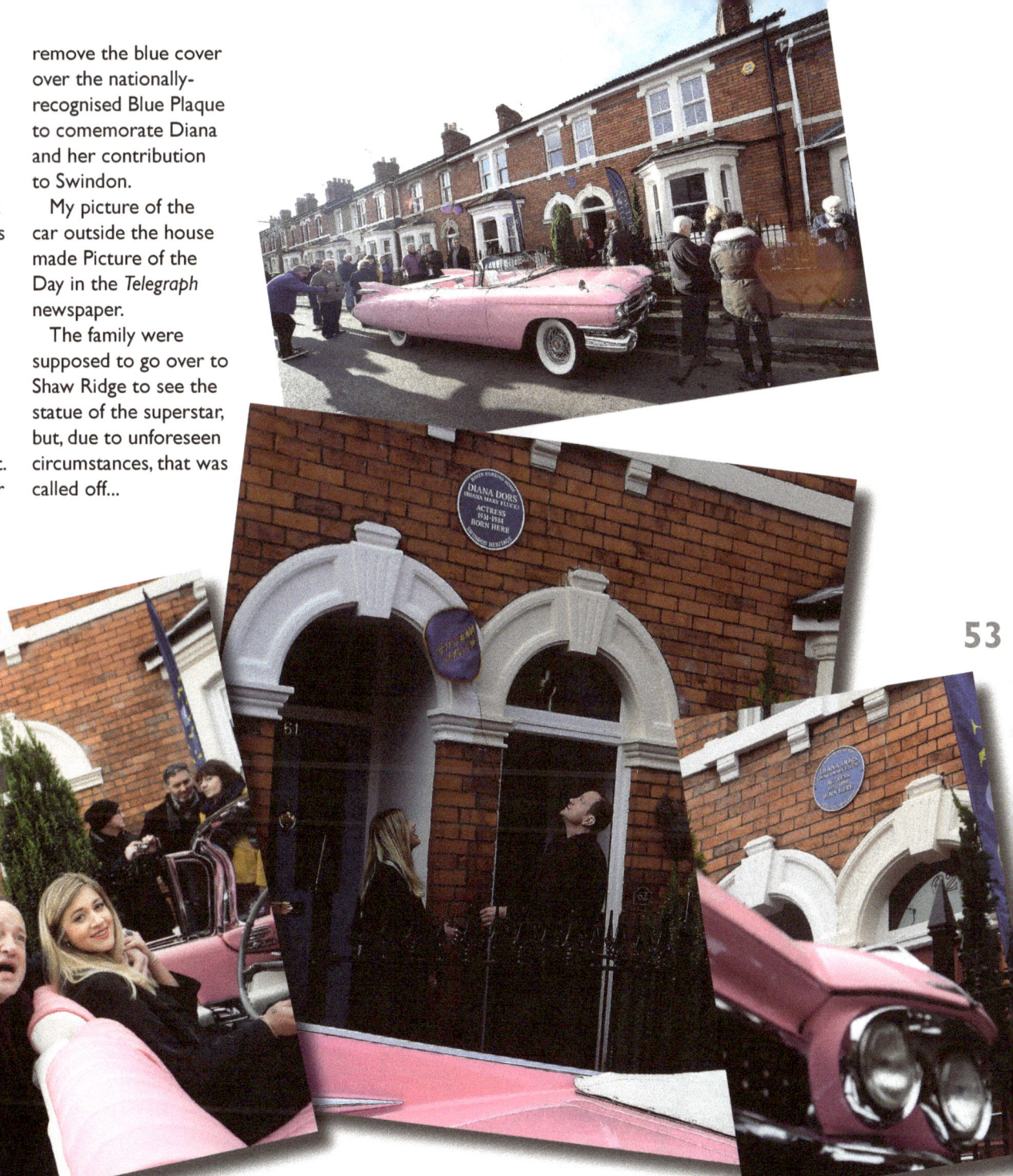

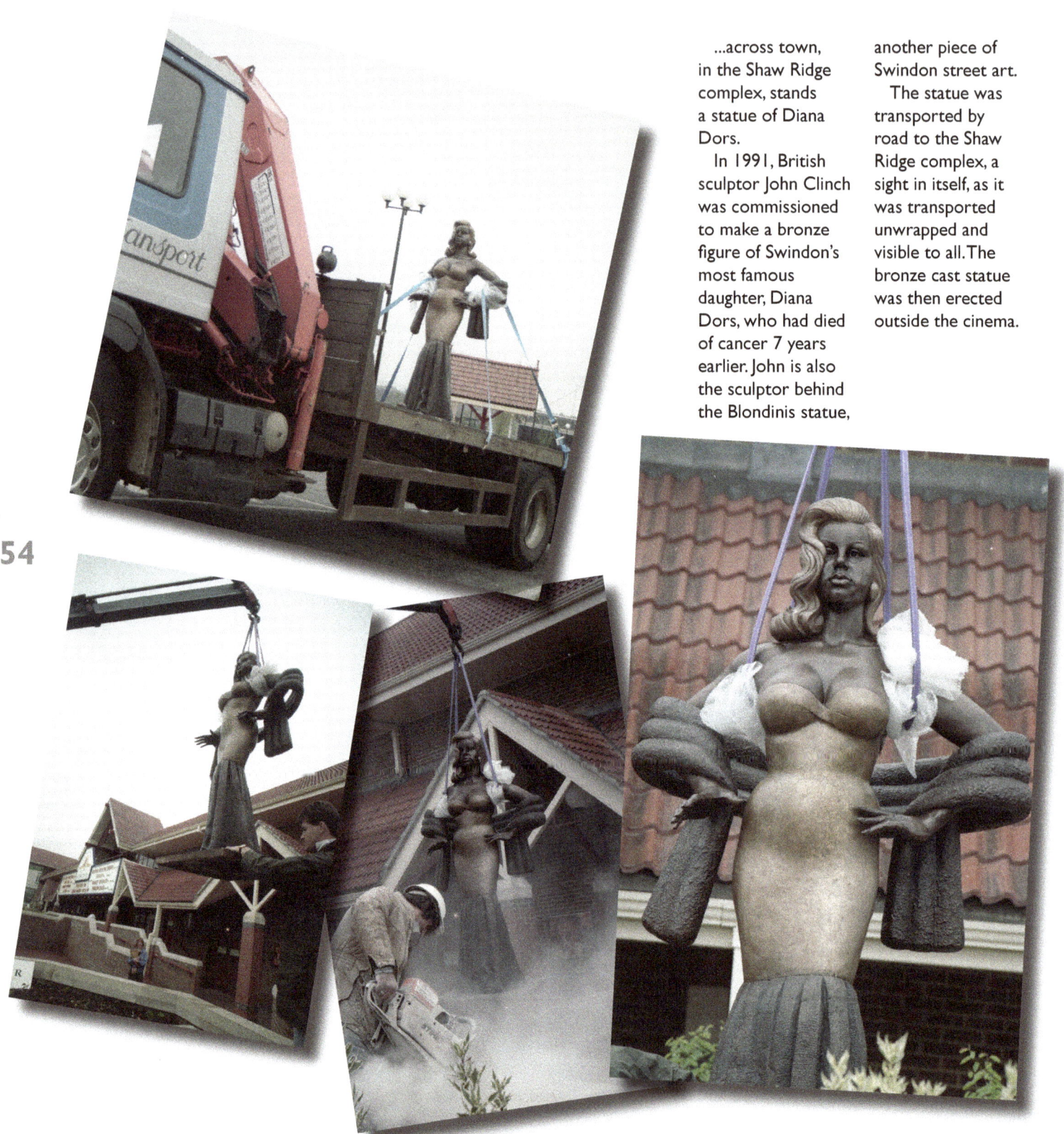

...across town, in the Shaw Ridge complex, stands a statue of Diana Dors.

In 1991, British sculptor John Clinch was commissioned to make a bronze figure of Swindon's most famous daughter, Diana Dors, who had died of cancer 7 years earlier. John is also the sculptor behind the Blondinis statue, another piece of Swindon street art.

The statue was transported by road to the Shaw Ridge complex, a sight in itself, as it was transported unwrapped and visible to all. The bronze cast statue was then erected outside the cinema.

A week later, when the dust from the cutters had settled, and with the help of several famous names from the world of entertainment including David Puttnam, the statue was unveiled by; yes... Jason and a very tiny Ruby.

Jason died on Sept 15th 2019.

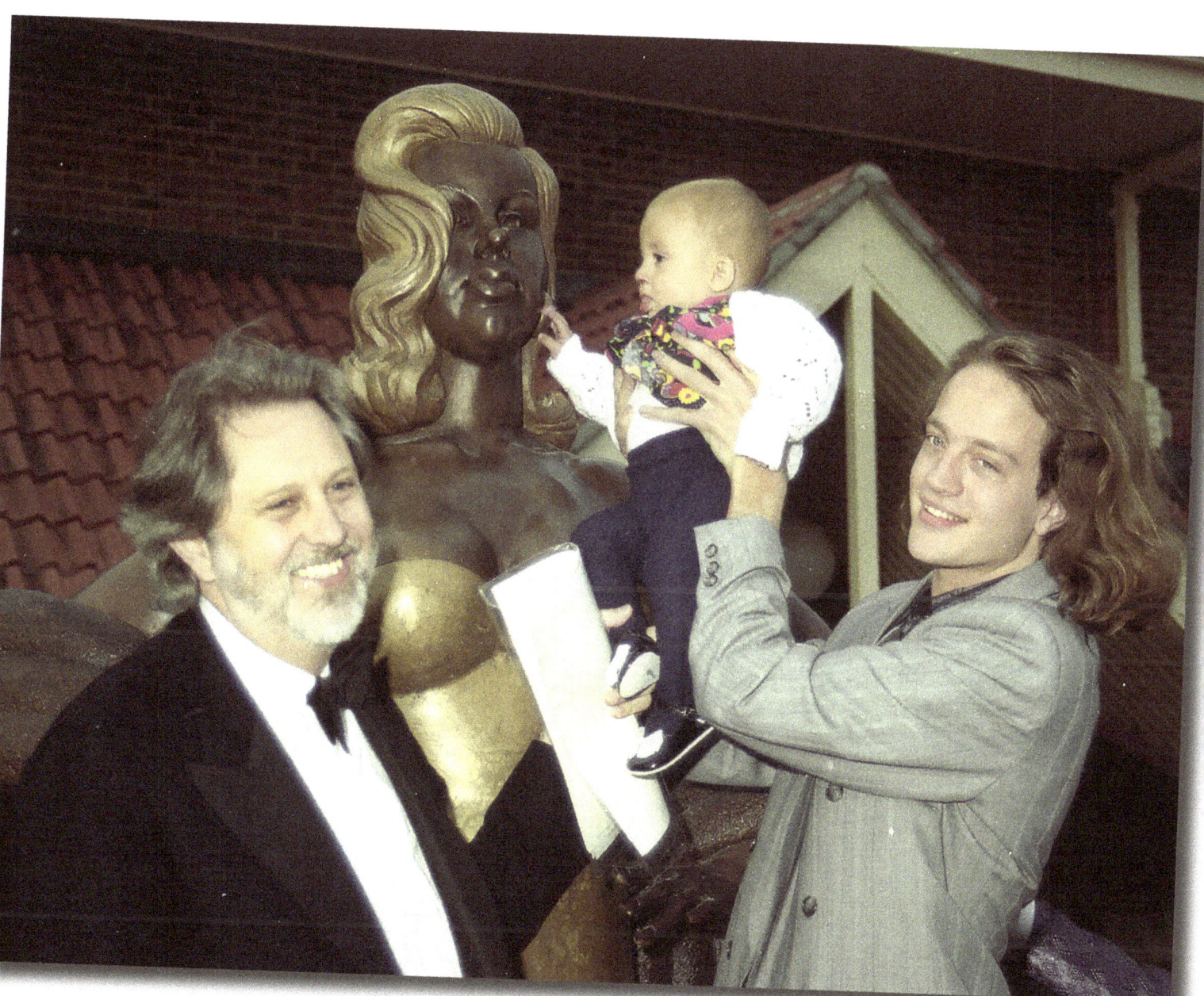

Diana featured in a Ken White mural in the Brunel Centre and Old Town....

Swindon's cultural fame extends beyond music and the stage; it flies high throughout the world.

Swindon artist **Ken White** is synonymous with Swindon's cultural heritage.

His most famous work, the Flying Red Lady, has adorned the Virgin Atlantic fleet of aircrafts, and many Virgin stores throughout the world. This also takes us back to a Miss Thamesdown, Anna Dinning, who worked for Virgin Atlantic as flight crew.

Ken White started out working in the Rail Works, and progressed to the carriage works in the signwriting section, He attended Swindon Art College with the likes of Gilbert O'Sullivan and Rick Davies of Supertramp, eventually leaving the works and taking up art full time.

My first recollection of Ken White was when I had to photograph him working on the St. George and the Dragon mural near where the Bruce Street bridges are now.

He was also responsible for the mural that circumnavigated the walkway in the Brunel Centre, where he depicted David Murray John, Brunel and Diana Dors. I recently found images of him working on a mural in the Oasis Leasure Centre too.

The Whale Bridge mural and the Prospect mural, which depicts many of the Swindon heroes, are still visible.

Ken still paints from his Old Town studio, where the boy from the Rail Works records life as it was 'inside', and his contribution to Swindon art scene has now been acknowledged with an exhibition in his home town's Museum and Art Gallery, as well as pictures in the place he worked; the STEAM Museum and Designer Outlet Village, which is housed in part of the old Rail Works.

Ken's work now stands alongside some of the great modern artists in Swindon's collection which is regarded as one of the finest in the country.

PS. He evens appears in a mural someone else painted...

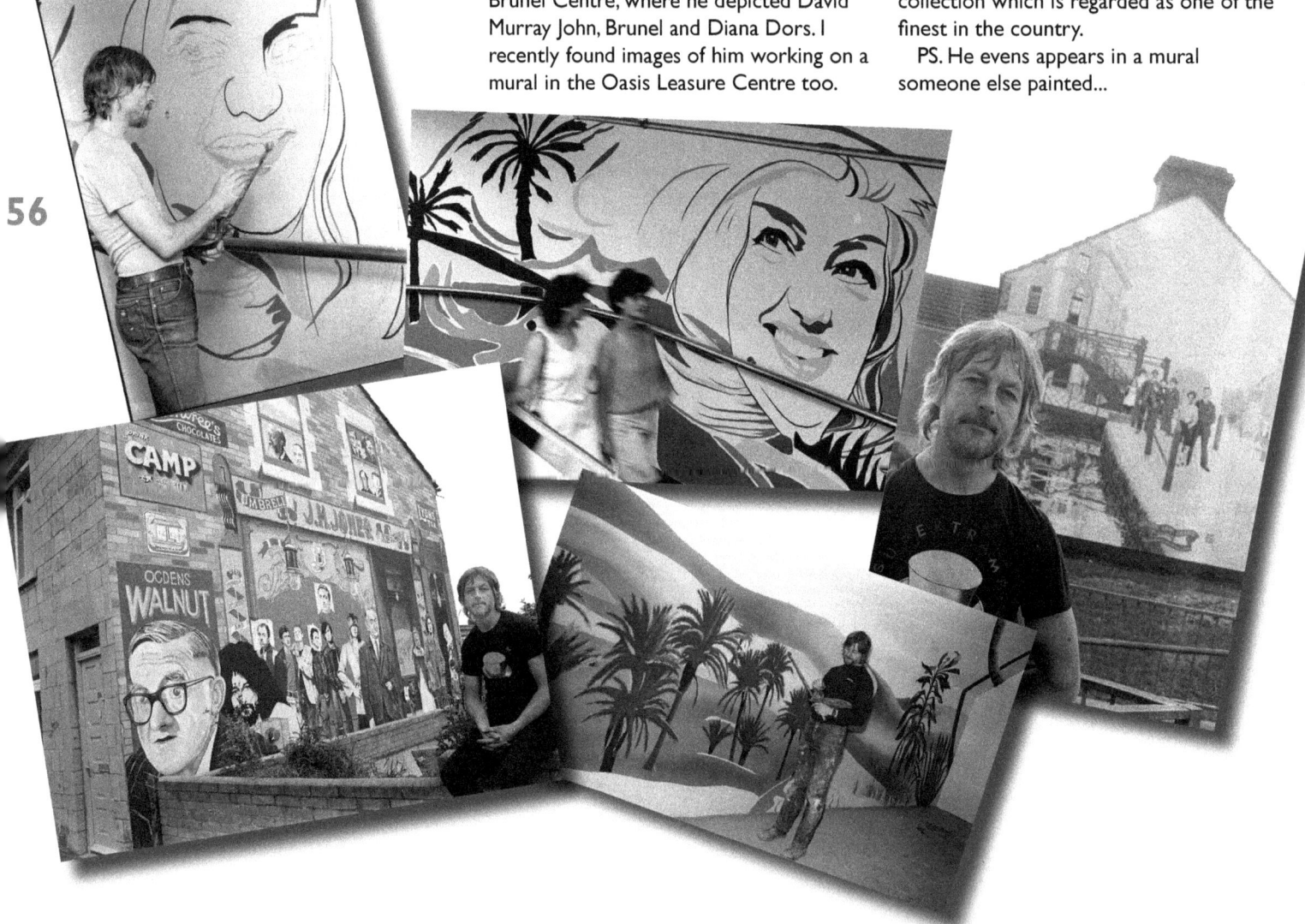

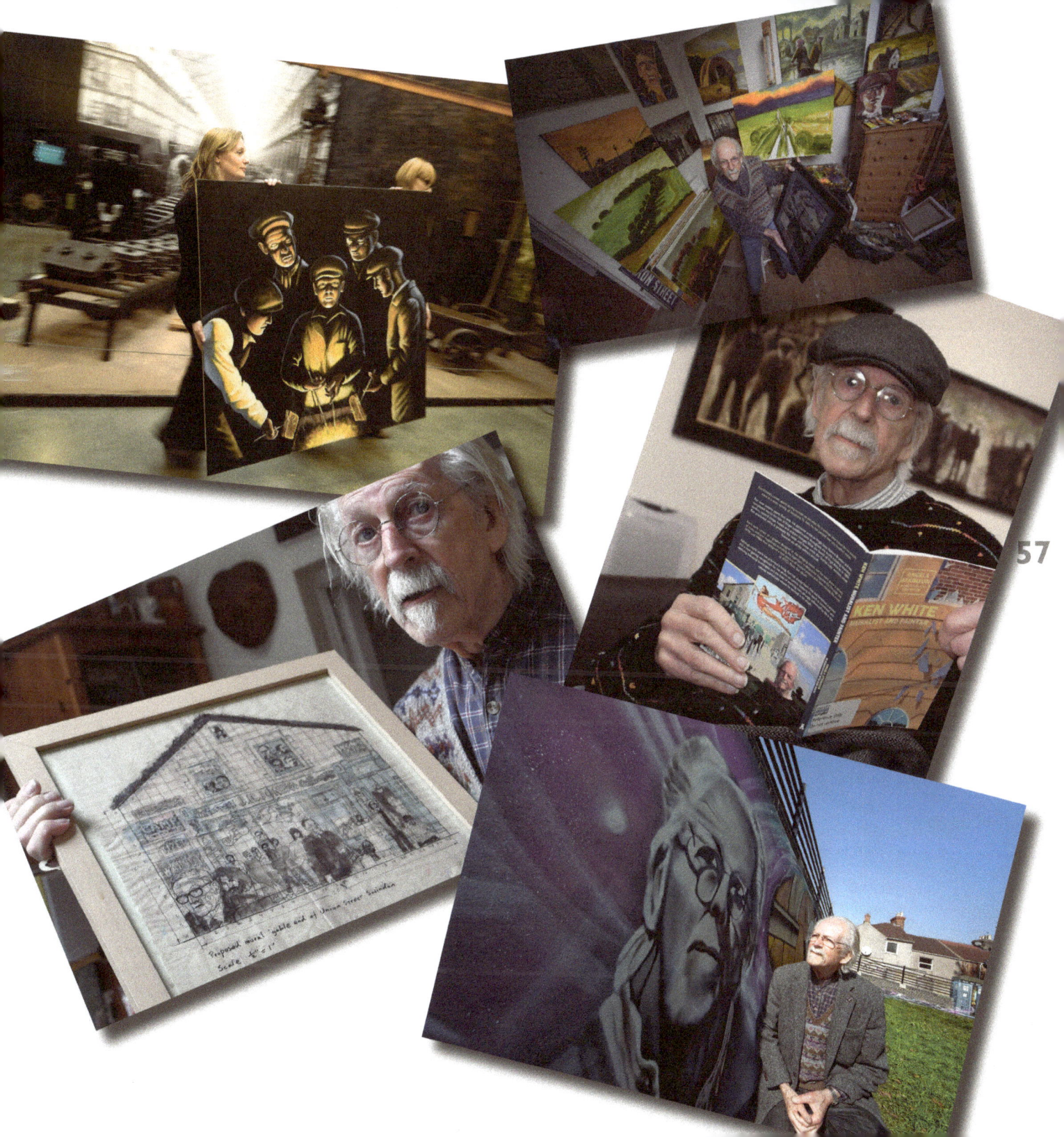

...One of the forgotton Swindonians is **Baron Marsh of Mannington** who unveiled a mural at the end of Iffley Road in 1982.

The mural celebrated the volunteering services in Swindon.

Lord Marsh was the son of William Marsh, a foundry worker from London, who worked in the Rail Works. Richard Marsh, MP for Greenwich, was the backbench MP responsible for the introduction of the forerunner to the Health and Safety at Work Act; the Offices, Shops and Railway Premises Act in 1960.

He served in the Harold Wilson government in 1964, in various ministerial positions including Minister of Transport. He went on to become Chairman of British Rail and Chairman of the Newspaper Publishers' Association (NPA).

In 1975, Baron Marsh's second wife Caroline died in a road accident in Spain in which the wife of broadcaster David Jacobs also lost her life; Marsh and Jacobs both survived the crash.

He died in 2011 in London aged 83.

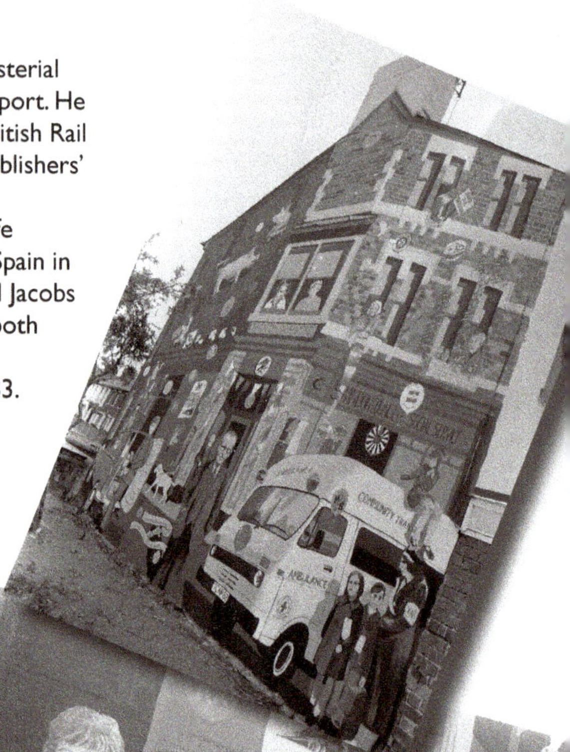

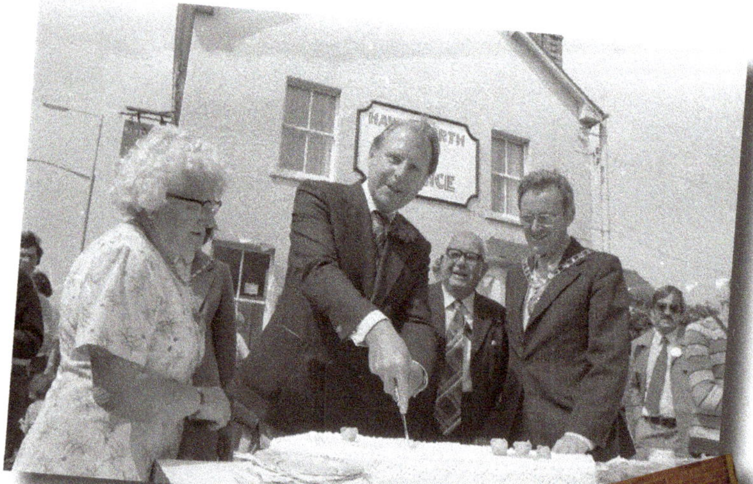

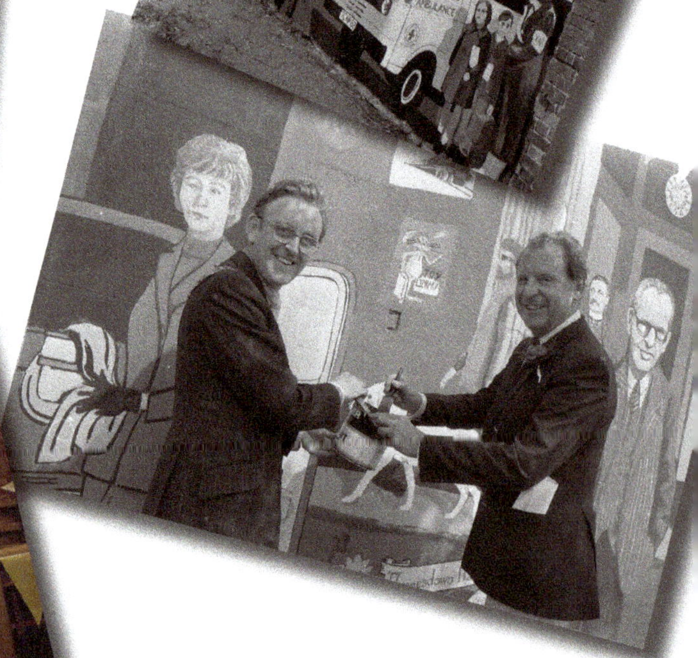

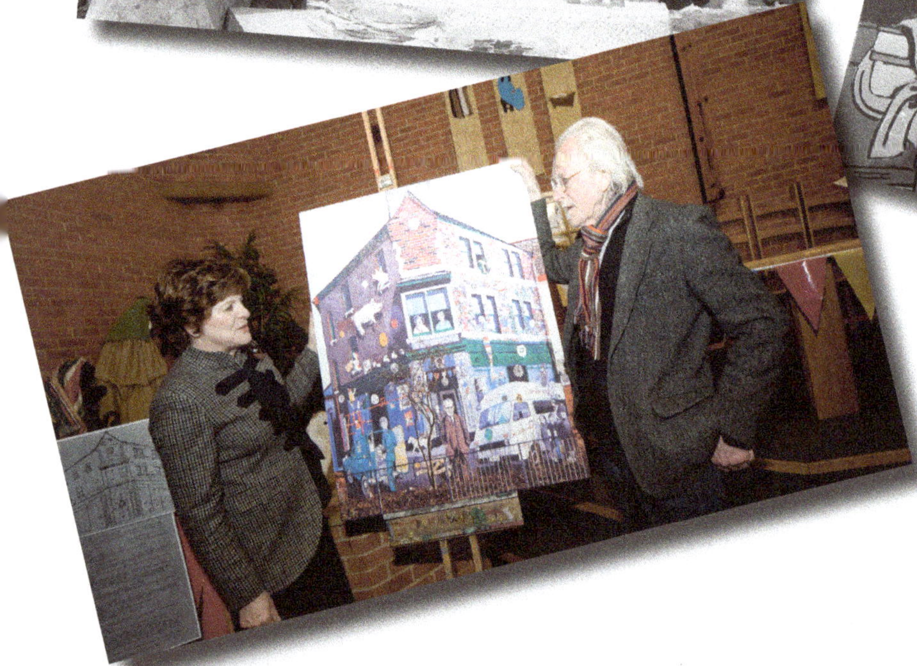

VAS or Voluntary Action Swindon, for which the mural was painted to celebrate their 50th year, celebrated their 80th year in 2012 with a party at the Pilgrim Centre and a visit from the Lord Lieutenant of Wiltshire, Mrs Sarah Rose Troughton, and muralist Ken White.

Murals are street art just as statues are...

Swindon is blessed with Street Art; not only the Diana Dors statue, but another John Clinch work the Blondinis, which coincidentally was possibly the last project carried out in the Rail Works, are among Swindon's art heritage.

Originally, the statue of the Blondinis performing stood in Wharf Green, but when the area was redeveloped and modernised they removed them, and eventually put them in the St. Mark's Park, where they perform alongside the tennis players to this day...

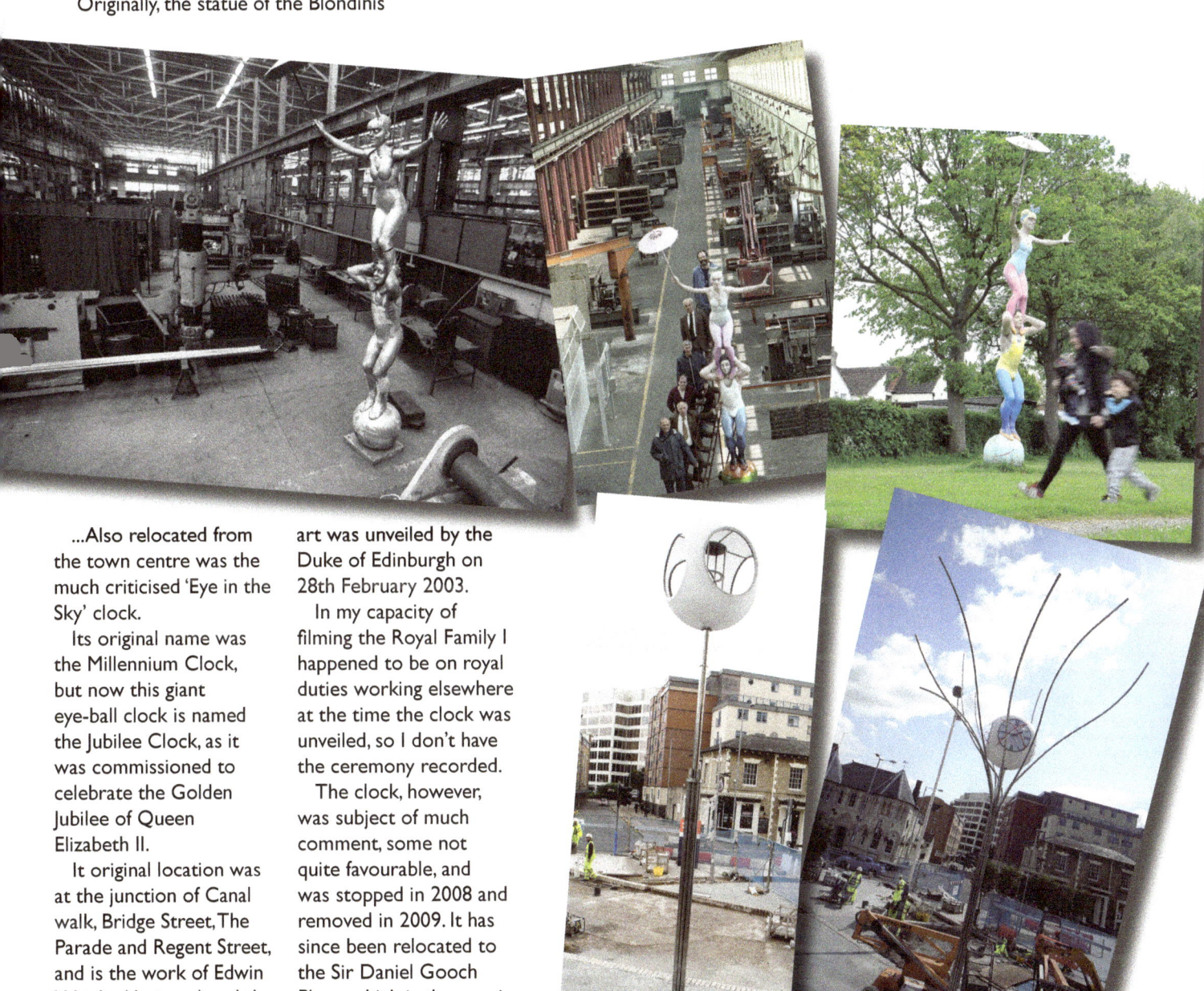

...Also relocated from the town centre was the much criticised 'Eye in the Sky' clock.

Its original name was the Millennium Clock, but now this giant eye-ball clock is named the Jubilee Clock, as it was commissioned to celebrate the Golden Jubilee of Queen Elizabeth II.

It original location was at the junction of Canal walk, Bridge Street, The Parade and Regent Street, and is the work of Edwin Wright (designer) and the Cumbria Clock Company.

This modern work of art was unveiled by the Duke of Edinburgh on 28th February 2003.

In my capacity of filming the Royal Family I happened to be on royal duties working elsewhere at the time the clock was unveiled, so I don't have the ceremony recorded.

The clock, however, was subject of much comment, some not quite favourable, and was stopped in 2008 and removed in 2009. It has since been relocated to the Sir Daniel Gooch Place, which is the area in front of the station....

....I don't supose there are many pieces of street art that have had two royal unveilings, but the 'Eye in the Sky' Station Clock has, in as much as the Duke of Edinbrugh unveiled it in the town centre; and Camilla, Duchess of Cornwall named the Daniel Gooch Place, where the clock now stands on 20th October 2016...

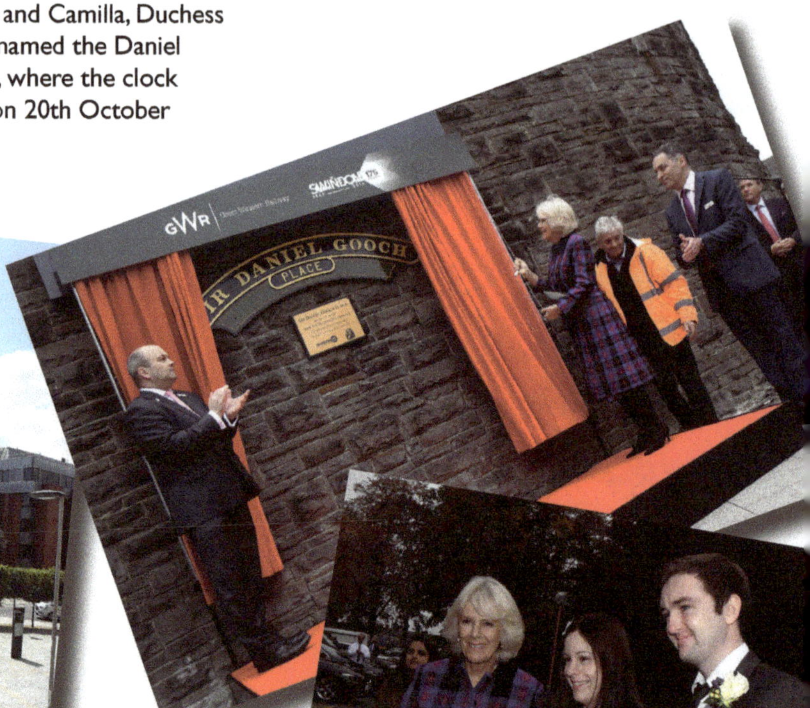

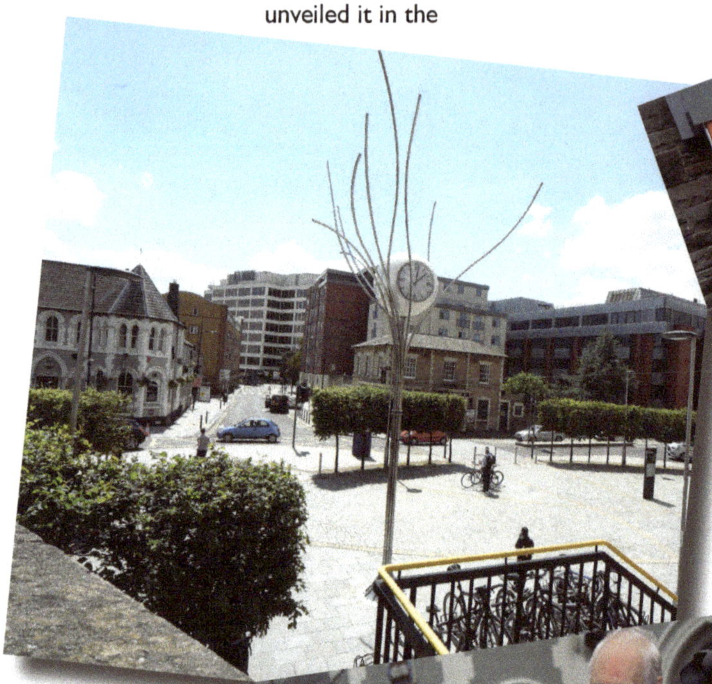

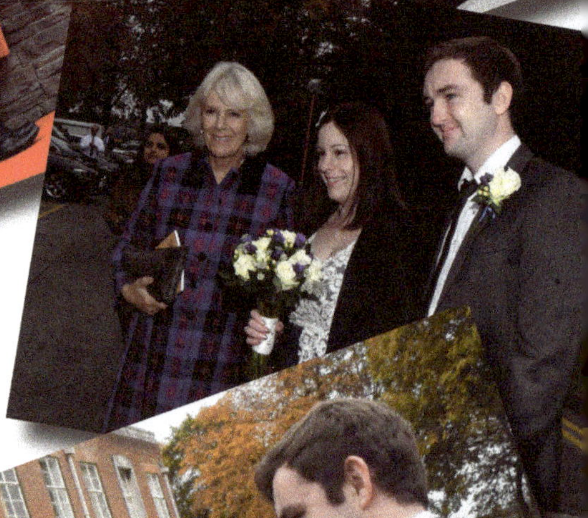

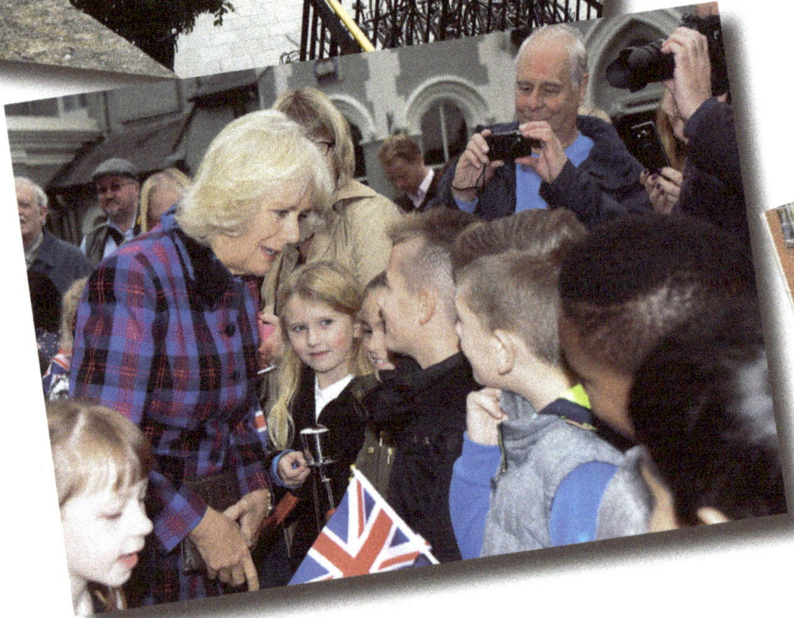

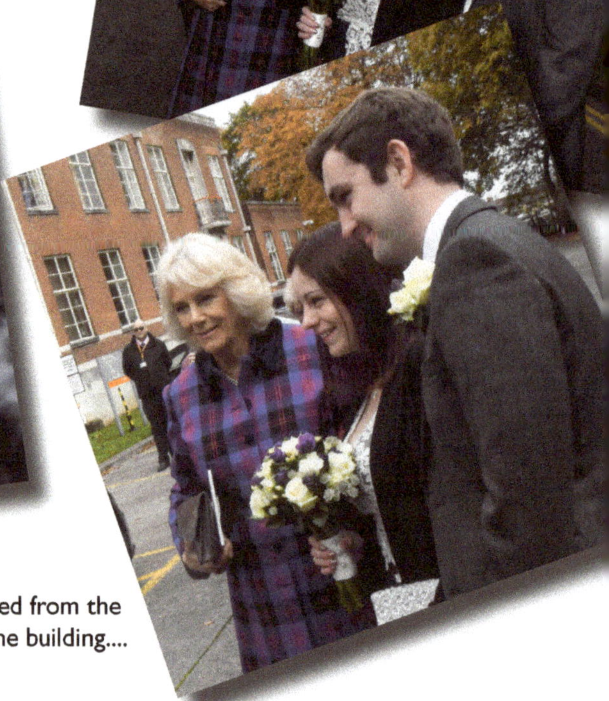

....Camilla then went on to pay a visit to the Council Offices in Euclid Street where she photobombed a wedding party that had just emerged from the Registry Office in the building....

...The Duchess of Cornwall has a house at Lacock on the Wilts and Berks Canal, so it's not surprising therefore that she's patron of the Canal Trust.

With this patronage in mind, she opened the stretch of canal that runs from Kingshill to the new Wichelstowe development and Waitrose store on a very wet day in July 2015...

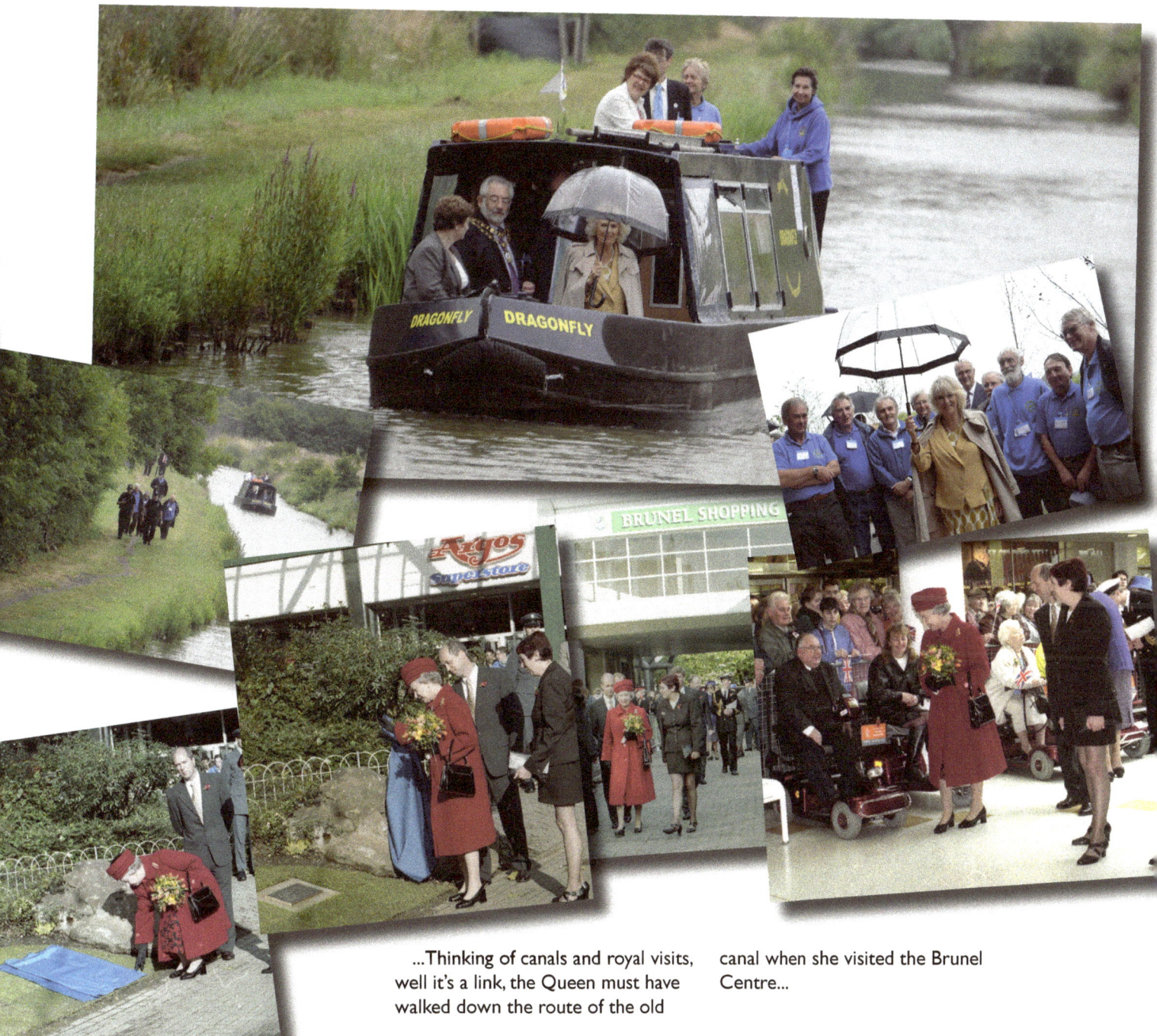

...Thinking of canals and royal visits, well it's a link, the Queen must have walked down the route of the old canal when she visited the Brunel Centre...

...The Queen, on another visit, opened the impressive Motorola factory on St. Andrew's Ridge at Blunsdon. One young man broke through the barriers and asked Her Majesty for an autograph, but royal protocol doesn't allow the monarch to undertake such showbiz activities as that and therefore there was a polite, 'I'm afraid not.' to the request.

The Motorola building came to the notice of a passing film researcher, and subsequently formed part of the James Bond film 'The World is not Enough' where it was transformed into a 'King Oil' plant at the centre of 'M's kidnap...

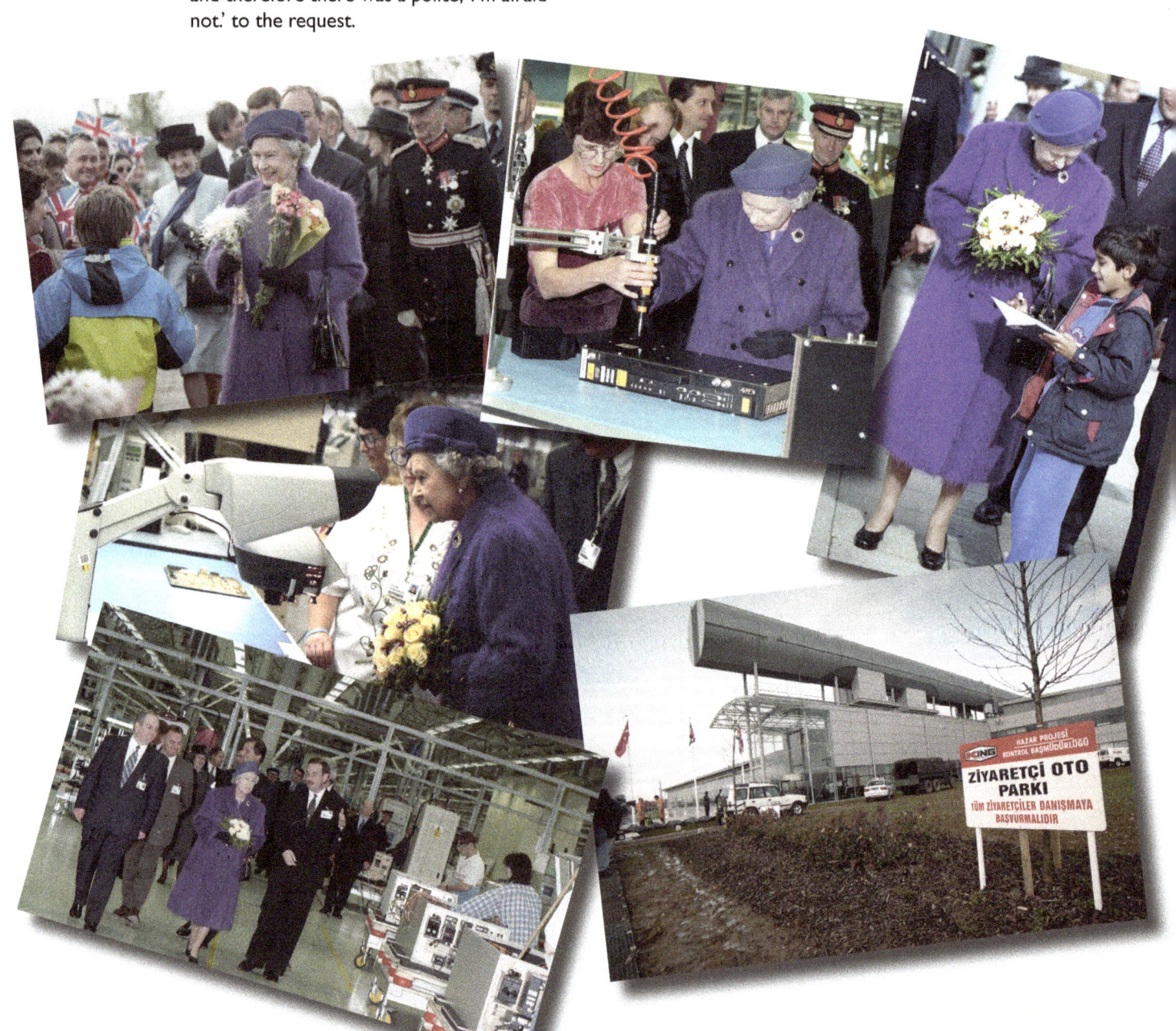

...The photocall for the **007** movie was early and, being local, I turned up early; which sort of confused the security staff on the gate. I was directed to a car park at the rear of the building, and had to walk to the press tent which was situated in front of it.

Our press conference with Pierce Brosnan, Sophie Marceau and Michael Wilson went to plan, and I joined the other photographers as they adjourned to the catering tent for a quick bite to eat. This also allowed them to process and send their pictures.

This was at the start of the digital era, and many of the snappers had digital cameras of some sort, so processing film was, in most cases, not needed.

I was still using film, so I decided to return to the office to process and send the images from there.

I discovered I had been parked in the wrong car park, as it seemed all the other press cars were alongside the catering tent, but mine was some way off round the back of the plant, which meant I had to cross the set to get to it.

On reaching the area in which they were filming, I noticed that Dame Judy Dench and some of the other stars of the film were being made ready for a take.

The part of the film they were shooting involved a helicopter which was airborne, so there was no problem with the sound of my shutter firing affecting the filming.

Dame Judy had her make-up completed; and then, with Colin Salmon and several other actors, she walked over to Pierce Brosnan at the entrance to the plant. Needless to say, I took several rolls of film of this, before departing with my exclusives.

Just a note to add to this photocall. There were two helicopters, one flying and one on a scaffold tower which too had its engines idling.

That chopper was being used for the jump scene where Pierce and Sophie jump from the helicopter onto the mountain in Azerbaijan. The jump was recorded in Swindon and with the aid of a 'green screen' made to look like it was taken in Azerbaijan.

Technology!!!

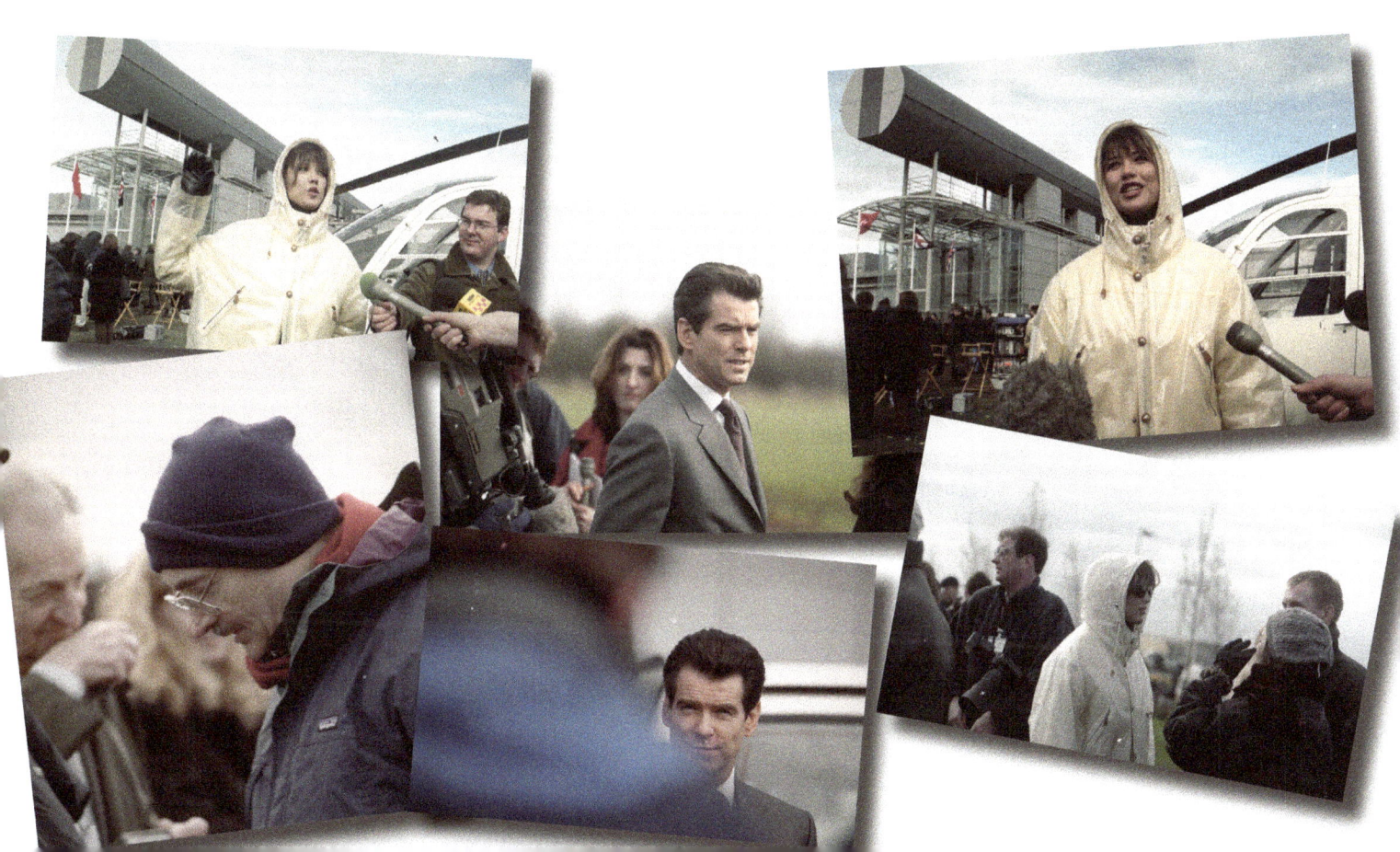

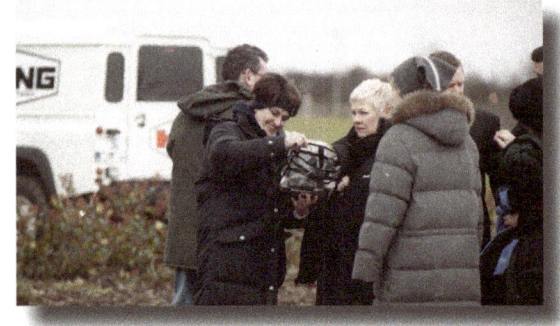
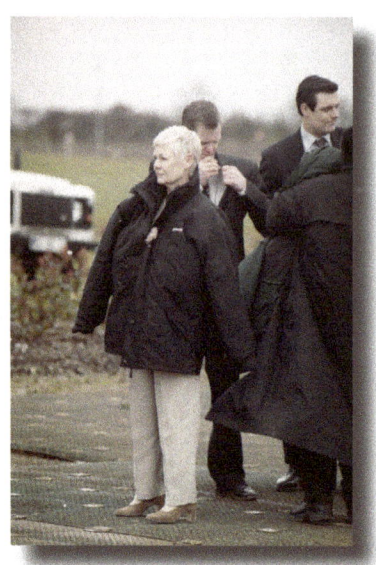
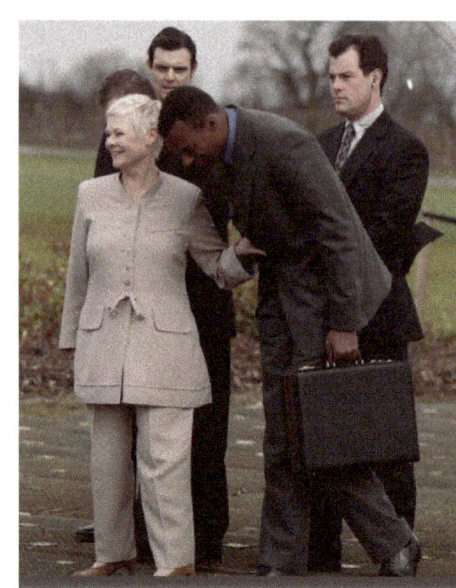
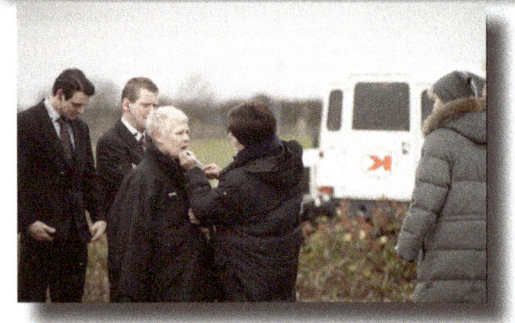
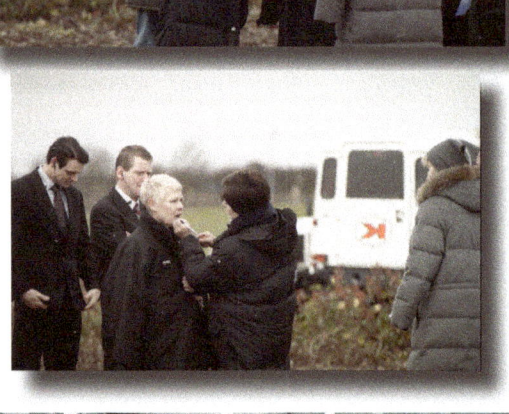
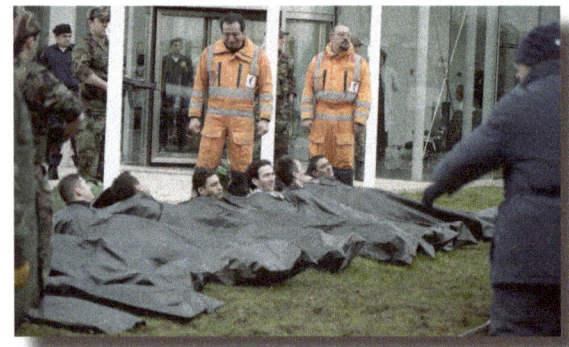
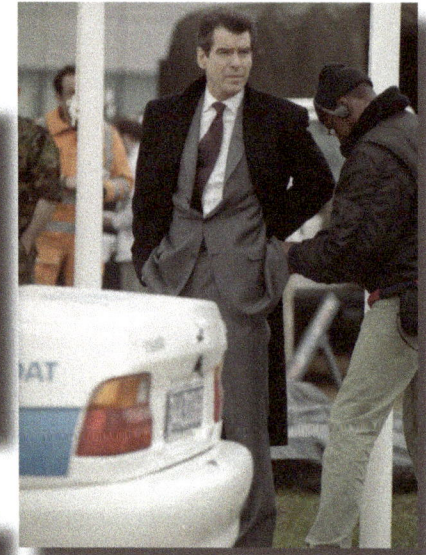
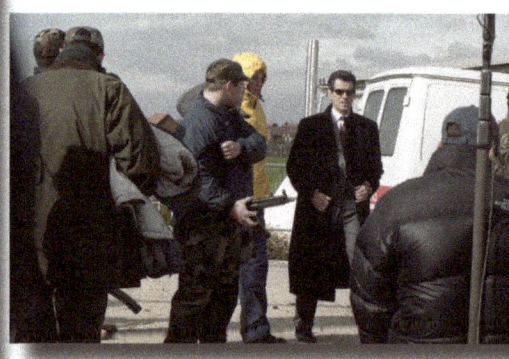
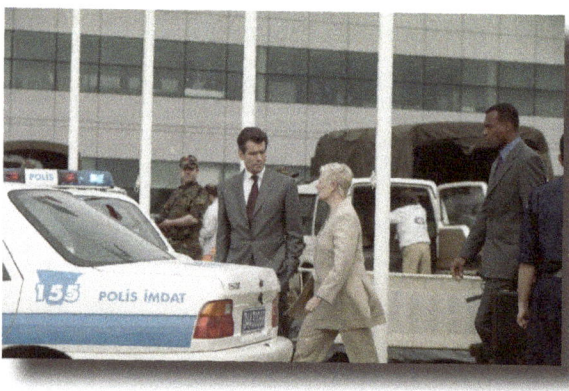
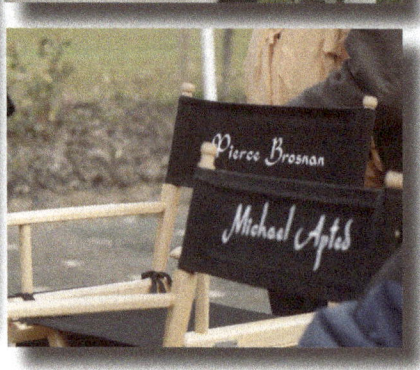
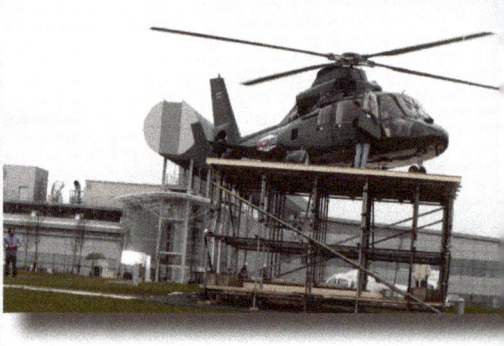

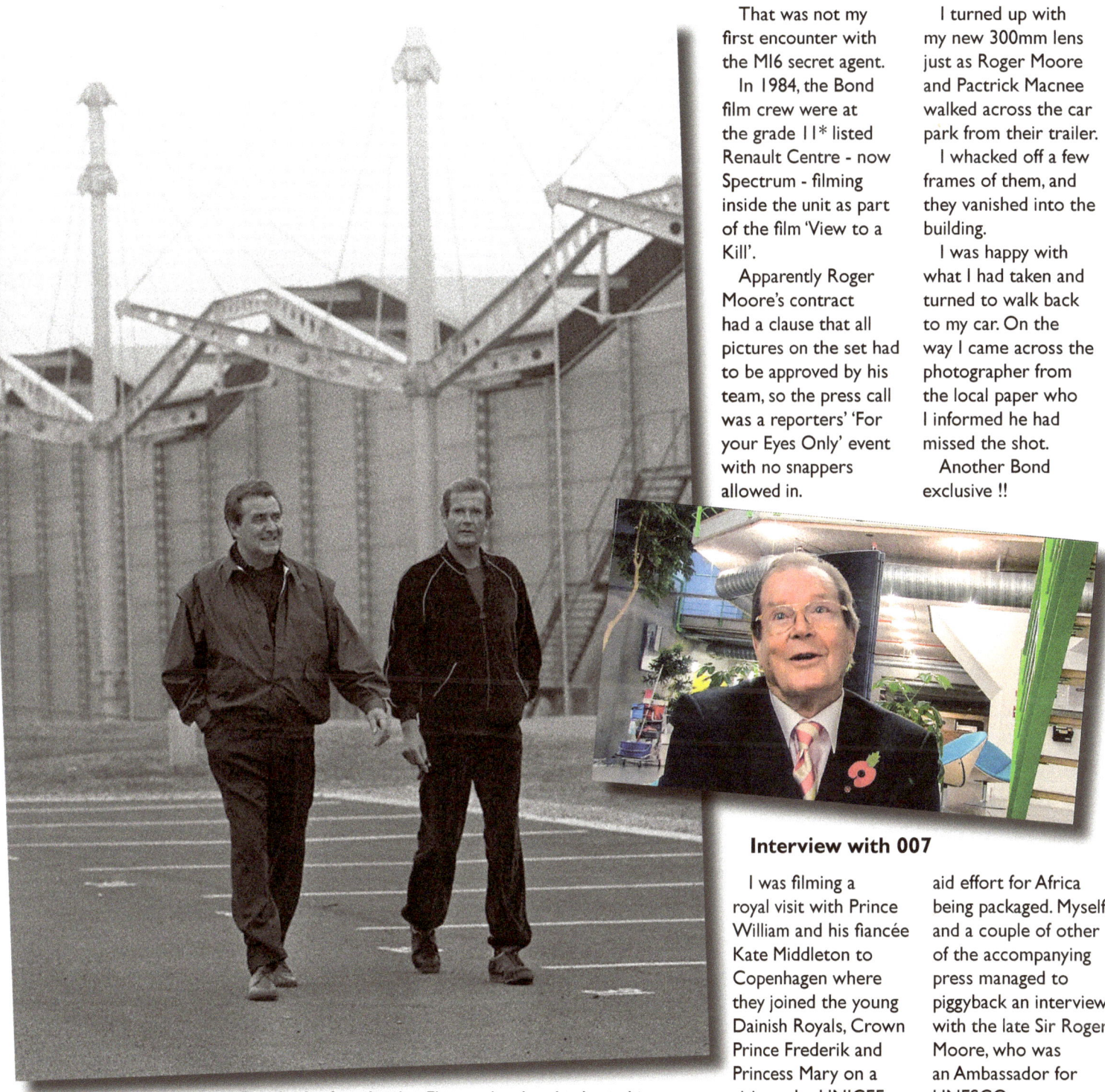

Beside the fact that Ian Fleming lived and is buried in in Sevenhampton near Highworth, Swindon has another connection with 007...

That was not my first encounter with the MI6 secret agent.

In 1984, the Bond film crew were at the grade II* listed Renault Centre - now Spectrum - filming inside the unit as part of the film 'View to a Kill'.

Apparently Roger Moore's contract had a clause that all pictures on the set had to be approved by his team, so the press call was a reporters' 'For your Eyes Only' event with no snappers allowed in.

I turned up with my new 300mm lens just as Roger Moore and Pactrick Macnee walked across the car park from their trailer.

I whacked off a few frames of them, and they vanished into the building.

I was happy with what I had taken and turned to walk back to my car. On the way I came across the photographer from the local paper who I informed he had missed the shot.

Another Bond exclusive !!

Interview with 007

I was filming a royal visit with Prince William and his fiancée Kate Middleton to Copenhagen where they joined the young Dainish Royals, Crown Prince Frederik and Princess Mary on a visit to the UNICEF warehouse to see the aid effort for Africa being packaged. Myself and a couple of other of the accompanying press managed to piggyback an interview with the late Sir Roger Moore, who was an Ambassador for UNESCO.

...As the stars flock to Swindon...

During the late nineties and early two thousands there was a shop that was the centre of celebrity signings.

The late Steve Goss ran **Infinitely Better** in the Brunel Centre, and he held frequent signings where film and TV celebrities would meet their fans and sign autographs for them.

Bond Girls and Star Trek stars were the regular attractions.

Maud Adams (Man with the Golden Gun, Octopussy, and a cameo in View to a Kill)(opposite page) Britt Ekland, Caroline Monroe, Maryam d'Abo, Trina Parks, Gloria Hendry. were among the Bond girls with David Hedison from Licence to Kill and the SIFI Film The Fly representing the men to appear.

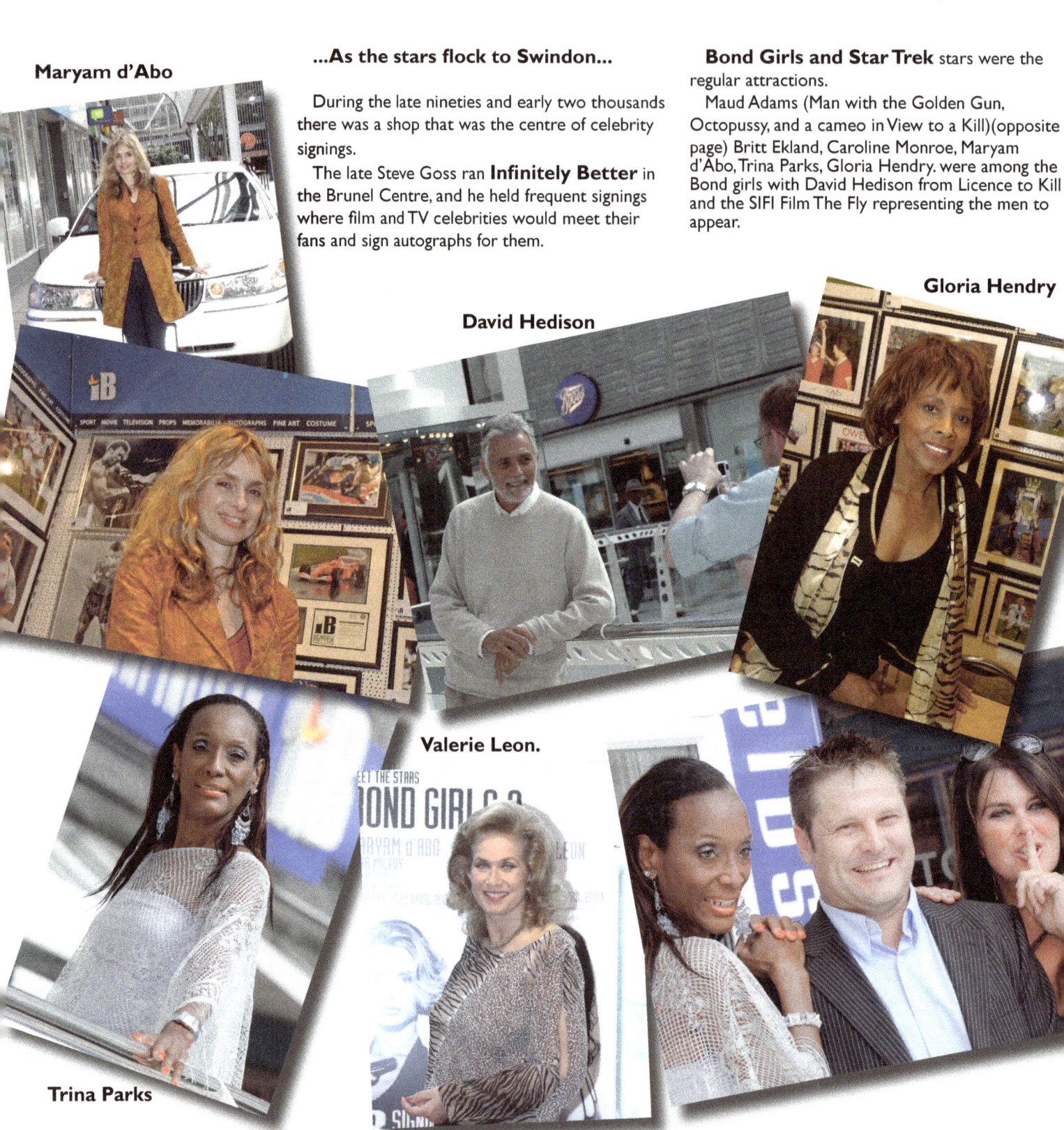

Maryam d'Abo

David Hedison

Gloria Hendry

Trina Parks

Valerie Leon.

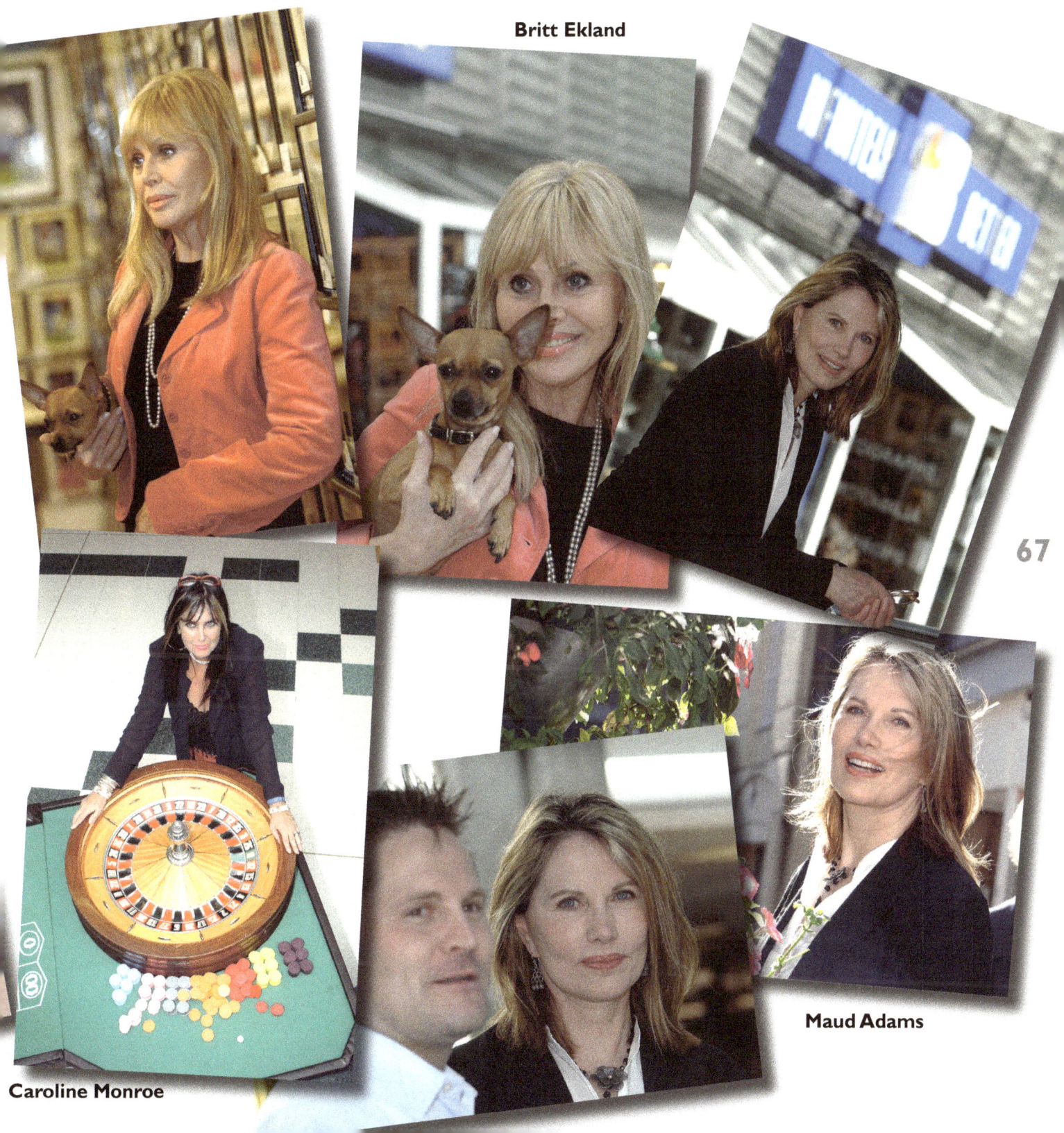

Britt Ekland

Caroline Monroe

Maud Adams

Stars of **Star Trek** Marina Sirtis, Dominic Keating and Alice Krige (the Borg Queen in Star Trek - First Contact film) transported, as did Nicole de Boer and Max Grodénchik from Deep Space 9 flew in to meet the fans; and Stargate didn't want to be left out so they also sent some of its cast on a couple of occasions. Peter Williams (Apophis) and Alexis Cruz (Shaara) of **Stargate SG-1** came.

Casts from horror movies were frequent attendees with Ingrid Pitt, Hellraisers and Kill Bill's David Carradine all showing up too.

On one occasion even some of the cast of **'Only Fools and Horses'** did a signing.

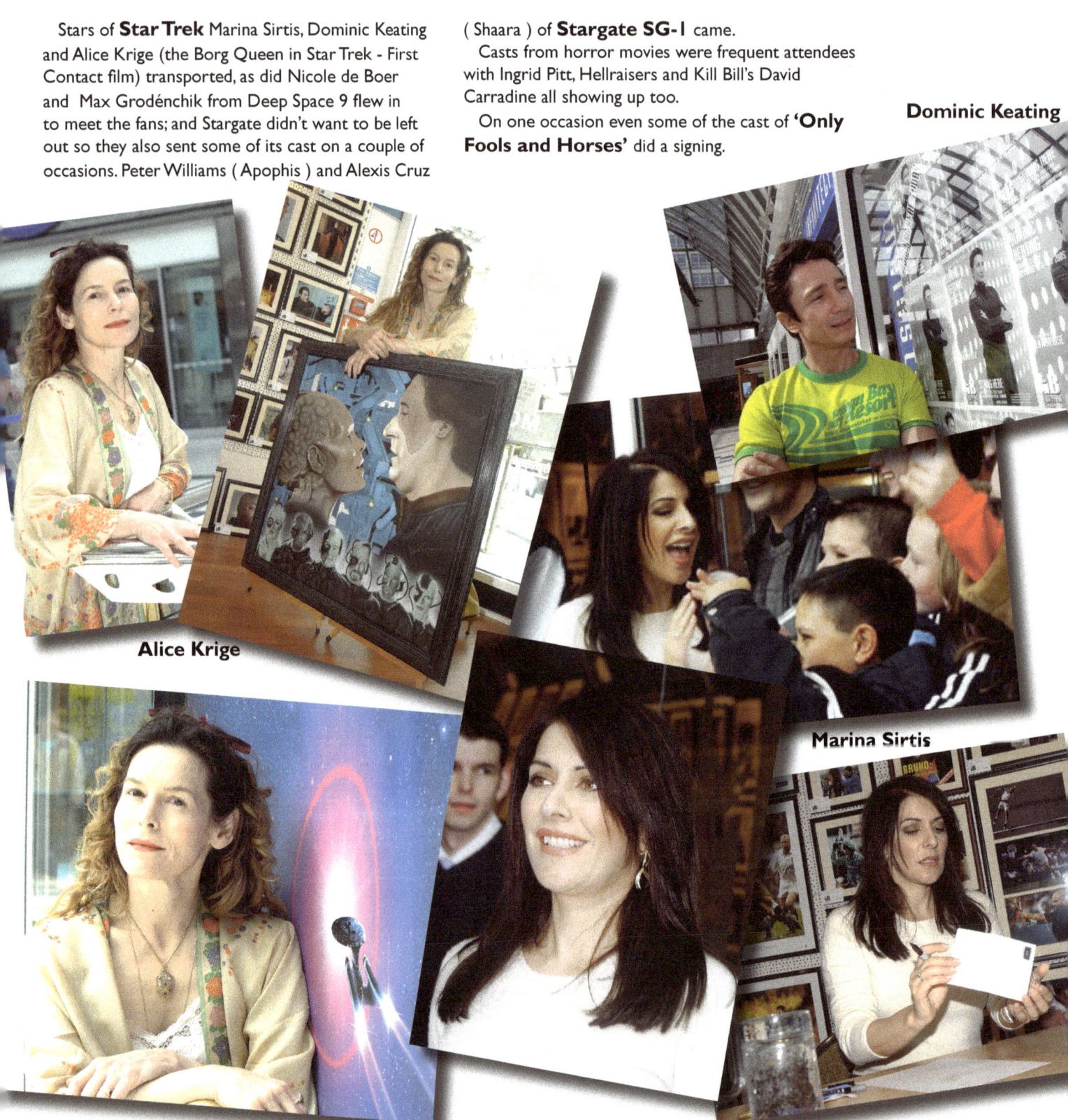

Alice Krige

Dominic Keating

Marina Sirtis

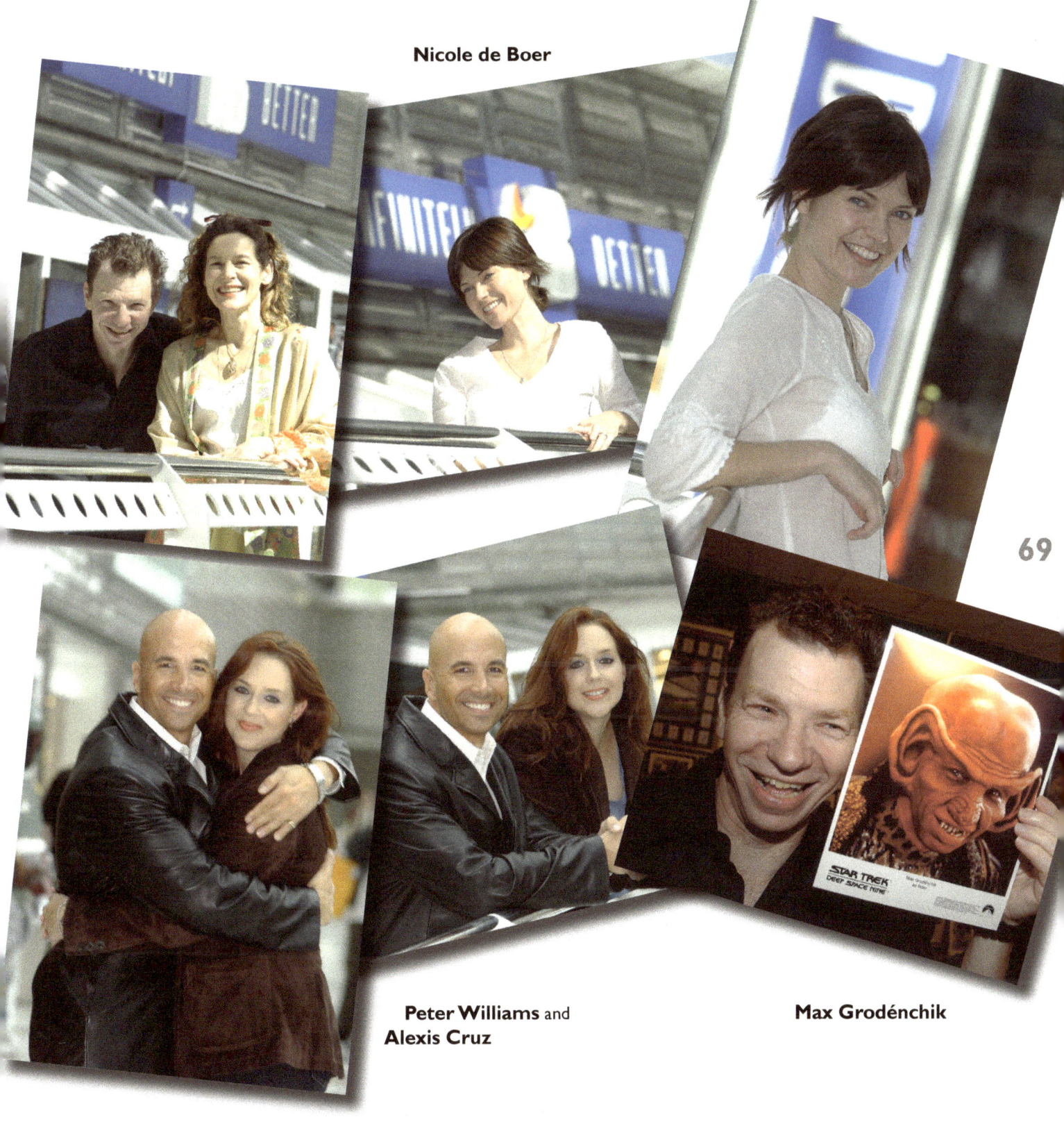

Nicole de Boer

Peter Williams and Alexis Cruz

Max Grodénchik

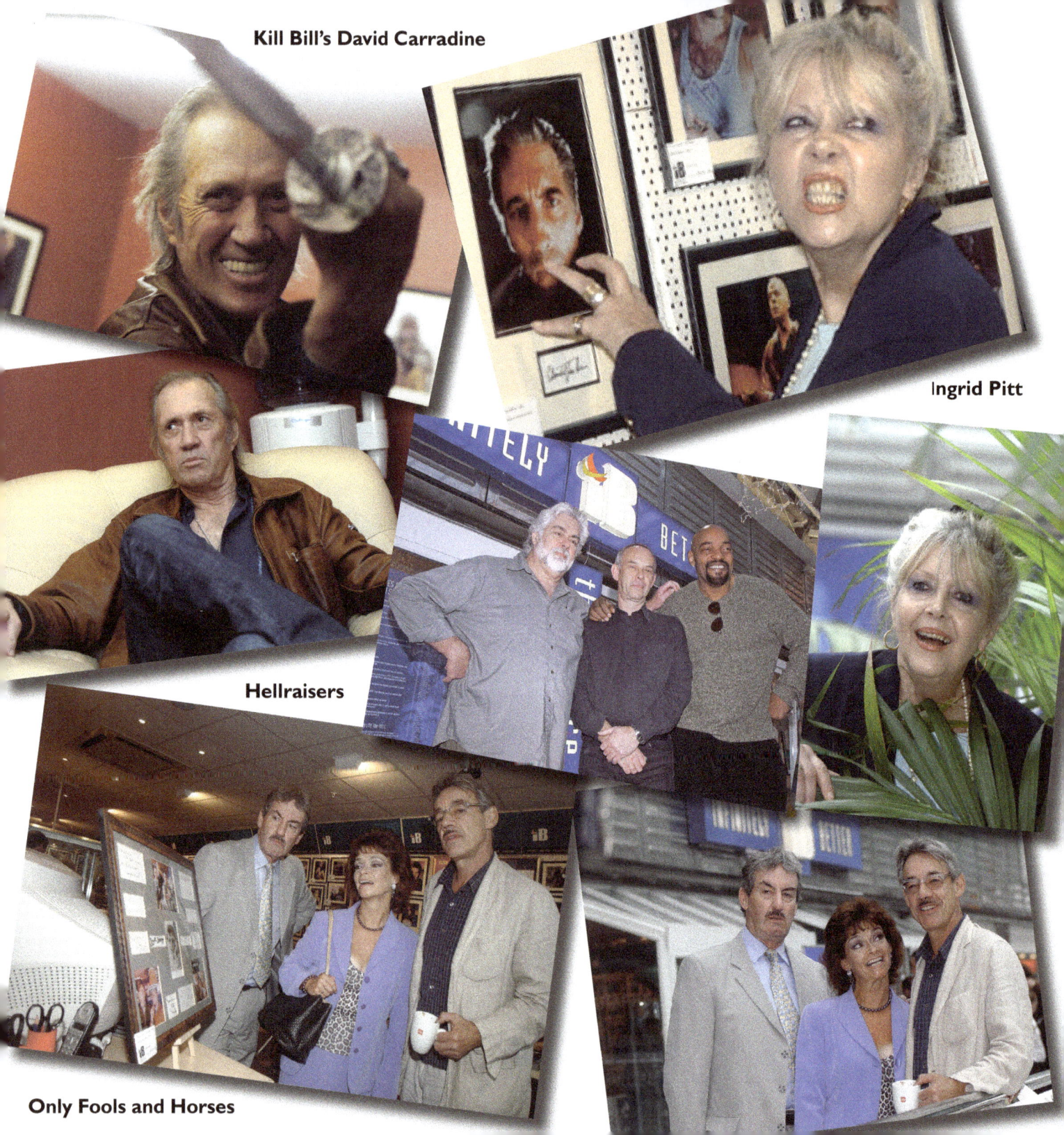

Kill Bill's David Carradine

Ingrid Pitt

Hellraisers

Only Fools and Horses

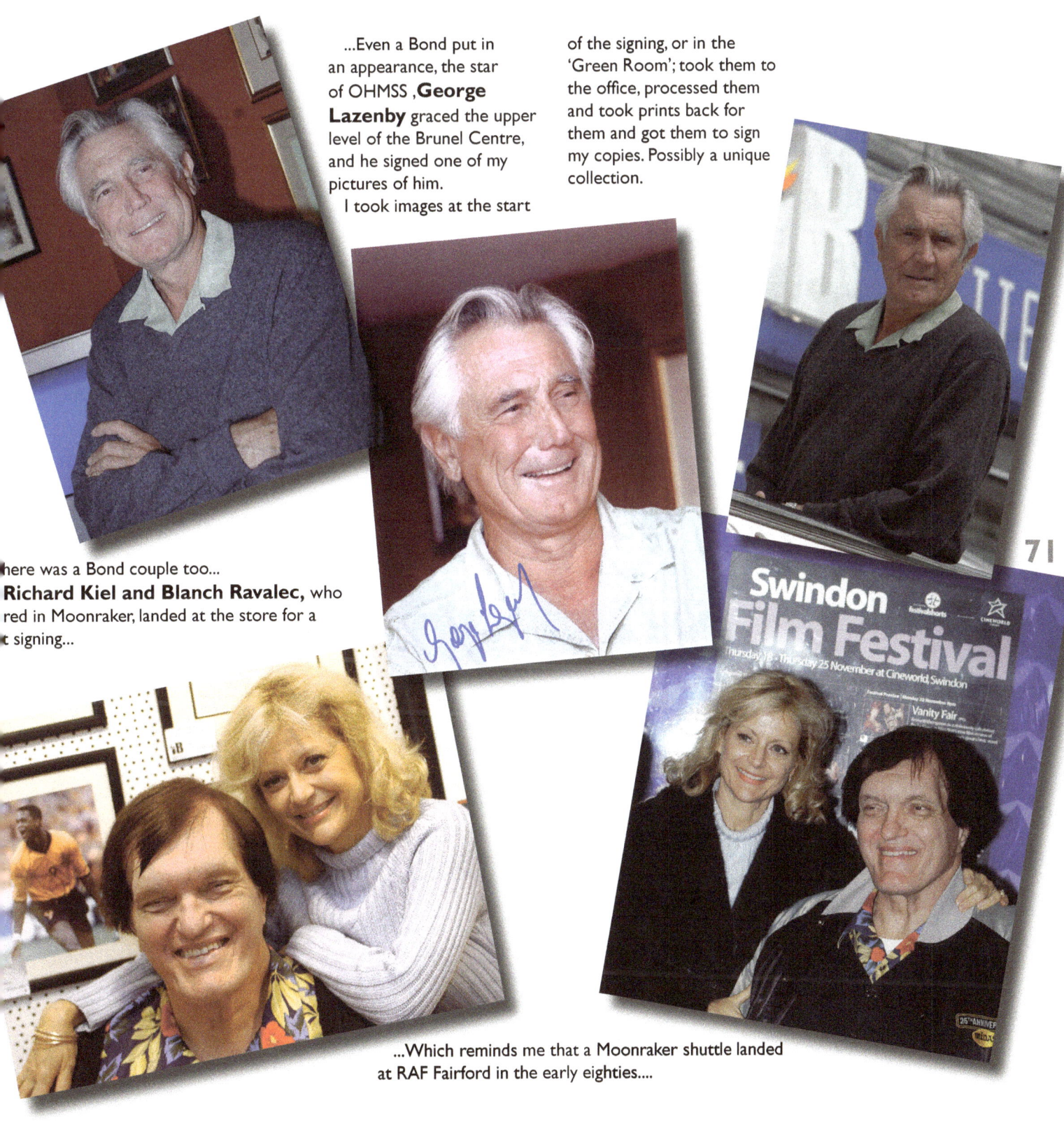

...Even a Bond put in an appearance, the star of OHMSS, **George Lazenby** graced the upper level of the Brunel Centre, and he signed one of my pictures of him.

I took images at the start of the signing, or in the 'Green Room'; took them to the office, processed them and took prints back for them and got them to sign my copies. Possibly a unique collection.

There was a Bond couple too... **Richard Kiel and Blanch Ravalec,** who starred in Moonraker, landed at the store for a signing...

...Which reminds me that a Moonraker shuttle landed at RAF Fairford in the early eighties....

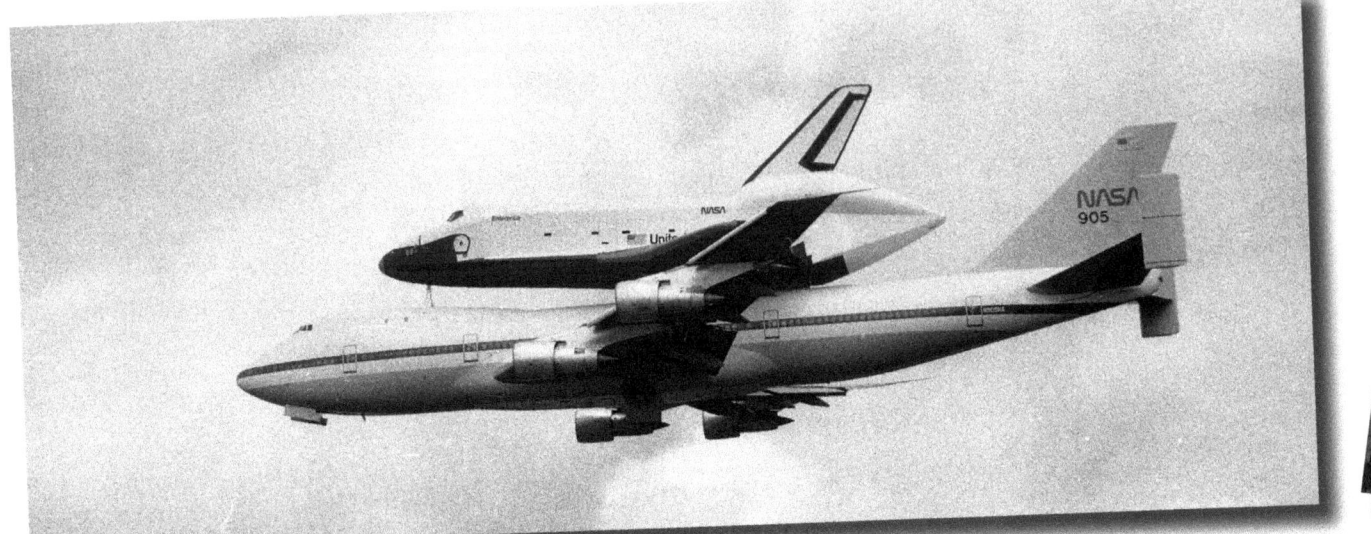

...The RAF base at Fairford is only about a fifteen minute drive from Swindon and, during the life of the **NASA Space Shuttle,** it was one of the emergency runways for the craft to divert to on take off, should there be a problem.

Should this have happened, I would have eight minuites to get to a vantage point to see it land. Needless to say, it never did need to abort to the Wiltshire / Gloucestershire base.

But the prototype shuttle did touch down there; on the back of a Boeing 747 Jumbo Jet on the 20th May 1983.

As you can imagine, there was a lot of press there to see it come in and land to refuel on its way to the Paris Airshow.

The RAF opened up the base to allow families to come in and watch the shuttle land and taxi. My family took advantage of this and made it a day-off school event.

The plane landed after an abortive approach, and taxied to where it parked, with the press held back.

One of the pilots was a lady officer, and in those days that was a rarity; particularly to the British press and of course the TV and reporters wanted to interview her.

The request to do this was denied and the VIPs were taken to the shuttle and the press left behind.

At the rear of the enclosure where we were held was a marquee with food on the tables.

Press and food; well you can imagine it, no interviews so we all tucked in.

As we waited outside the tent for the VIPs to return my friendly press officer turned to me and said, 'That's f***** it, that food was for the VIPs!'

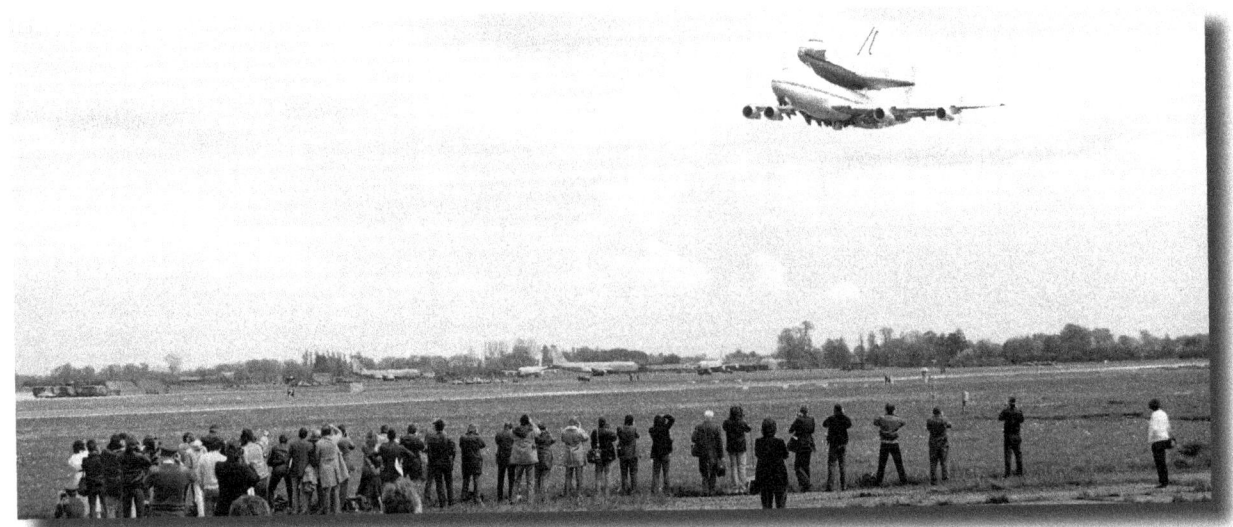

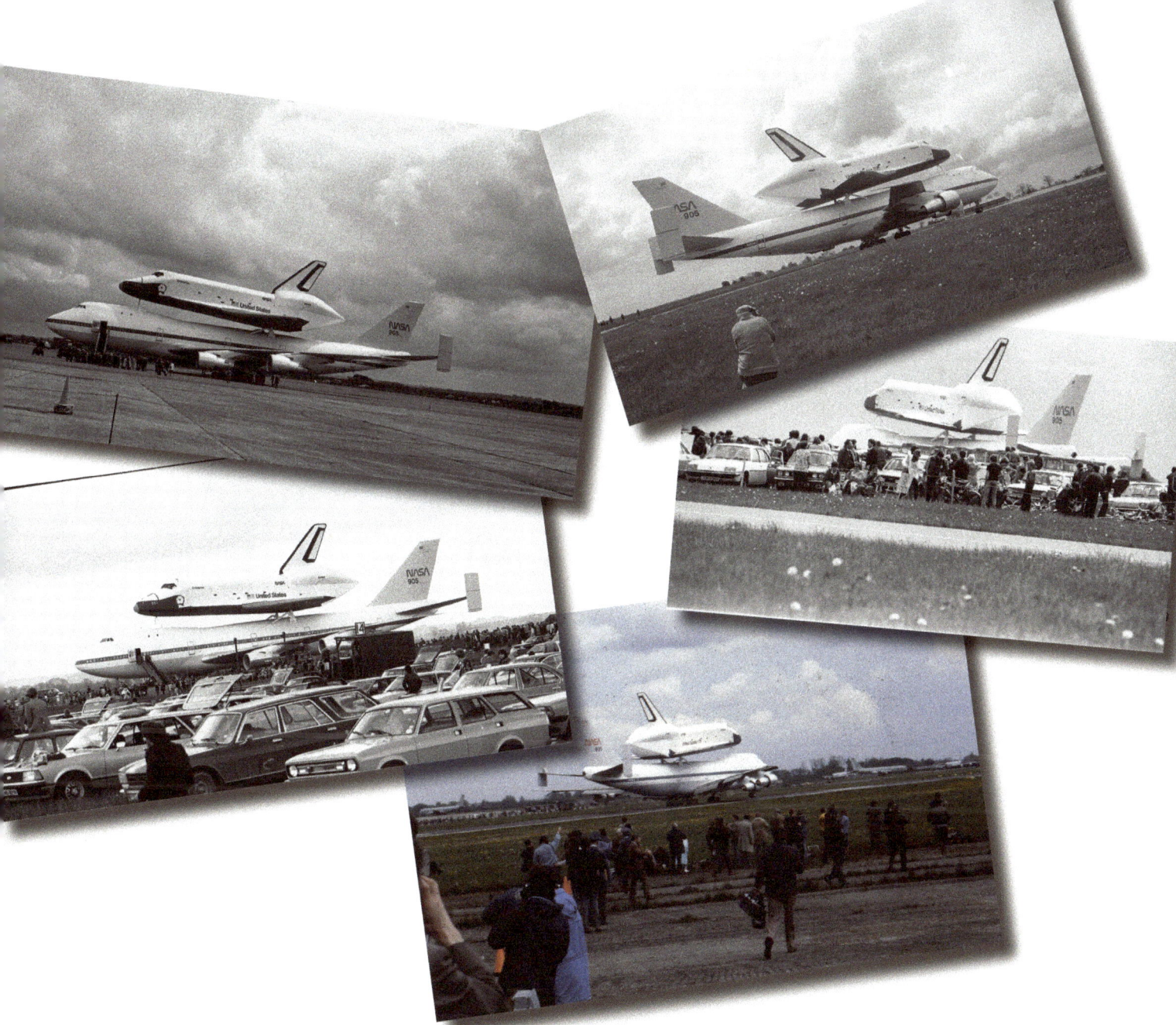

One last thing about the day, a good friend and mentor the late Bob Barclay, who was staff photographer for the *Daily Star*, arrived late; that was not unusual for Bob, and he was ferried to the press area in one of the base's trucks.

As they got to the runway crossing point at the Welford end of the runway the shuttle was on approach and they were not allowed across.

Bob jumped out of the truck and took his pictures from there, which were much better than any of us managed to get.

Fairford is often COLD

....**RAF Fairford** is the home of the Royal International Air Tattoo annual event and, over the years, I have taken many notable images on its runways and taxiways.

One snowy winter's day in January 1985 I was contacted by one of the Sunday picture desks, and asked if I could get some off-beat snow pictures.

My first thoughts were to contact RAF Lyneham to see how they were clearing the runways, as the Hercules aircraft were still flying round, but the response I received was as cold as the weather.

So I called my friend in the Fairford press office.

In a previous existence he had been a press photographer in America, but had been seconded into the Air Force for the Vietnam war. Photographers were used as door gunners on sorties during that conflict.

On asking how they were clearing the runways I was told, 'By tanker with a blade fitted to the front,' and that I should get in my car, come on over to the base, and he would show me.

Eventually, I managed to get to Fairford and was duly given the American coffee and cookies treatment before going out to the taxiway, which had several large aircraft parked up along it.

As we walked along following the snowplough, two squaddies, one with a gun and one with a shovel, jumped out in front of us and said, 'Don't cross the red line.'

There were a few inches of snow on the ground and no sign of a red line, so the one with a shovel started to expose the said red line with said shovel.

The two of us looked at each other and took several paces back and started taking pictures.

The resulting images showed the USAF clearing the runways of Fairford of snow with a shovel.

Jeff's pictures went round the world on the cover of the USAF magazine, and mine were used in the national papers too.

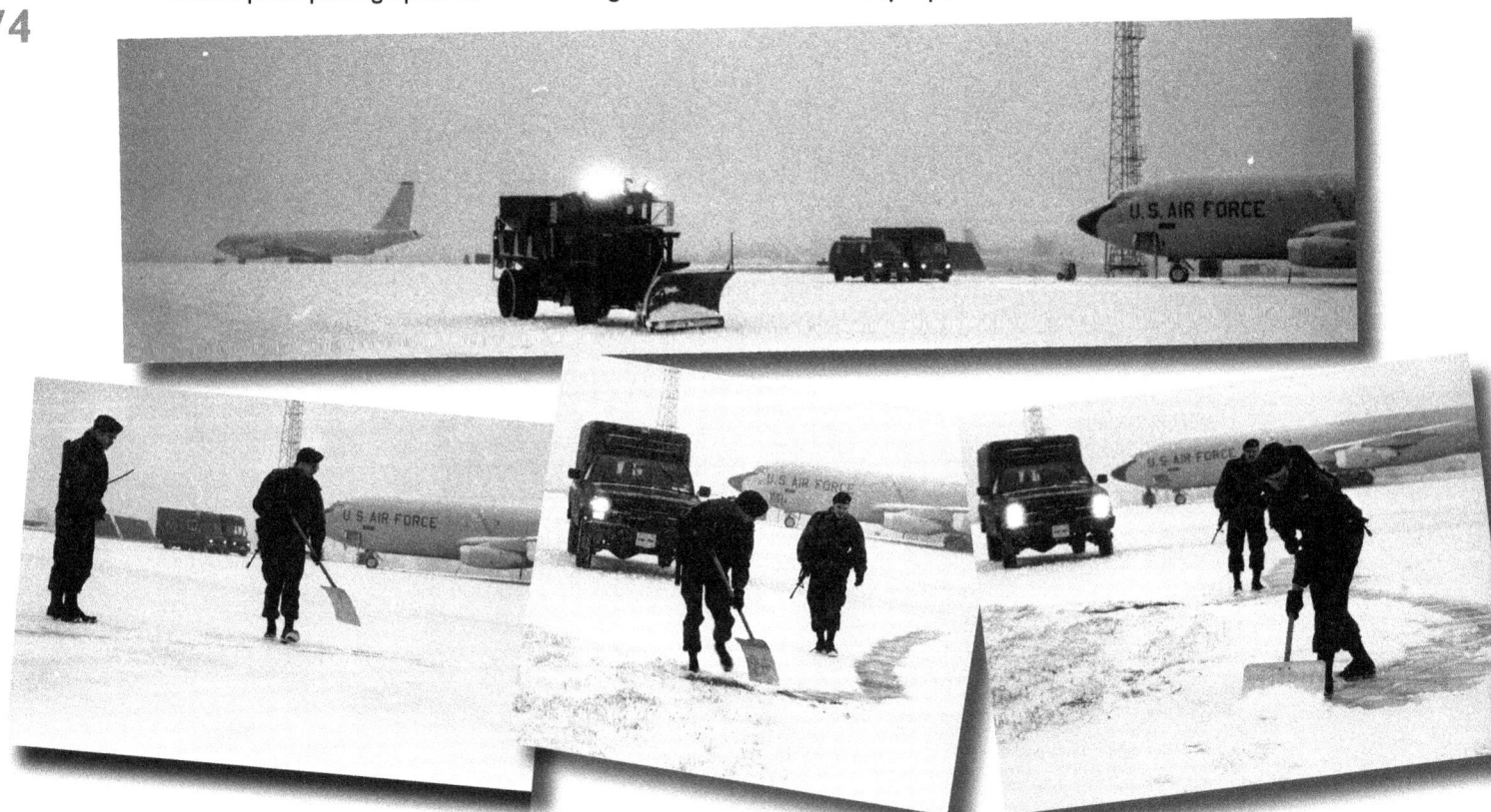

Sometimes it's WET

Before the annual RIAT event was established, it was biennual, with the USAF putting on an open day in the alternate years.

The various wings of the USAF and National Guard would line up along the taxiway with their aircraft, and give out burgers and proper American Budweiser beer which they had imported from the States, rather than the European brewed equivalent which we had over here.

I obtained a super BBQ sauce recipe from the Texas National Guard that I still use today, when the British weather permits.

One year, the rain was so hard that the show was almost abandoned, and people were sheltering under whatever plane was to hand. I found a father and son sheltering under a F1-11. This led to a set of images that went on to the cover of the USAF magazine.

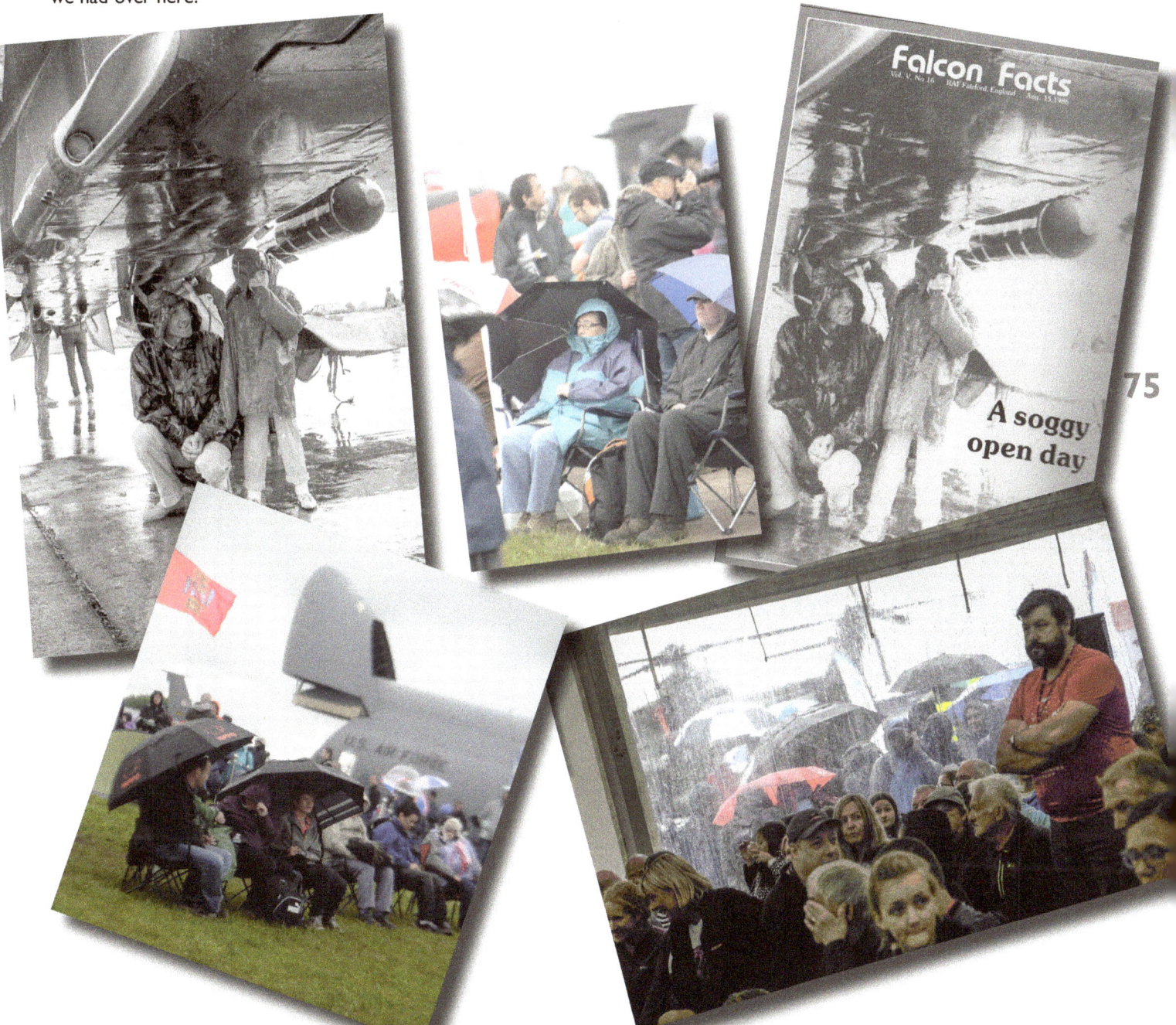

Sometimes it's HOT

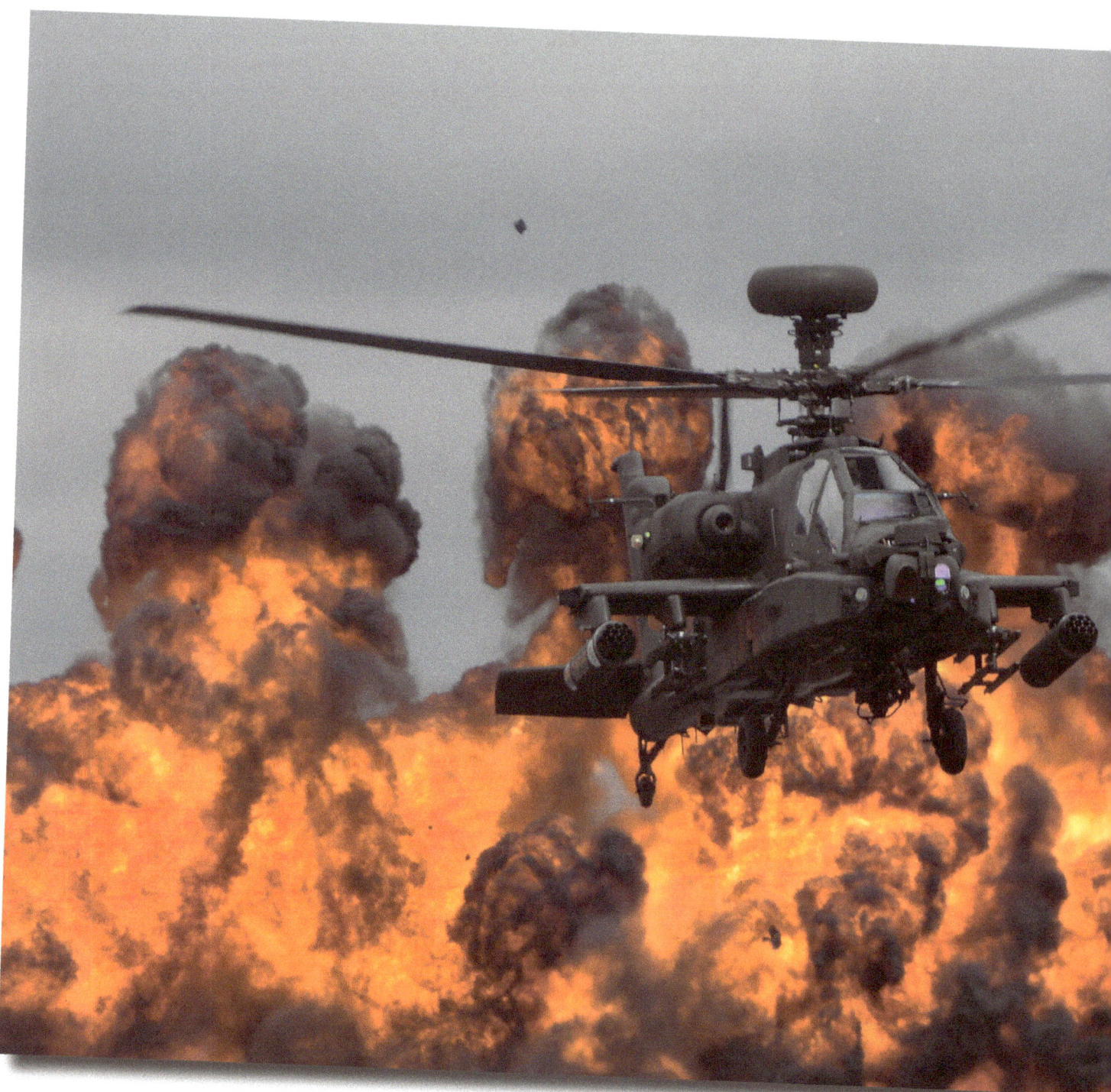

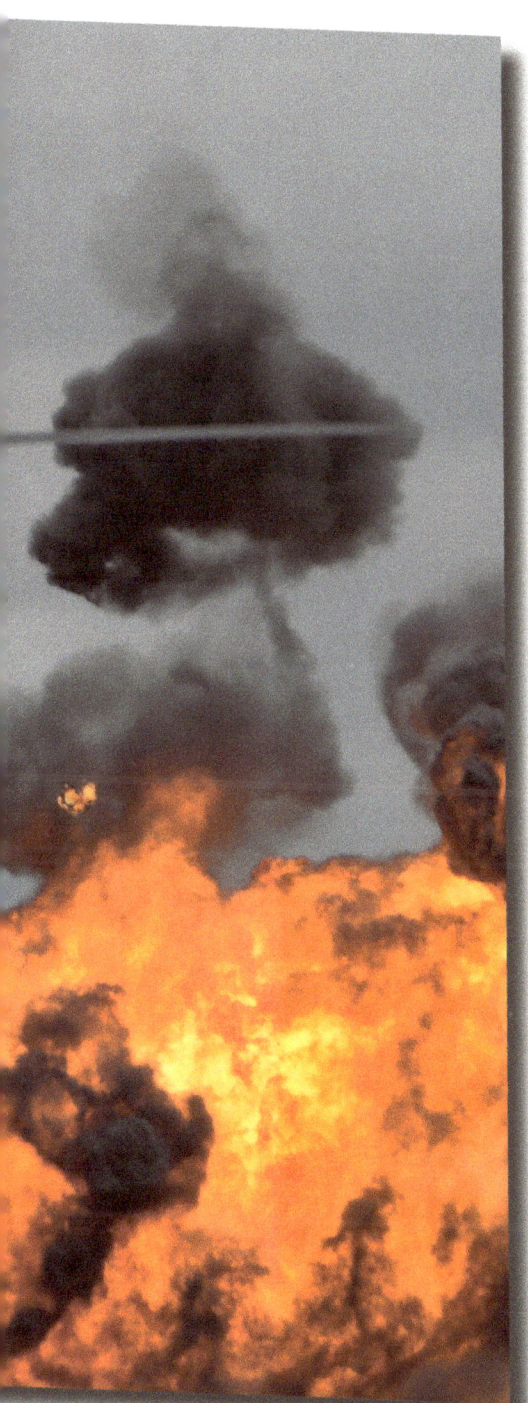

Sometimes you just have to be in the right place at the right time, as my young photographer found during the 2016 and 2017 Royal International Air Tattoos.....

Rachel Davis, a young photographer who was working with me and helped me cover the 2017 RIAT show, dashed into the media tent, grabbed her camera and my lens, and ran back out.

Some minuites later there was the thump and ground-shaking explosions of the Apache display team demonstration taking place on the far side of the runway.

A little time later Rachel returned, sat at the laptop and brought up a set of images on the screen that literally blew me and another national agency photographer away.

'I have wanted to do that picture for five or six years,' she said.

I questioned what was different this year and got the reply, 'I've got a press pass'.

Rachel's picture was made National Association of Press Agencies News Picture of the year 2017, and she was presented with the award at the prestigous dinner in London by journalist, author and broadcaster Eve Pollard.

Rachel was the first lady winner of the annual award.

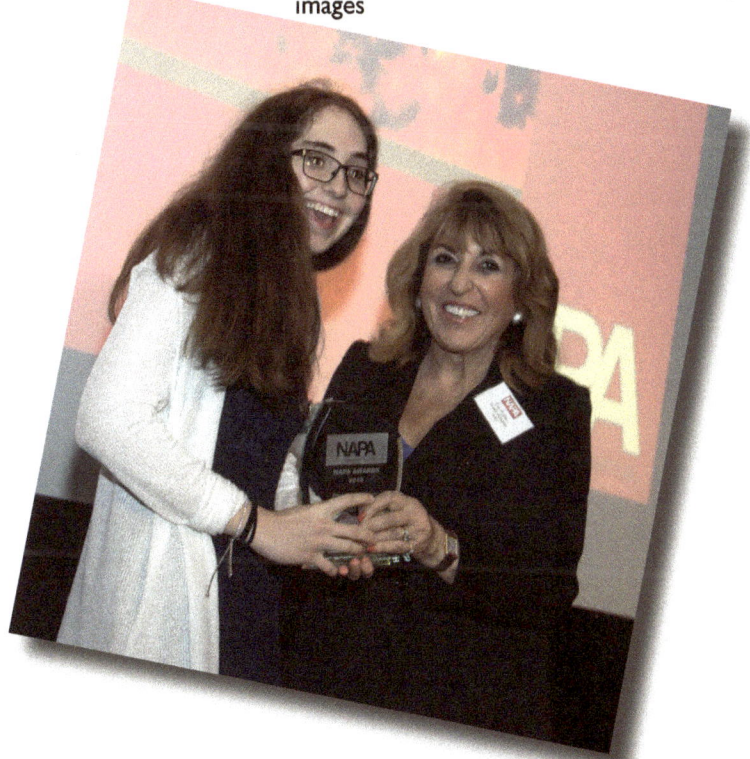

RIAT has royal patronage, as suggested by the name.

Prince Charles attended in 2014 and was presented with the Swindon aviation artist David Bent's book on the Red Arrows by the the team leader (Red 1) Jim Turner.

It turns out that this image was the only one that showed the cover of the book.

During RIAT back in 1991, I was walking near the VIP tents and noticed a royal protection officer.

I then noticed two young boys with balloons walking around in the cordoned-off area.

Yes, it was Princes William (in hoops) and Harry (blue polo shirt). Apparently the boys, with their mother Princess Diana, had decided to turn up at very short notice while on a day out.

They later went on to have some rides on the fair on Wootton Bassett Road opposite The Runner.

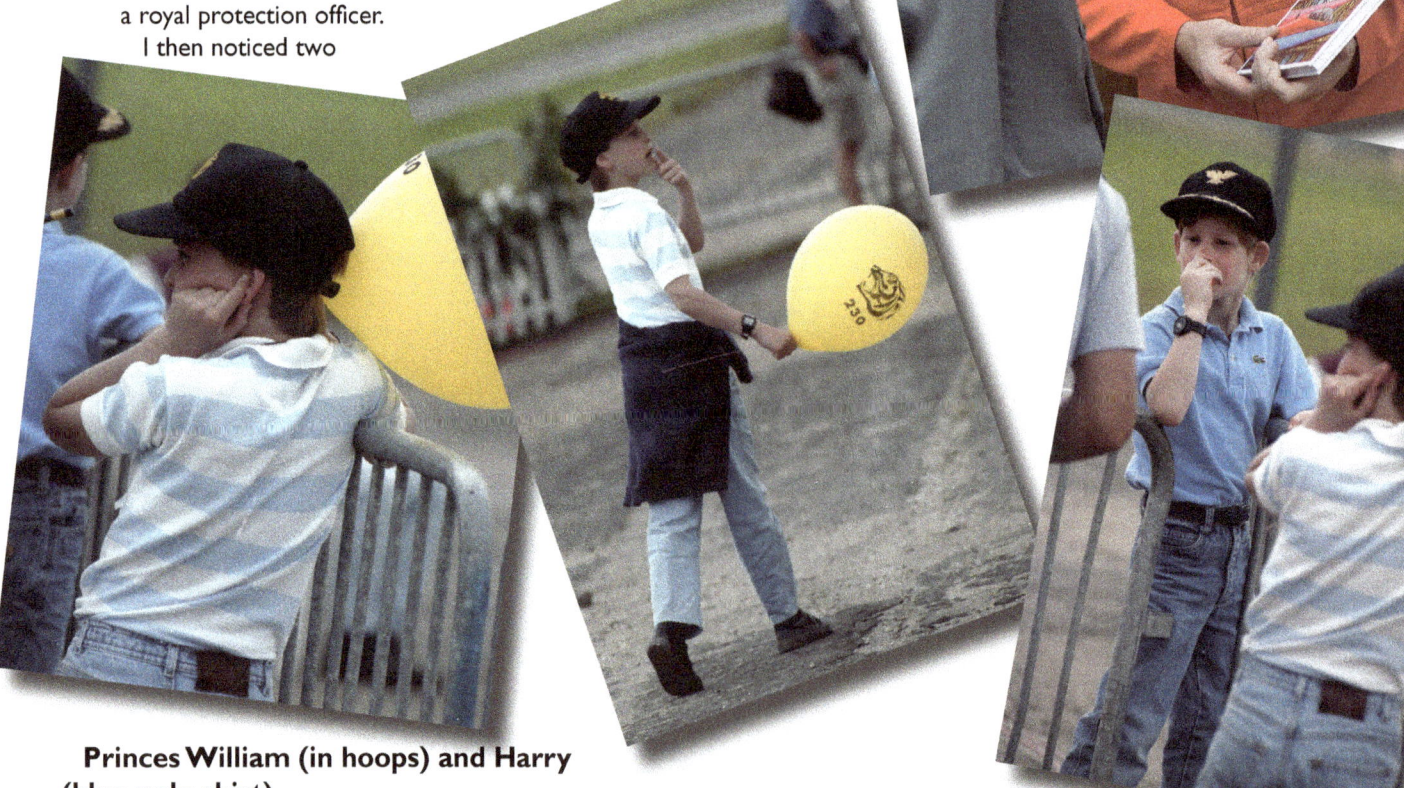

Princes William (in hoops) and Harry (blue polo shirt)

History has a habit of repeating itself...

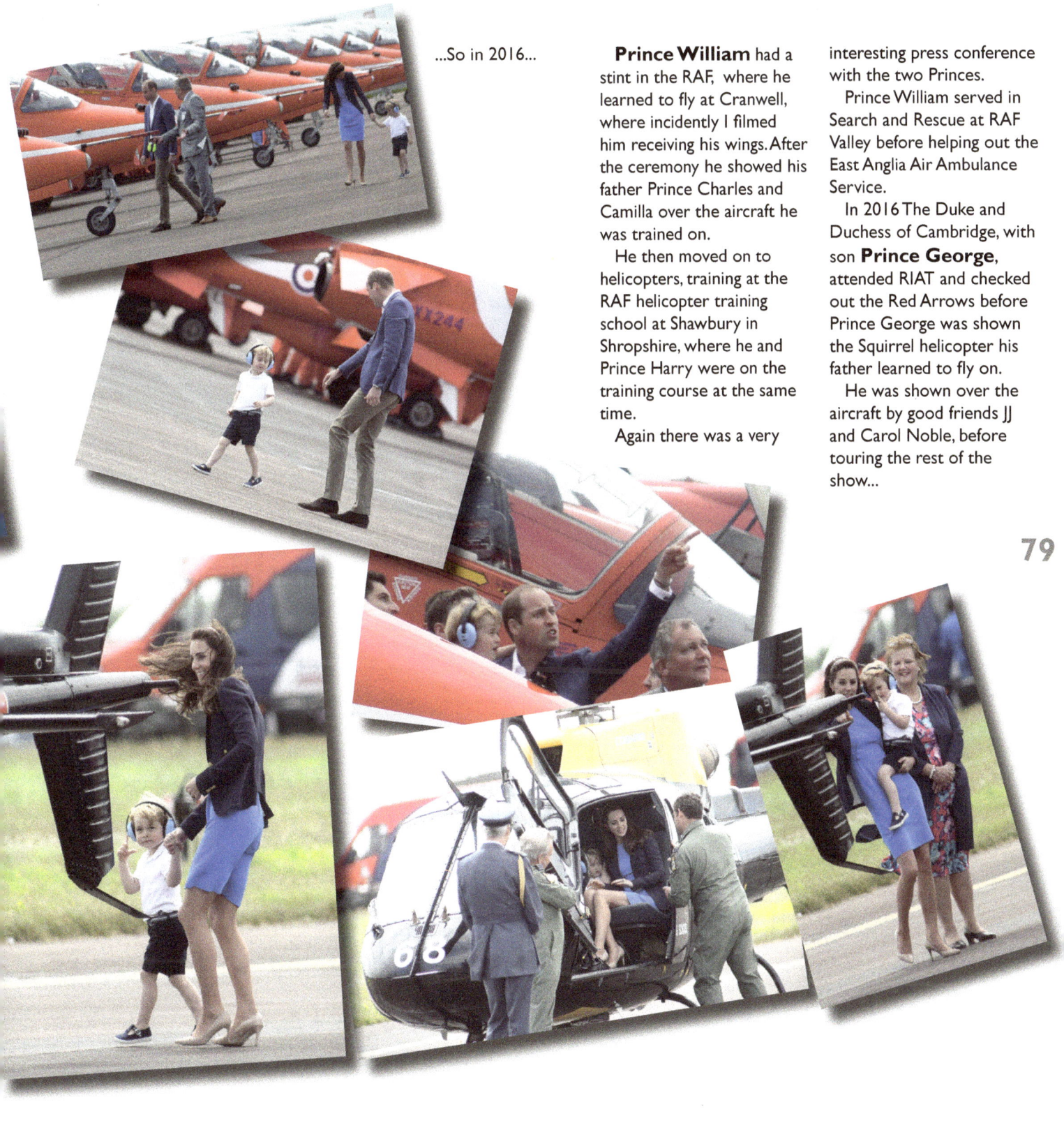

...So in 2016...

Prince William had a stint in the RAF, where he learned to fly at Cranwell, where incidently I filmed him receiving his wings. After the ceremony he showed his father Prince Charles and Camilla over the aircraft he was trained on.

He then moved on to helicopters, training at the RAF helicopter training school at Shawbury in Shropshire, where he and Prince Harry were on the training course at the same time.

Again there was a very interesting press conference with the two Princes.

Prince William served in Search and Rescue at RAF Valley before helping out the East Anglia Air Ambulance Service.

In 2016 The Duke and Duchess of Cambridge, with son **Prince George**, attended RIAT and checked out the Red Arrows before Prince George was shown the Squirrel helicopter his father learned to fly on.

He was shown over the aircraft by good friends JJ and Carol Noble, before touring the rest of the show...

79

...Rachel, sitting at the laptop, looked up, paused, grabbed a camera and left the media tent at a run. Once again she proved her press photographer credentials as she had seen the royals ascending the steps into the Australian transport aircraft parked outside the media tent. Her efforts produced a superb set of images of the royals touring the show, which finished up in several international magazines.

The badge that Prince George is sporting is the artwork of ... ...yes; Swindon artist David Bent.

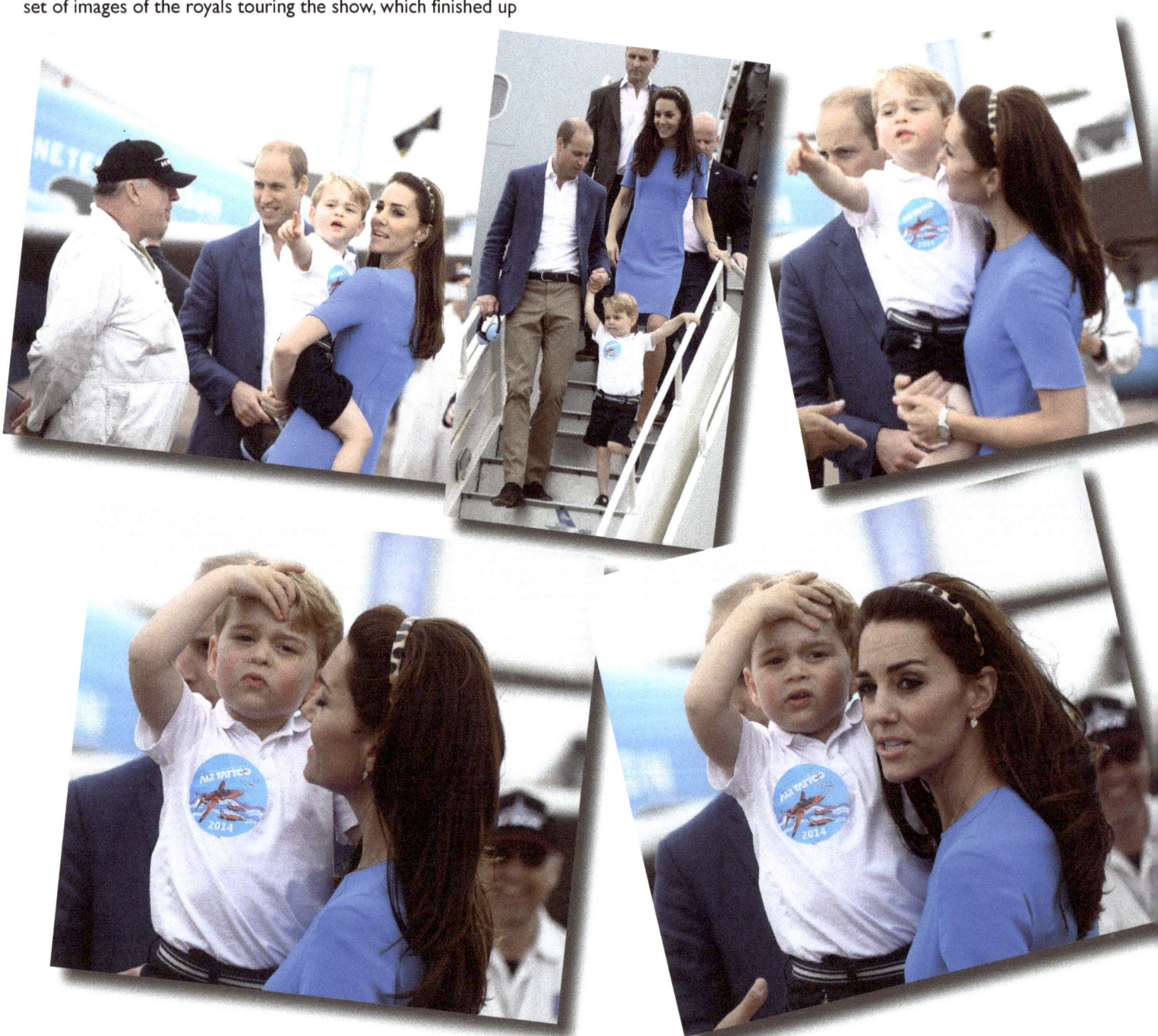

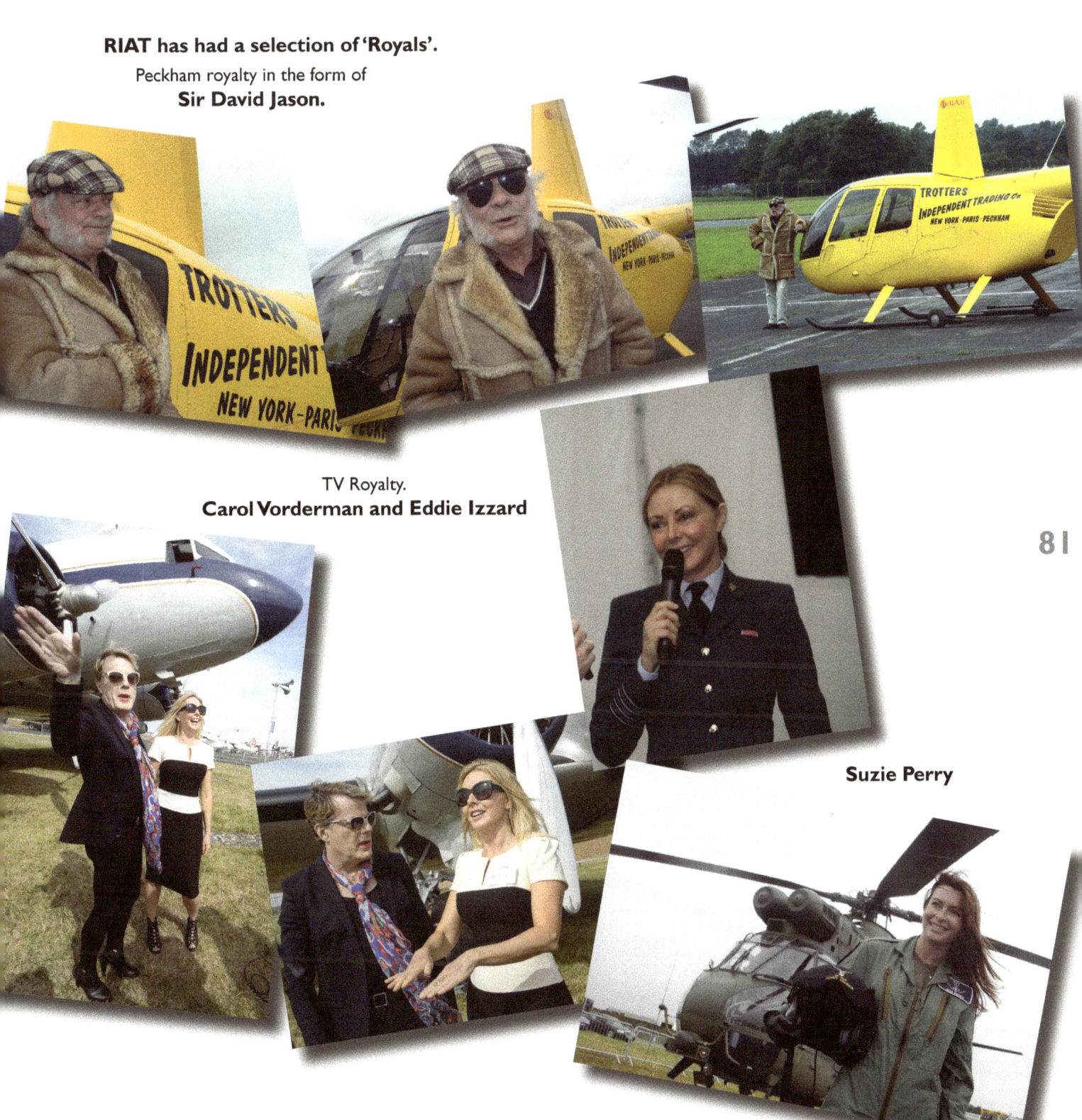

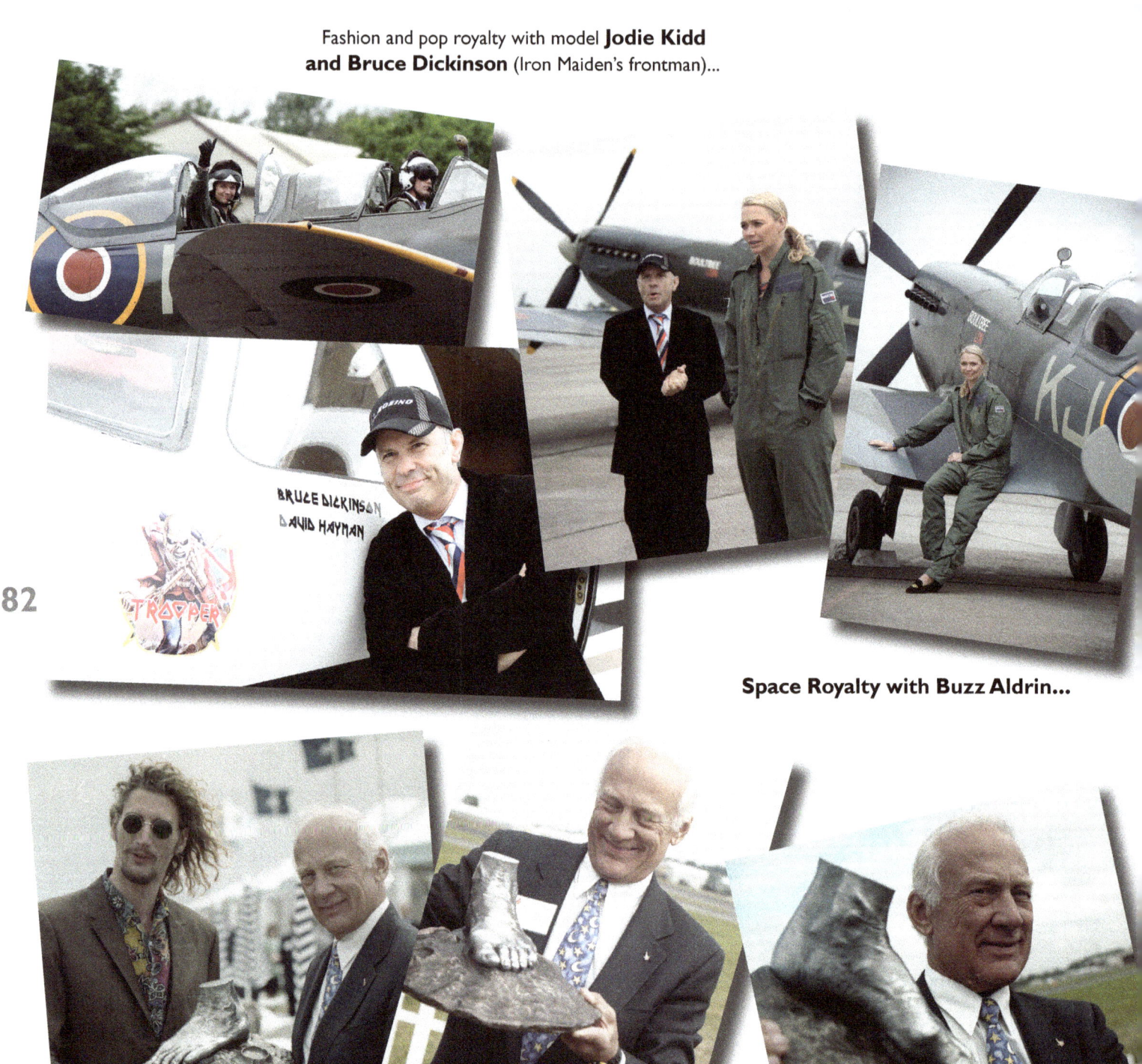

Fashion and pop royalty with model **Jodie Kidd** and **Bruce Dickinson** (Iron Maiden's frontman)...

Space Royalty with Buzz Aldrin...

...and Tim Peake....

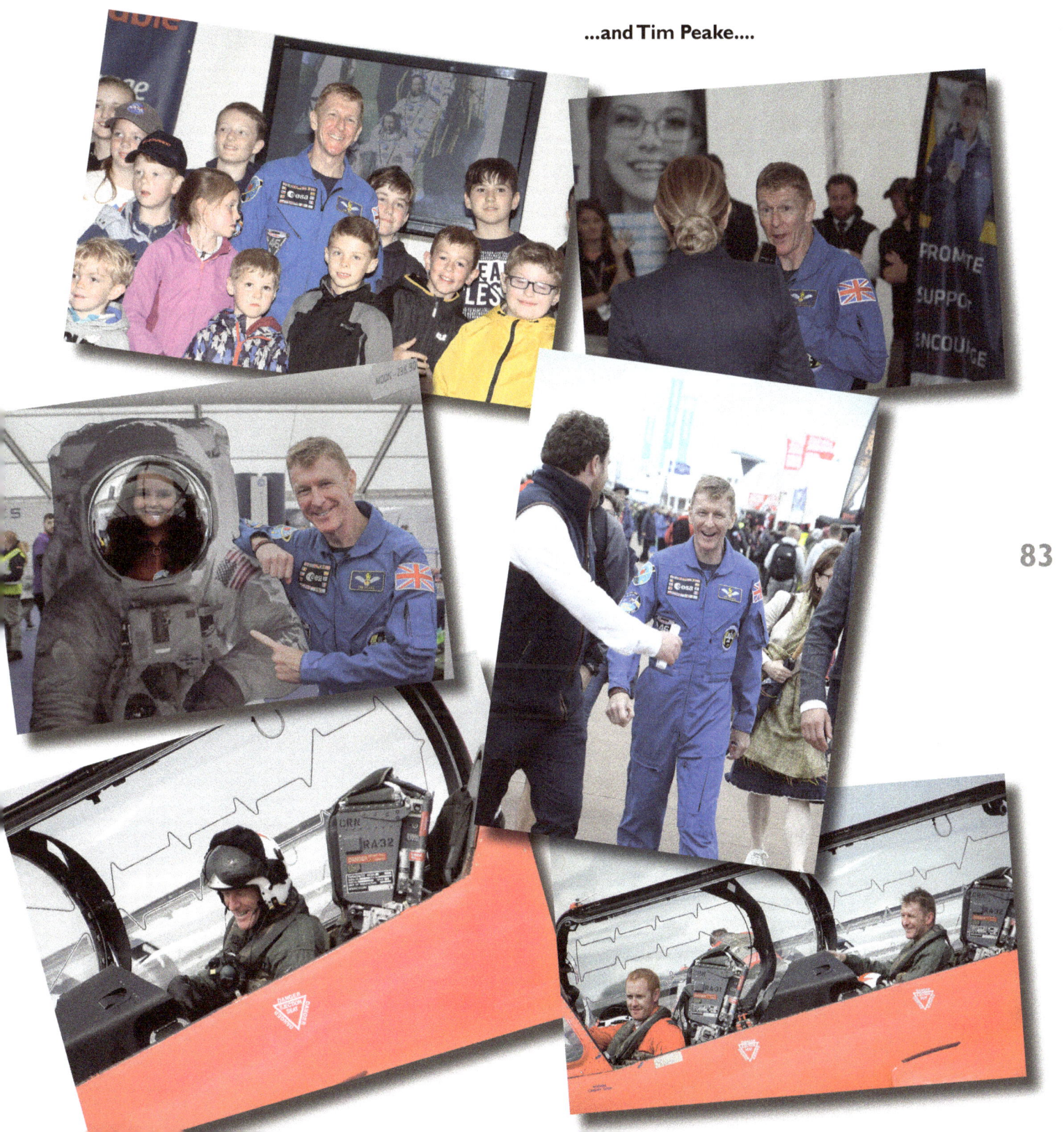

Aircraft Royalty

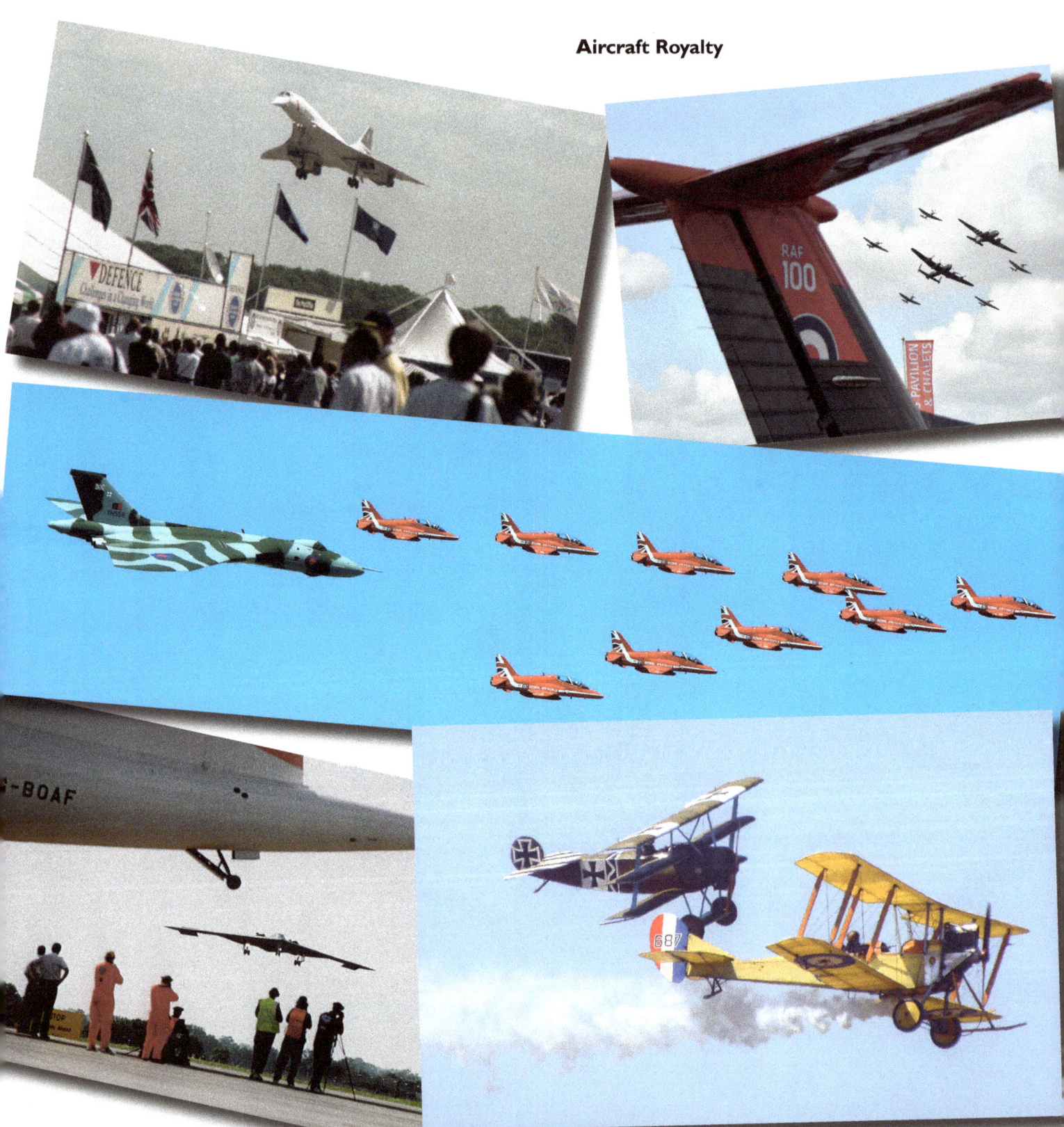

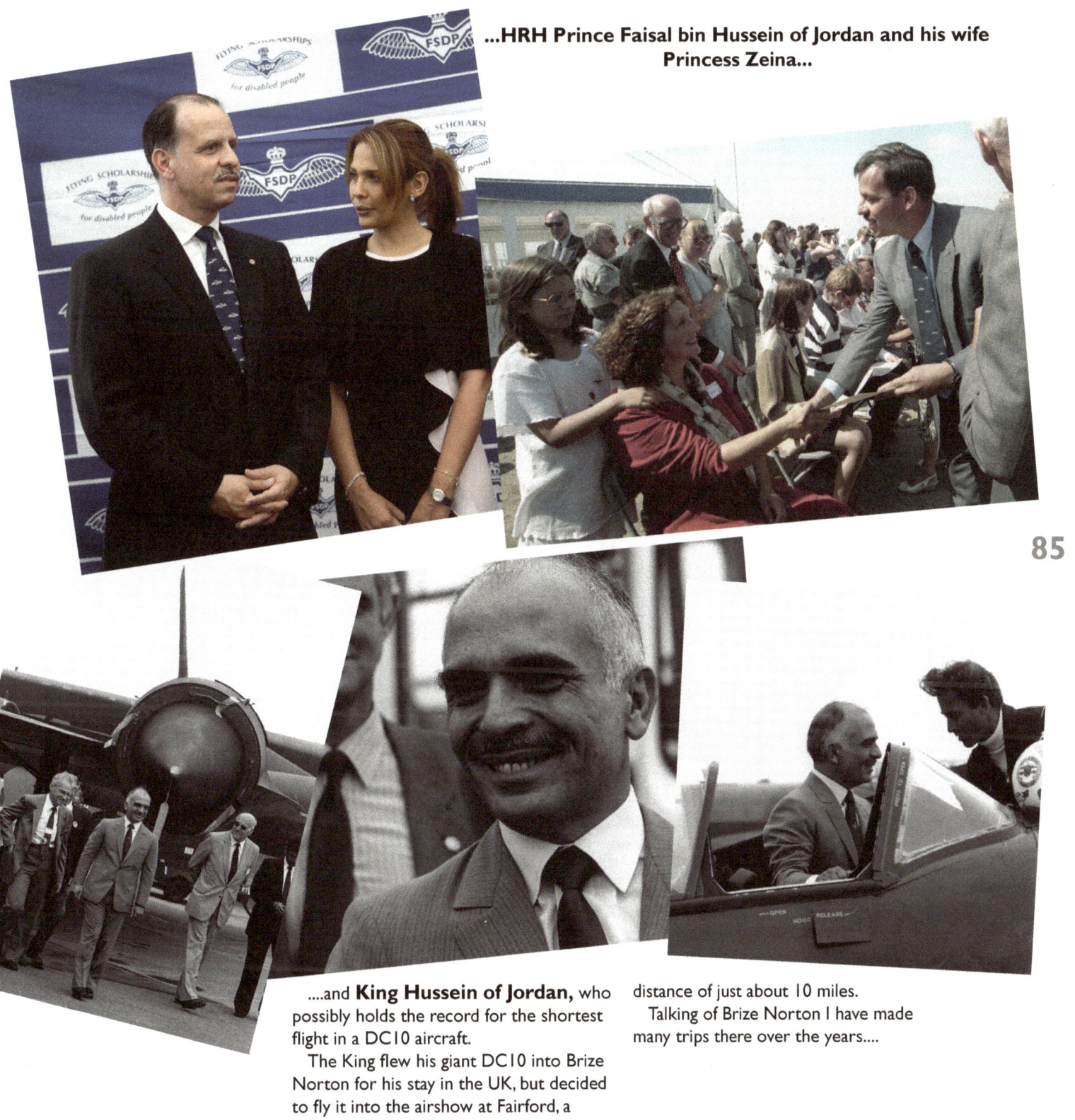

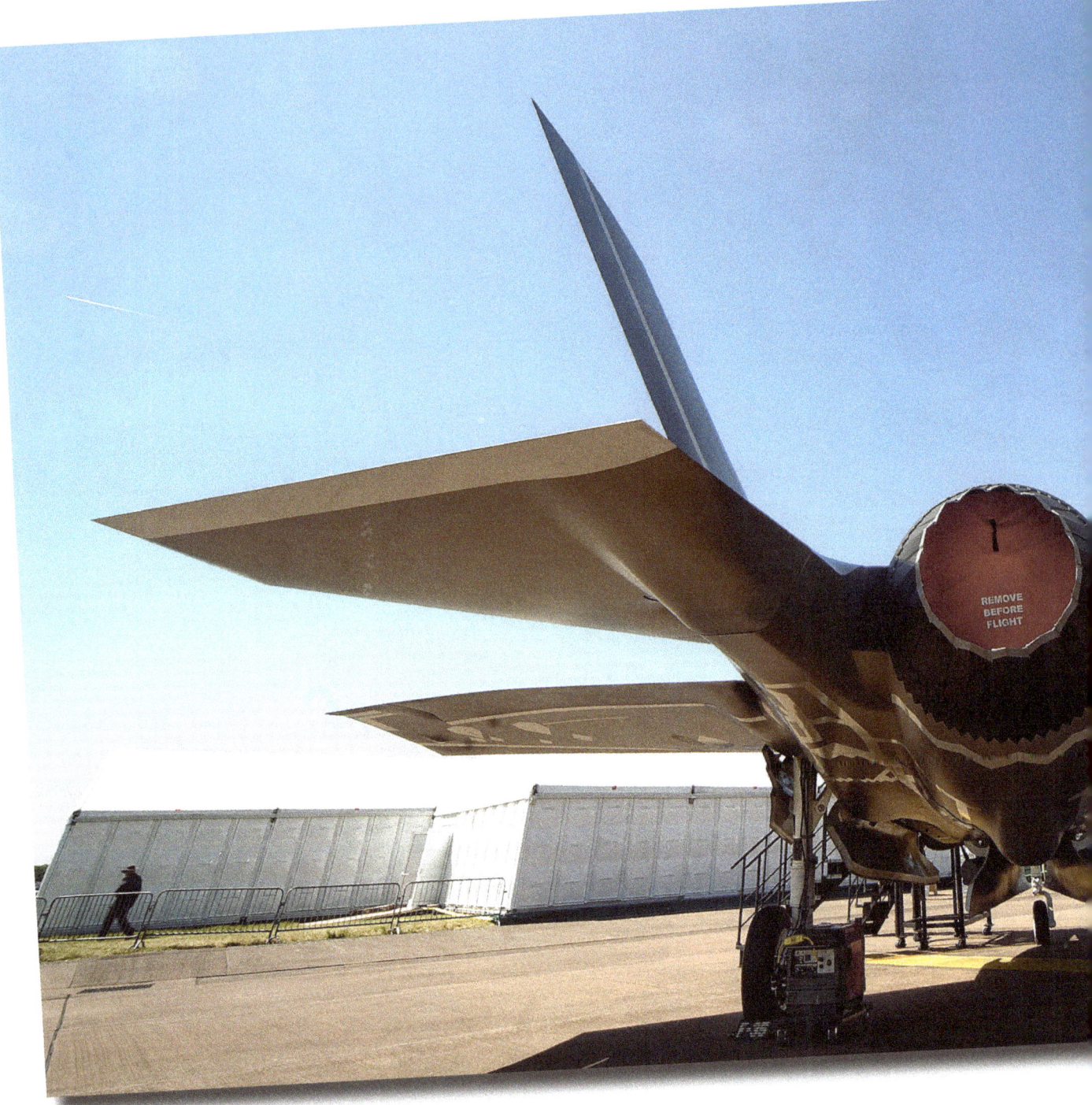

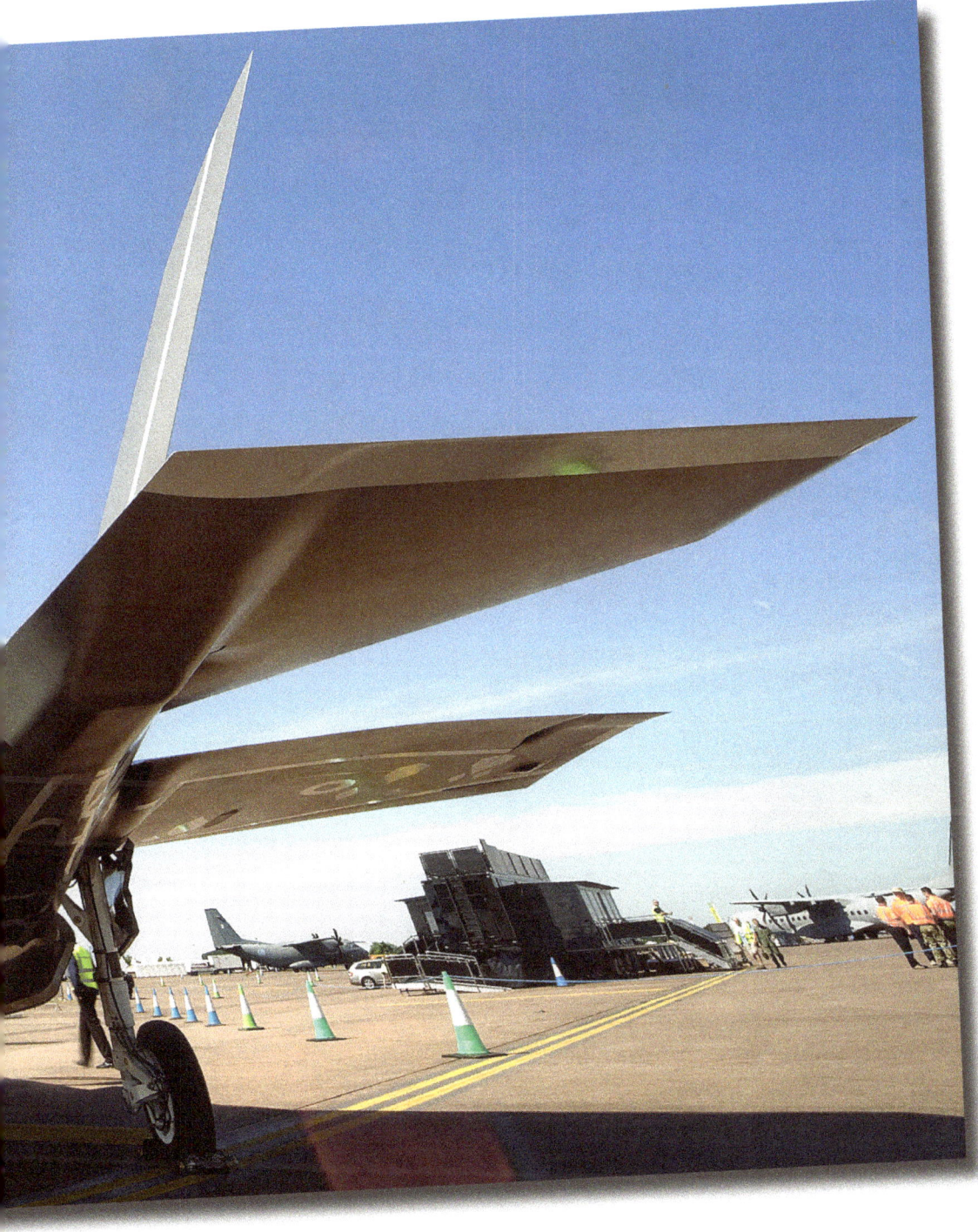

...The mock-up of the stealthy F35b fighter that has entered service with the RAF in 2018 looks better from the rear, except if you photograph it refuelling, as I discovered on a trip to Brize Norton......

...There was always a friendly rivalry between RAF Brize Norton and RAF Lyneham as to who could get the greatest press coverage.

Several events at Brize Norton stand out above all others that are in the depths of the archive.

But the archive is a living entity and, as such, I am including recent stories.

Like most jobs it started with a phone call, this time from Jeremy Flack, whom I have known for many years and is a leading avation photographer with many books to his credit.

'Fancy a flight?' he said,' and is your passport up to date?'

The reason for the call was that his passport had expired and there was a place on a flight in one of the new Voyager tanker aircraft to refuel Eurofighter Typhoons and the new stealth F35b fighters over Scotland and the North Sea.

A 5am start is not my favourite lead into the day, but, hell, go for it!

We had a virtually empty 390-seat aircraft and our own steward, an endless supply of tea, and a meal as we circled over the North Atlantic and then over the North Sea.

The pictures were spectacular and made national coverage...

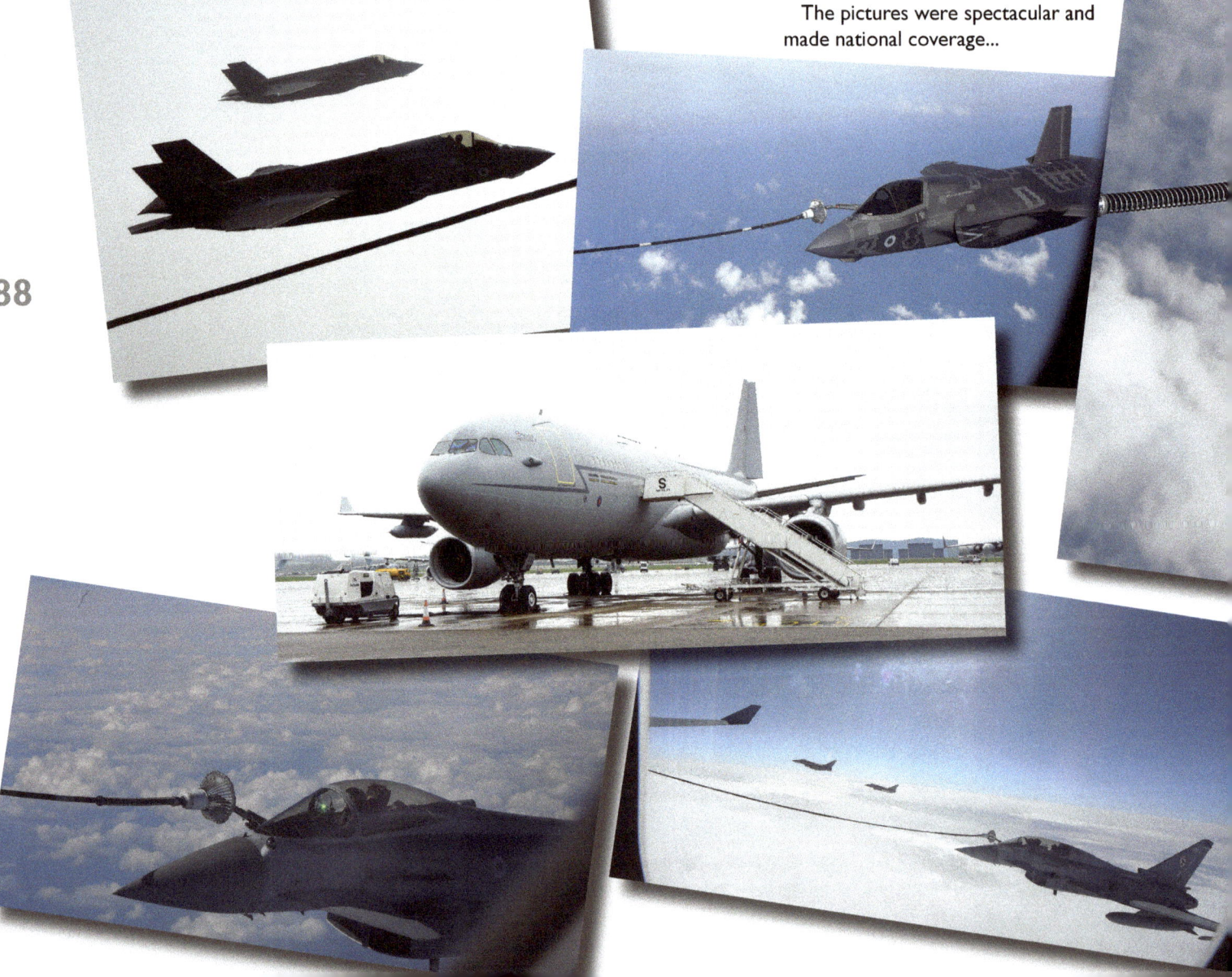

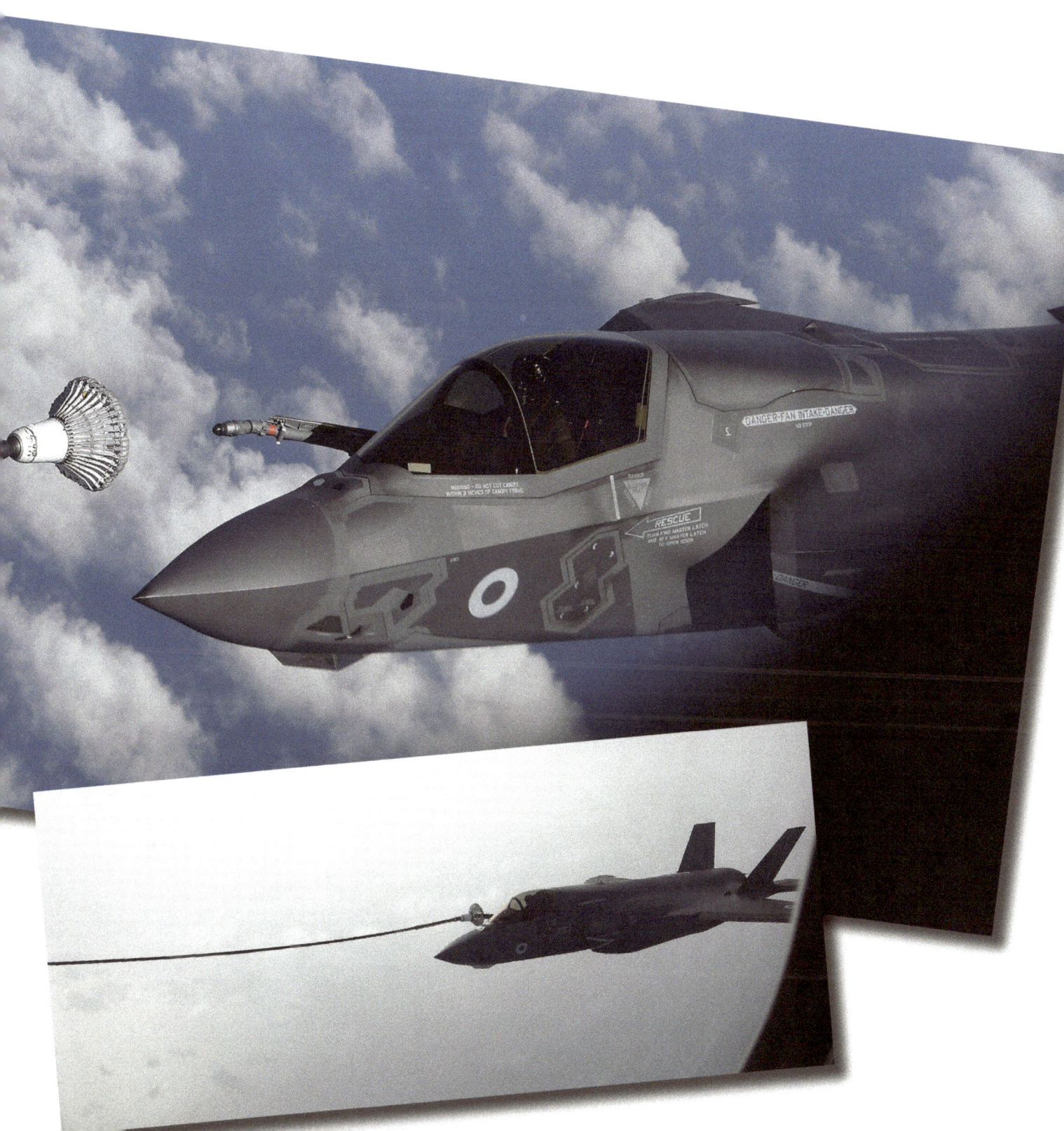

..The first of the two historical events I remember was in May 2004 when I received a call from the Community Relations Officer (CRO) about their 'Fear of Flying course', which was about to have a rather interesting participant.

The 2005 UK Eurovision contestant Javine Hylton didn't like flying, so she was put on the course and the press was duly invited.

She was helped into a flying suit before she toured the RAF Transport Tri Star aircraft and then went for a flight.

As regards Eurovision; she finished with 18 points, in 22nd place, ahead of France and Germany...

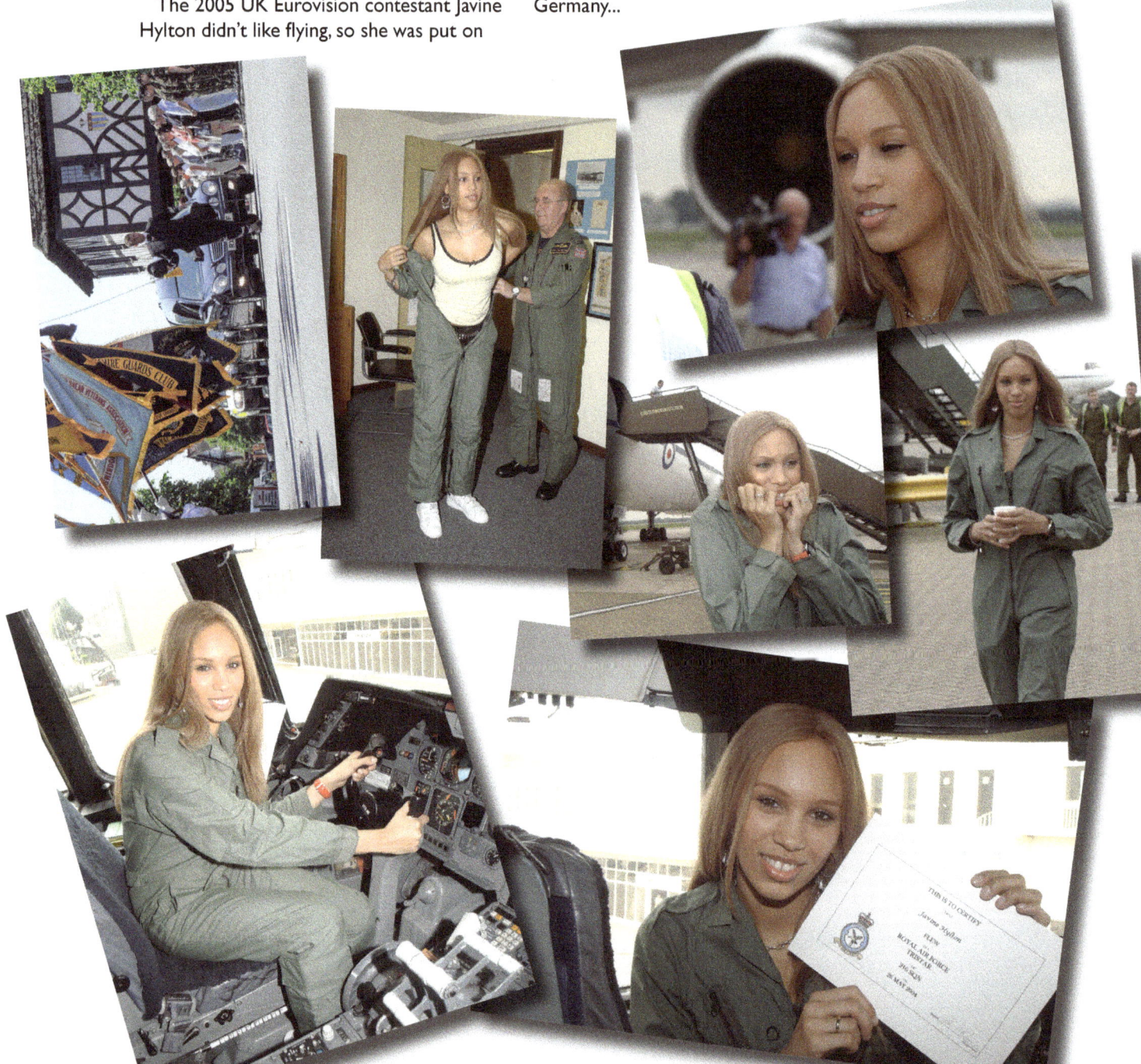

...The second, and possibly the most interesting of my foreign sorties, was on 4th March 1996 when I was asked to go on a flight to pick up some troops from Sarajevo and deliver them back to their base to Germany.

It turned out ours was the first 'commercial type aircraft' to land at Sarajevo in Bosnia Herzegovina after the Serbian troubles.

The VC10 was fully fuelled at Brize with the intention of taking off from Sarajevo for the return flight, stopping in Aviano, northern Italy, for refuelling. The reason for this was that the only fuel at what remained of the airfield was in fifty gallon drums, and that made it impossible to refuel the VC10!

This weighed heavily on the period we were on the tarmac, because if they shut down the four engines we would be stranded there, as they had no means of restarting them. To overcome this they left one of the engines running on tick-over. This meant we only had an hour before we needed to lift off.

My collegue Jeremy Flack, who had been to Bosnia during the troubles, decided we should go up to the top of the control tower and get some general views (GVs) of the place.

Now here was a problem; we had flown directly from the UK into Sarajevo, so didn't have the correct press passes, as the NATO press accreditations were issued by the authorities in Split, over the border in Croatia.

Jeremy had an old press pass, and we eventually convinced the French Foreign Legion, that were guarding the airfield, who we were and why we were not accredited; they then relented.

On reaching the top the view was chilling. We could see the war damage done to the town and what war does to a place, as shown in my images from the tower.

The image of the VC10 on the tarmac was printed up and presented to the Brize Norton Commanding Officer. It took pride of place on his office wall.

In all the seriousness of the visit, there was a lighter incident.

The local TV news channel had sent a crew who were determined to do the piece to camera on the infamous bridge in the town centre.

They blagged their way to the town centre using a very expensive taxi, did their piece, and returned; only to find that they weren't allowed back into the airport by the Foreign Leigon, for the same reason we had experienced.

The plane started its engines, and eventually they got the guards to understand that, if the plane left, they would have to find them accommodation and pay for it.

The steps were returned to the aircraft, the door opened and a couple of Central Television's finest made it back on the flight with milliseconds to spare...

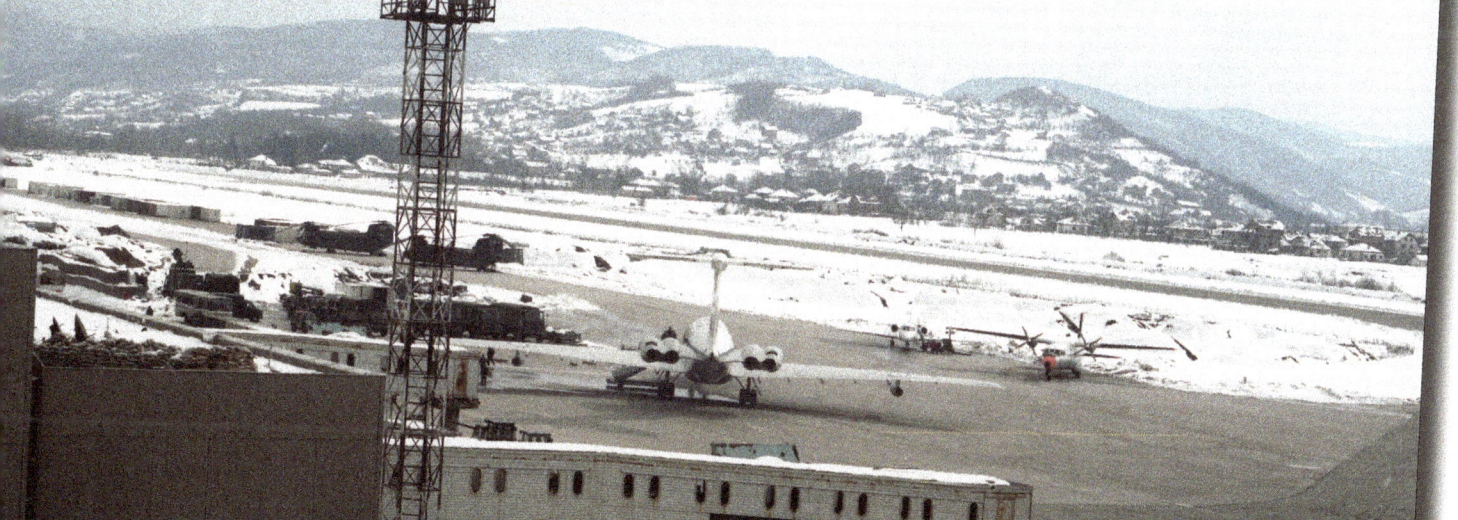

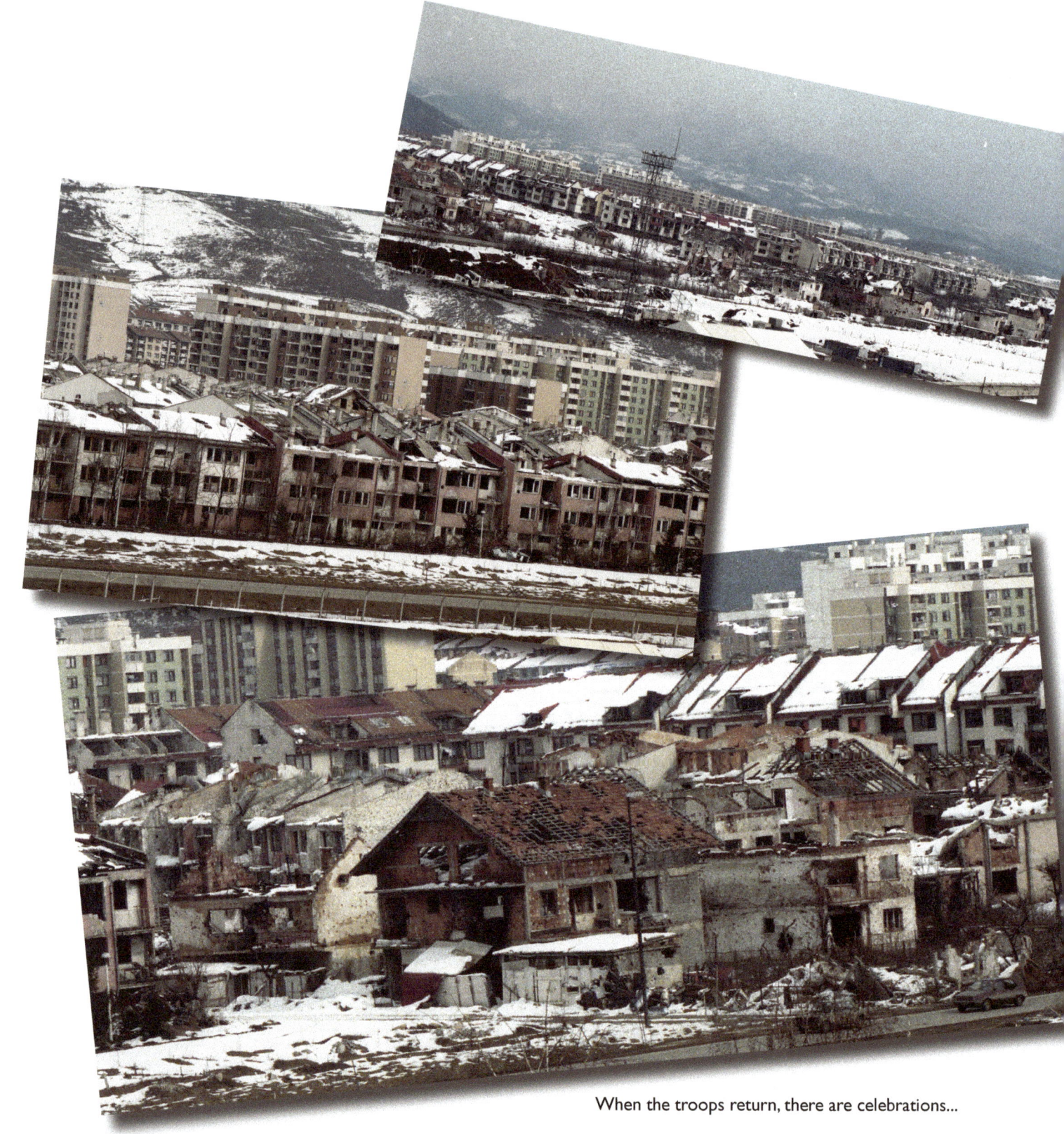

When the troops return, there are celebrations...

...as the **Falkland heroes** found on their return to Brize Norton, where Pomagne was the 1980s version of Prosecco, although I think one Welsh Guard may think staying in the South Atlantic may be a better option...

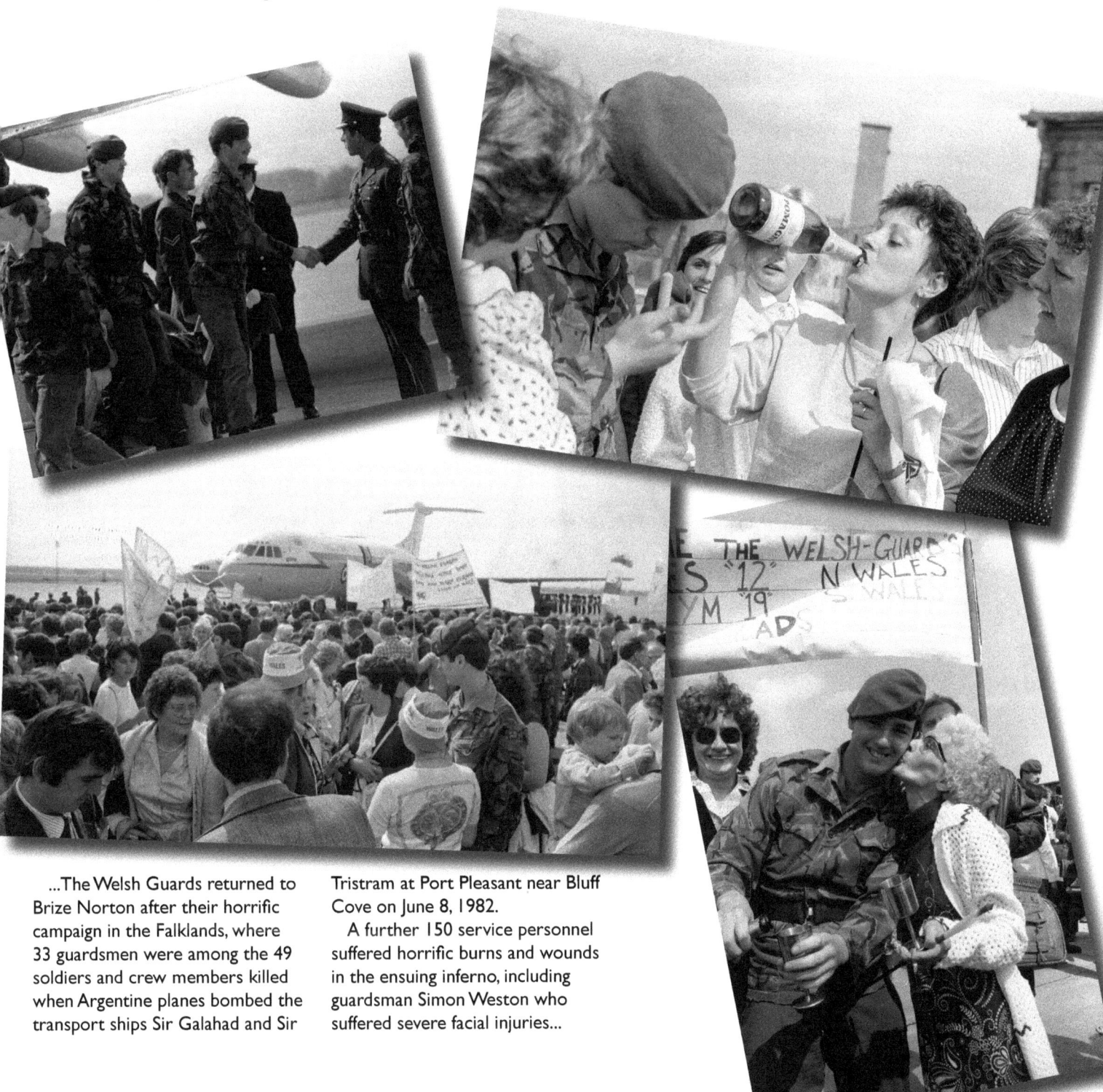

...The Welsh Guards returned to Brize Norton after their horrific campaign in the Falklands, where 33 guardsmen were among the 49 soldiers and crew members killed when Argentine planes bombed the transport ships Sir Galahad and Sir Tristram at Port Pleasant near Bluff Cove on June 8, 1982.

A further 150 service personnel suffered horrific burns and wounds in the ensuing inferno, including guardsman Simon Weston who suffered severe facial injuries...

...But, as with the Falklands conflict, every war has casualties. Who can ever forget the members of the public from far and wide who joined the residents of **Wootton Bassett,** as it was then, and the members of the British Legion who, as the solitary bell tolled, stood in the town centre as a tribute to those fallen heroes as they passed through the town on their way to the John Radcliffe Hospital, after being repatriated at RAF Lyneham.

In 2011 Wootton Bassett was made Royal Wootton Bassett in a ceremony with Princess Anne, as a mark of honour for the respect shown by the town to the fallen.

When RAF Lyneham closed, the ceremonies ceased and were taken over by Brize Norton...

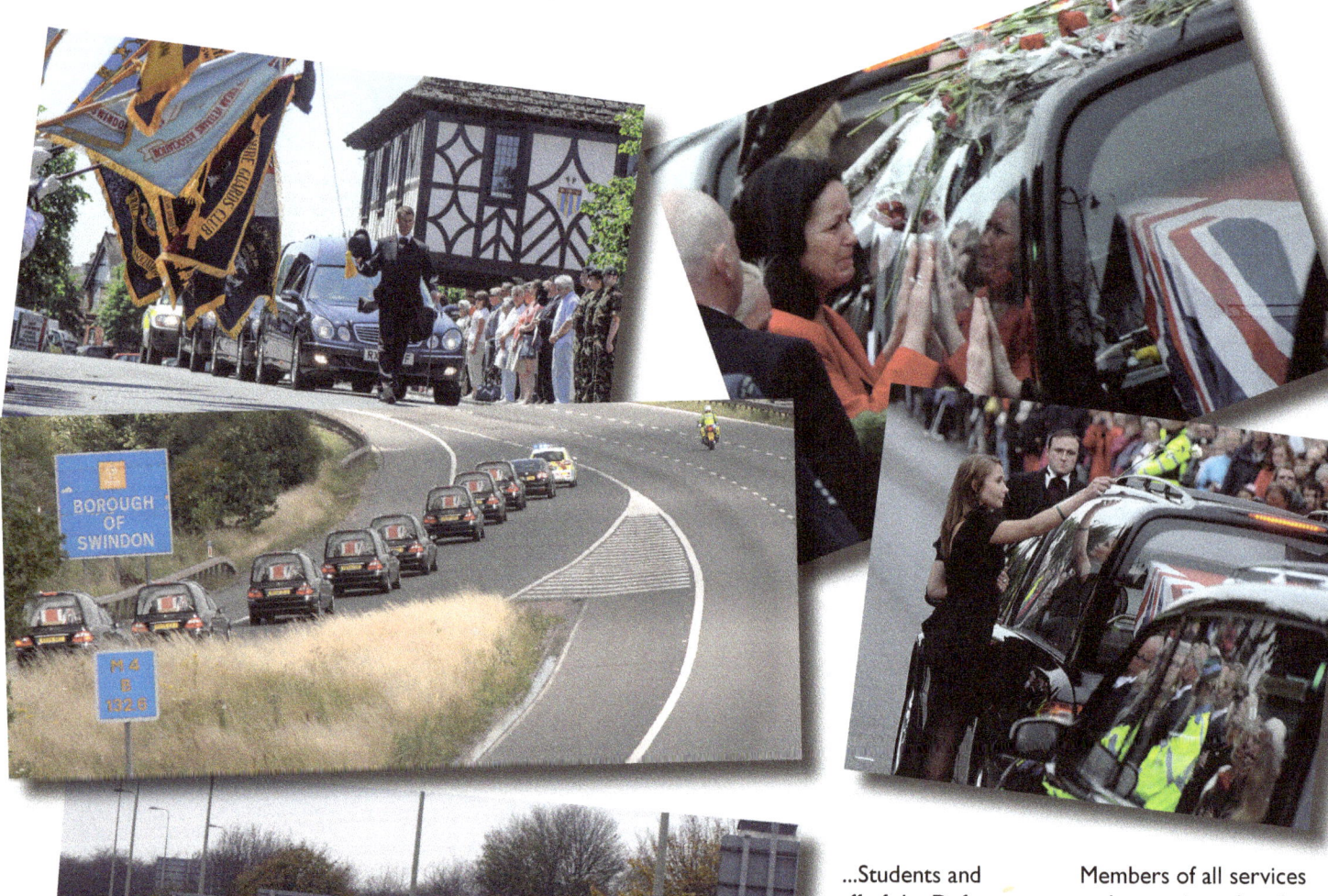

...Students and staff of the Defence Academy of the United Kingdom lined the A420 at Shrivenham as the cortege passed.

Members of all services and countries saluted as the fallen made their way to Oxford.

But all these repatriations were first flown into RAF Lyneham...

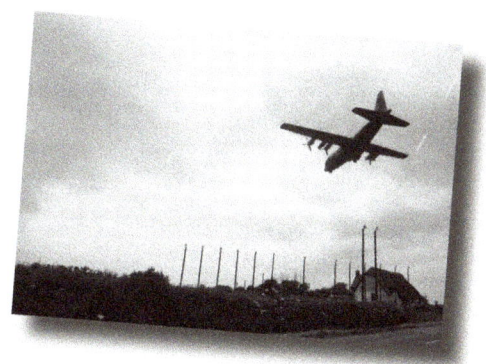

...I miss it, you know; that drone of the majestic workhorse of the air, the Lockheed C130 Hercules, as it flew in and out of the Lyneham air base on missions or training sorties.

Living on the ten-mile turning point of the eastern approach to the base, the 'Fat Alberts' as they were known seemed to keep you company day and night.

Now that the base has morphed into an Army Training School and the runway has been decommissioned, the sky is eerily quiet, with just the odd helicopter passing over, and planes travelling to the airfields at Brize Norton or Fairford causing you to look up.

Lyneham has featured in quite a few events over the years: the various anniversaries of the lumbering Hercules transport aircraft, the various missions undertaken to, among other scenarios, the Ethiopian famine and Falklands conflict.

Of course there were the world famous, solemn, repatriations through Royal Wootton Bassett and numerous Royal visits associated with the base.

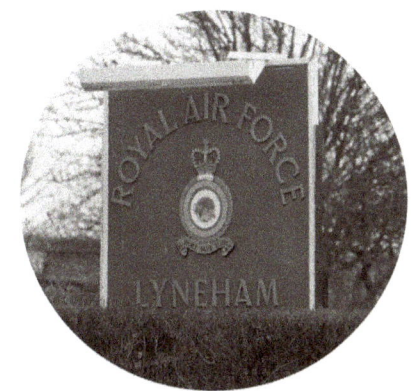

But, on 19 October 1991, the biggest event RAF Lyneham had seen took place.

It was dark, very wet, and a rather awful day to be standing on an exposed airbase amongst the largest press pack seen in years, waiting for an RAF transport plane to land with a rather important passenger. Amongst the press was a young lad who was with us for work experience from a local school. He was to have an experience that he will remember throughout his days.

The chain of events all started several months earlier, when on 8 August after 1,943 days in captivity, TV journalist John McCarthy arrived at the Wiltshire base to a very large reception, and massed ranks of the media. His girlfriend Jill Morrell, who had campaigned relentlessly for his release, was there to greet him.

After his release from captivity in Beirut, McCarthy was taken under army escort to the Syrian capital of Damascus, where he was reunited with his father and brother, and gave a statement to the press.

In it, he confirmed the 'good health and good spirits' of his fellow hostages including the Archbishop of Canterbury's special envoy Terry Waite, whom he praised for giving him the strength to survive the ordeal.

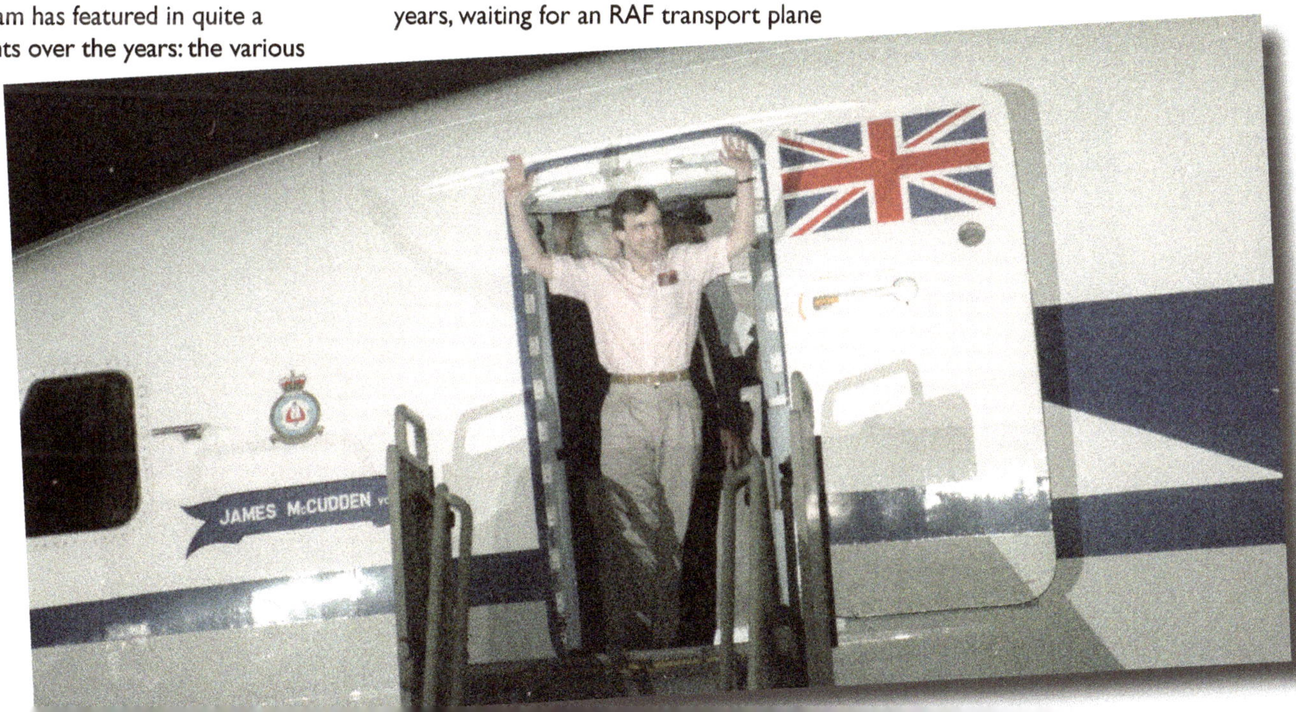

The plane, an RAF VC10, landed at the base, and **John McCarthy** emerged into the floodlights. He raised both arms in a salute to freedom, and descended the steps from the aircraft. He was greeted by the base commander Group Captain Ian Corbitt, and gave the obligatory press conference. He was then transferred into the hands of the medical staff from RAF Wroughton's Princess Alexandra Hospital to undergo rehabilitation.

On 11 August we returned to Lyneham for a ceremony of international standing that surpassed many Lyneham had ever seen.

John McCarthy publicly handed a sealed letter to the United Nations Secretary General Javier Perez de Cuellar from his former captives in Lebanon.

De Cuellar had made the trip from New York to the amazement of McCarthy who said, in his book *Some Other Rainbow*:

'Perez de Cuellar had agreed to come to Lyneham to save me flying to New York, which was a huge relief – although I was amazed that such an important man would rearrange his schedule to suit me.'

He went on to say, 'I was still enough of a journalist to appreciate how infuriating it must have been for the press not to have the opportunity to talk to me. A few questions after the meeting with de Cuellar would both fulfil my pledge to Islamic Jihad to make the hand-over as public as possible and give the press something more than the limited briefings from the RAF and WTN.'

The hand-over was public, the press conference took place, and we made sure that the images went worldwide.

Several weeks passed, and fellow hostage, WW2 fighter ace Jackie Mann, joined McCarthy back in the UK. He was accompanied on his return to the UK by his colourful wife 'Sunnie'. They descended into Lyneham, and were greeted by the Group Captain. This was a rather lower key event, but still significant in the history of Lyneham. I must admit that I did not go, dispatching one of my photographers to cover the event instead.

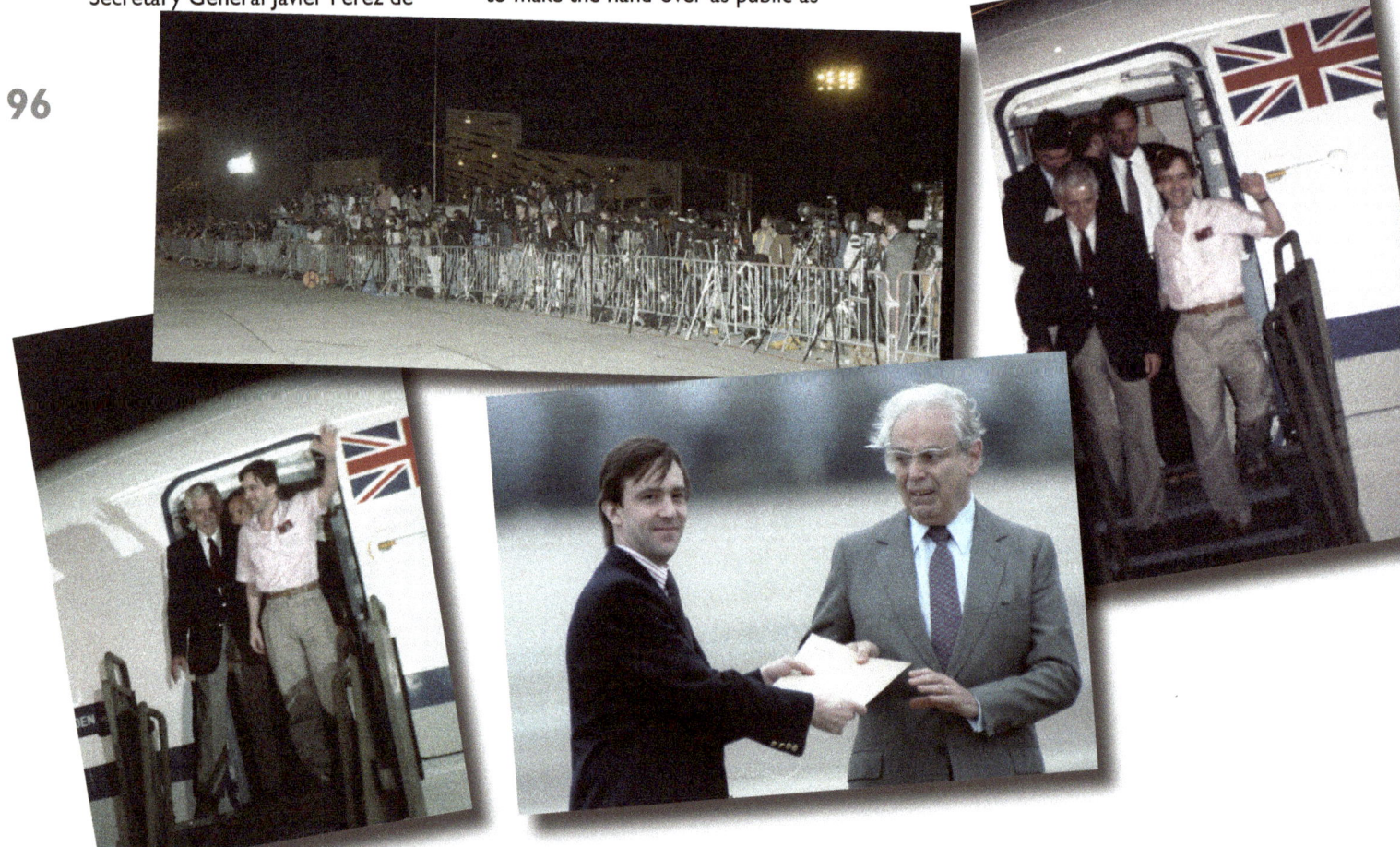

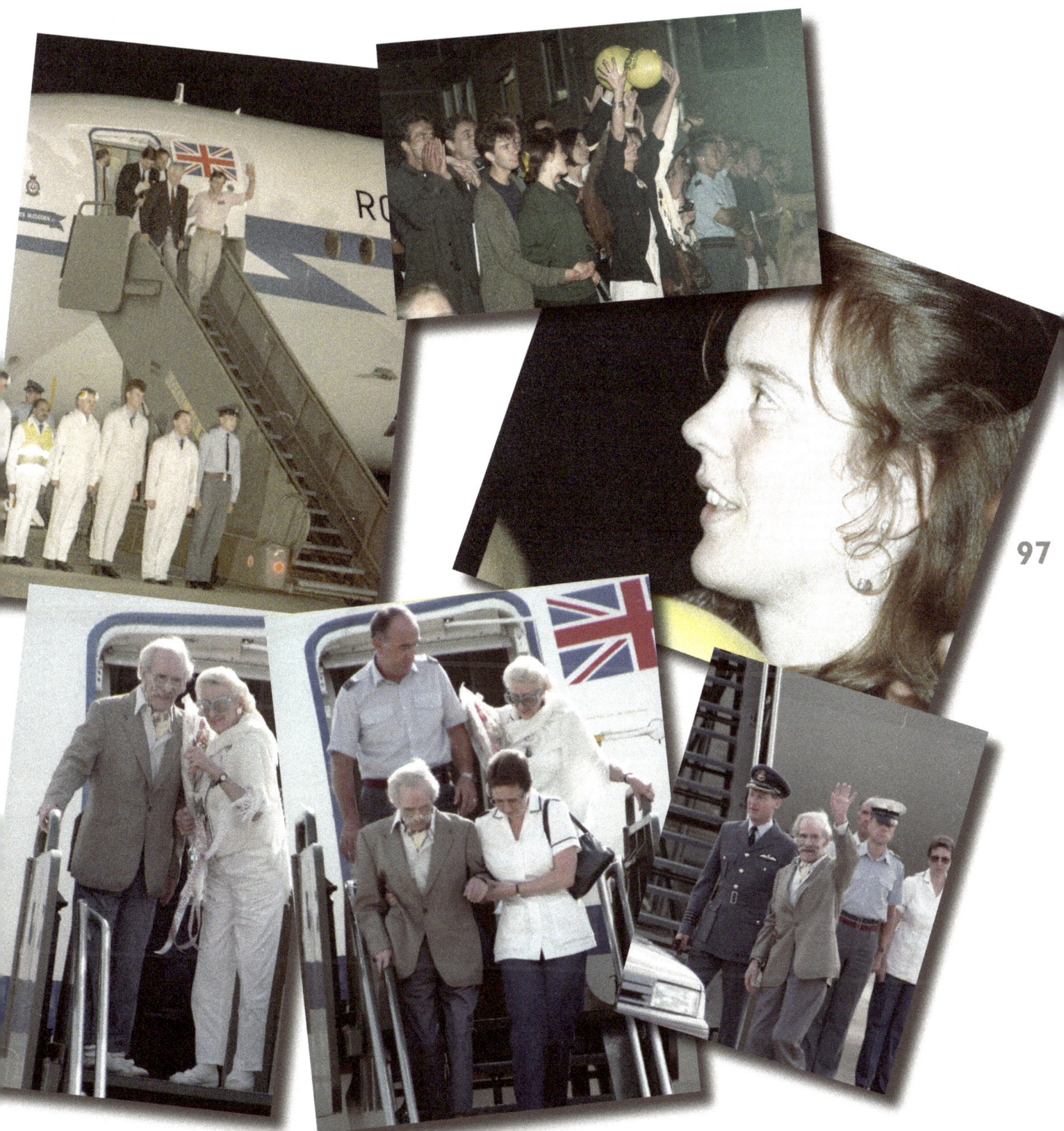

It was on the 17 October 1991 when there was a newsflash saying that Terry Waite had been released, and was on his way to freedom. Twitter had not been conceived, the Internet was in its infancy, so we only had Ceefax and Teletext services on our small office television. The newsflash sent us into an immediate conference, as we knew that the next day would be chaos.

I remember turning to our work experience lad and saying, 'You had better tell your parents you might be late home tomorrow, as you will witness one of the major events in history.'

And it was.

The John McCarthy press pack was large, but Terry's was much bigger. They even had Sir Trevor McDonald on the roof of the terminal doing a live broadcast; a very rare and expensive event in those days.

Hundreds of photographers, reporters and technicians arrived at the base and were put in one of the hangars. Our work experience lad was put in charge of looking after several thousands of pounds worth of kit, while the press pack consumed copious amounts of tea and biscuits which were served as we waited for the plane to arrive.

The VC10 (incorrectly announced as a DC10 by Sir Trevor) pulled up, and the Archbishop with his advisors climbed the steps and boarded the plane. Shortly after that Terry appeared and did the obligatory wave. He descended the steps into the Lyneham gloom.

From then on it was mayhem.

My photographer departed back to our Swindon office as soon as Terry's foot hit the tarmac, so that he could beat the many other snappers, some processing their film on the base with portable labs and sending images of their pictures via very basic and expensive negative scanner transmitters over RAF-provided phone lines.

We were all trying to get the first pictures out. Myself and the young lad followed an hour or so later with the images from Terry's press conference.

That in itself was a major event, as Terry proceeded to tell his story; and what a story it turned out to be.

We had two wire machines in those days, but only one was a colour machine, so we were able to send our images quite quickly for the first editions and upgrade to colour for later editions if required.

Sending a picture on the old wire network meant you had to stick a caption strip on the edge of the print; there was no metadata in those days.

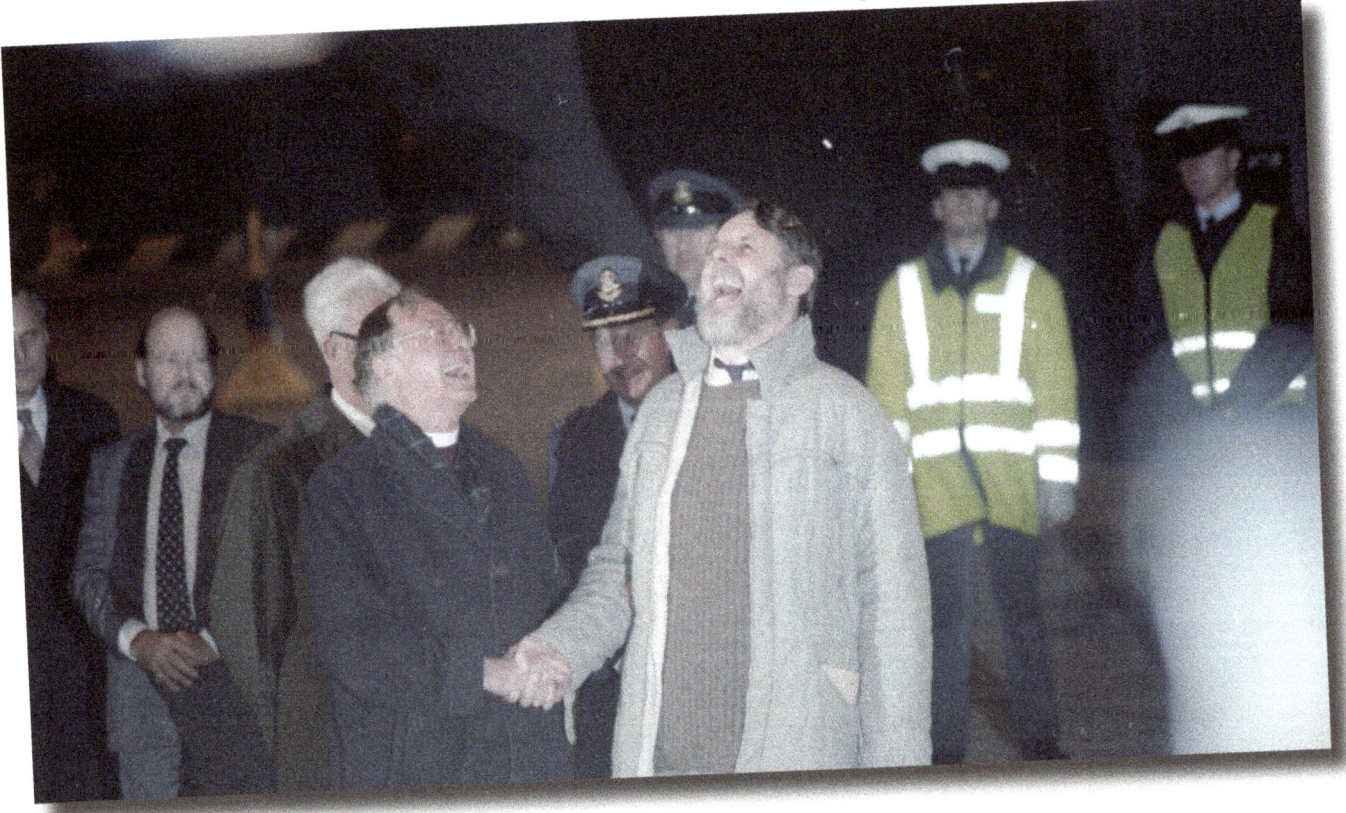

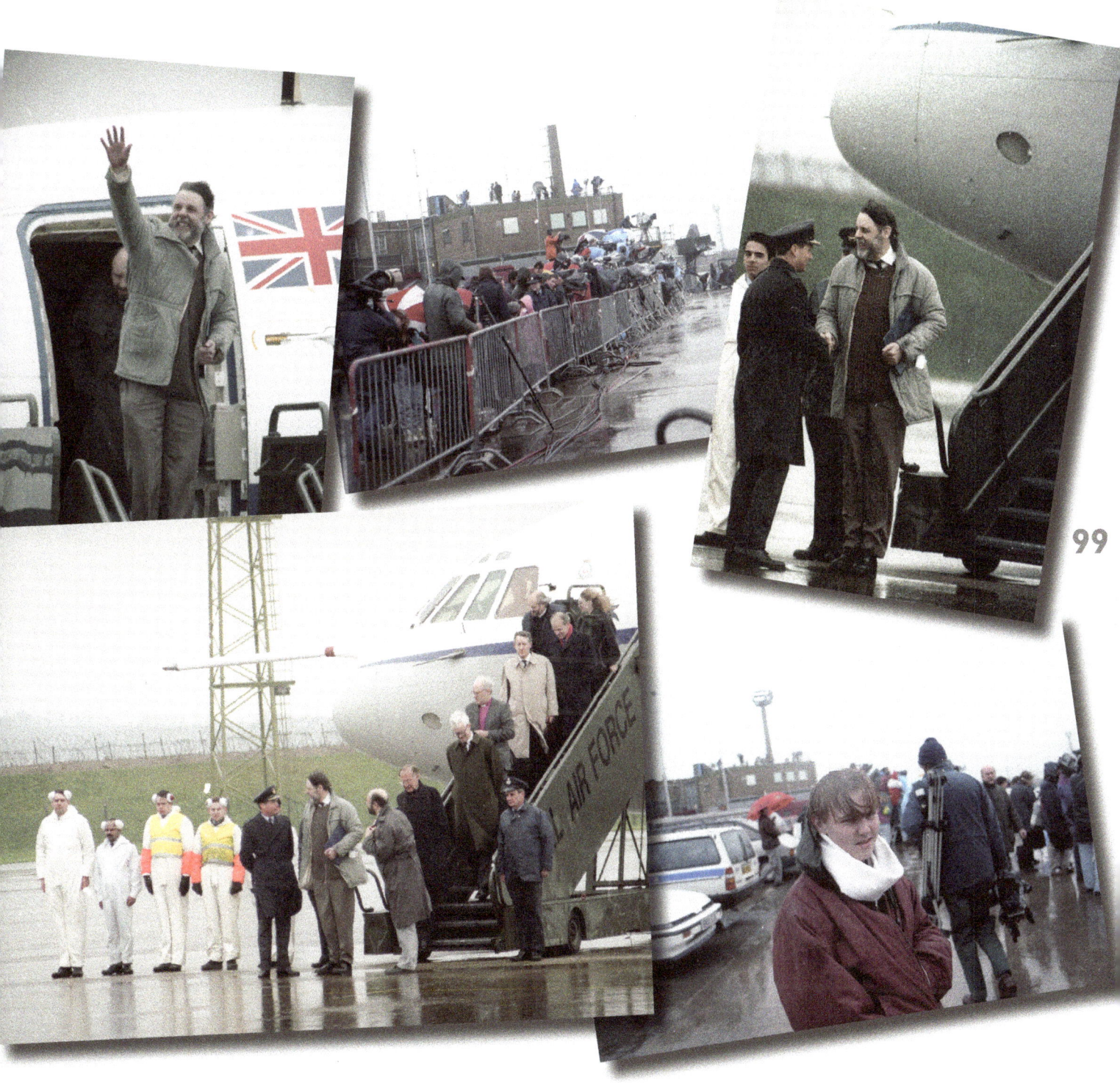

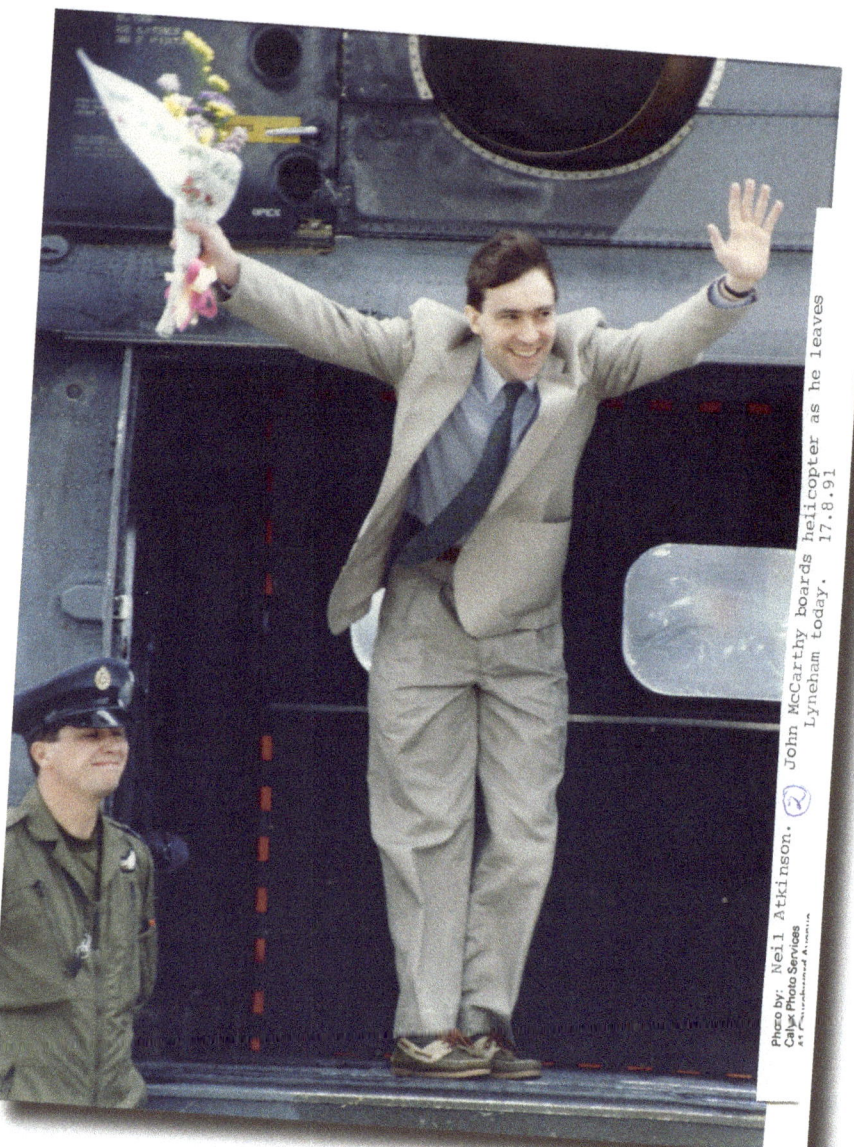

I will try to explain how we transmitted pictures around the world, to the present generation where now pictures taken one second appear the next all over the world.

The picture is of the 'wire print' of the arrival of John McCarthy at RAF Lyneham. to meet with United Nations Secretary General Javier Perez de Cuellar on 11 August 1991.

The image was taken on colour negative film, and the colour print was produced from the selected negative. It is a 6" x 8" colour print with the caption STUCK on using glue.

The image was then placed on the cylinder of a telephoto transmitter machine, or a 'wire machine', which by NGA union dictat could only be operated by one of their members.

A Post Office telephone engineer in the local telephone exchange would have to plug your 'wire line' into the national 'wire network' and an engineer the other end would have to connect the receiving newspaper wire line to the said network.

The machine was started and the cylinder rotated at 2 revolutions per second. Each time the bar holding the print passed a beam of light emitted by the transmission unit there would be a 'PING'; this was to synchronise the receiving machine with your transmitter. This is where the expression 'to ping a picture' originates from.

After 30 seconds, the operator pressed the transmit button and the beam of light would slowly traverse the image, sending an analogue squeal down the line.

After 6 minutes the picture had been sent and you could load the next picture on the cylinder, if you were sending a monochrome image.

If you needed to send colour you changed the filter from Cyan to Magenta and repeated the sending process. You then did the Yellow scan, meaning that a colour picture took over 25 minutes to send.

Including processing and printing, you were talking of about an hour to send one colour print to one newspaper.

How times have changed!!!...

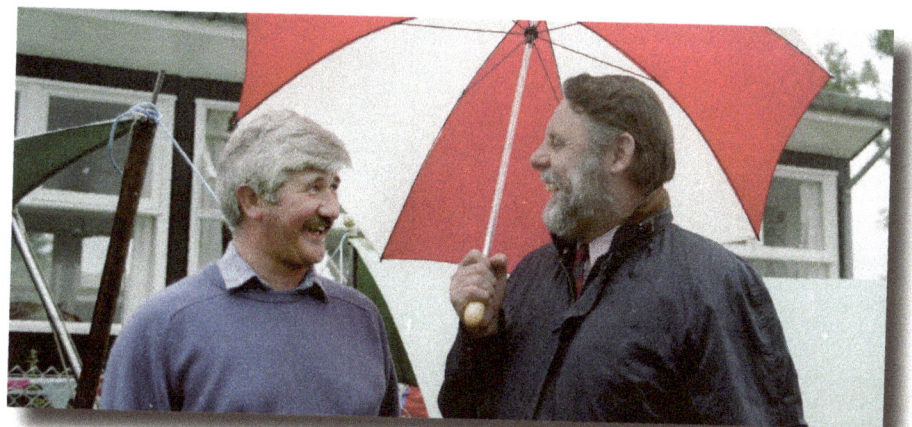

...John McCarthy left Lyneham after his rehabilitation in a flurry of publicity a few weeks after he set foot in the base, and our work was used nationally, as was that of Jackie Mann's departure.

Terry Waite left the base more quietly a few weeks after he arrived.

As a follow-up, I was commissioned to take the first pictures of the psychiatrist Gordon Turnbull, who was in charge of their rehabilitation, at the Wroughton hospital, and have taken pictures of him since; on one occasion with Terry Waite at the Broad Town Fete.

On 1 July 2011 the last planes flew out of the Beehive (as Lyneham became known locally) to be stationed at Brize Norton in Oxfordshire, closing the RAF era there.

So they are gone. No more low-flying over my roof, no more photocalls, and being entertained in the Officers' Mess.

On one visit, covering an all-night shift with ground crews loading sacks of emergency food for Africa, a bedraggled press pack of photographers and TV crews were shepherded into the Officers' Mess by the press officer and served breakfast by formally-dressed stewards with the silver service. It was a very bizarre but memorable event in the annals of the Lyneham air base.

The base has now been re-commissioned as the REME training establishment and houses the regimental museum which is in what was the Officers' Mess.

The Comet gate guardian gone; replaced by a wall with a plaque that was unveiled by the Regiment's Colonel-in Chief, HRH Prince Philip, Duke of Edinburgh.

The Duke met children from the Lyneham School before pulling the cord to reveal the slate plaque on the Cotswold stone wall, built where once stood the Comet. As the curtains parted, so another chapter opened for the once busy airfield.

The 'bees' have moved to Brize, but many more stories cover the history of the base and have yet to be told...

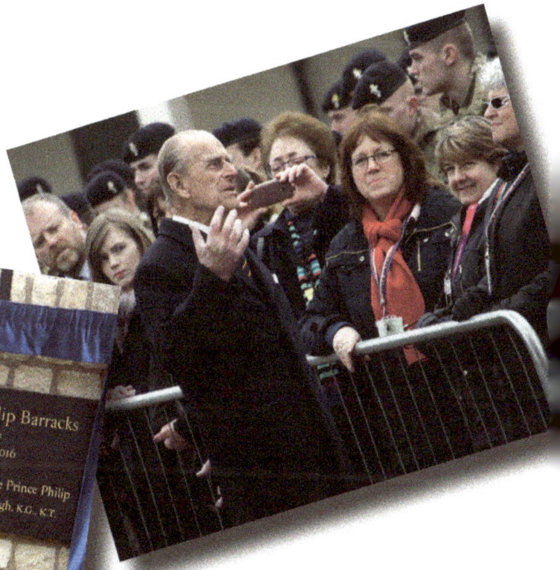

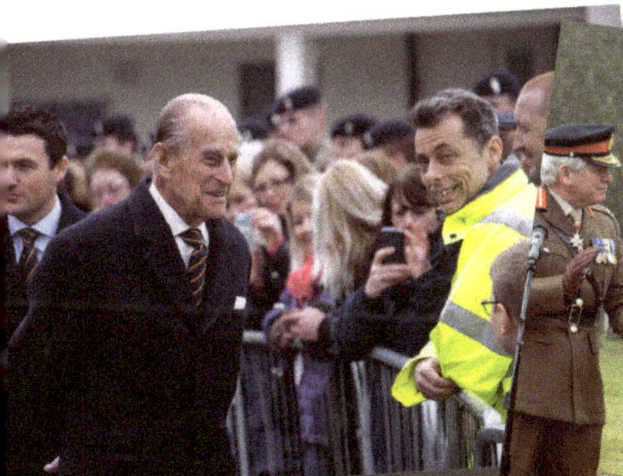

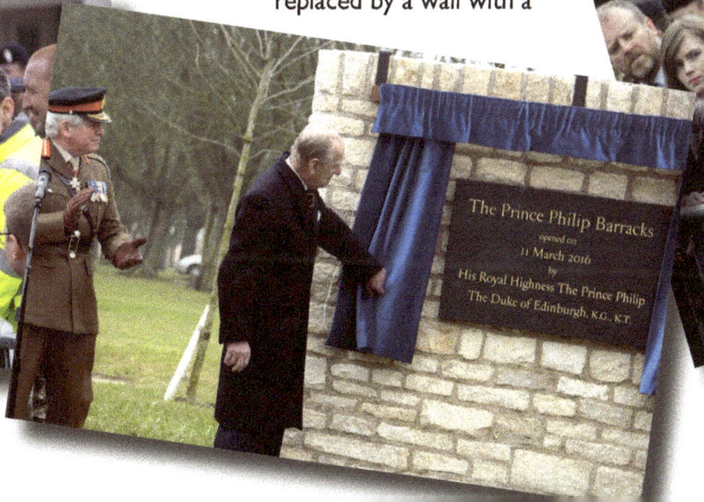

...The hostages were treated by Wing Comander (now professor) Gordon Turnbull at the Princess Alexandra's Hospital at Wroughton. The hospital has now gone, existing only in the archive.

Heroes from the Falklands were treated there, but their expertise with injuries of conflict helped victims of another major news story; the Hungerford shootings.

It was a quiet day in August 1987, and I was just turning off the M32 onto the M4 having delivered some negatives to the *Western Daily Press* in Bristol when my carphone sounded.

In those days it was a large dashboard-mounted unit with a small suitcase in the boot and you had to be connected by an operator. The Pye Olympic was the same unit that was used by taxi companies.

This call was from *The Times* and the picture editor told me that a man had just started shooting up the town of Hungerford and could I get there soonest.

Needless to say I rather hammered it to Hungerford. I don't think speeding was an issue, as I was overtaken by many police cars on the way.

I fitted into the last space in the pub car park at the bottom of the High Street, grabbed the cameras and legged it up to where the road was cordoned off.

I met up with some other photographers, a TV stringer, as well as a reporter from the *Daily Express* and somehow we found an alleyway that the police had overlooked and left unguarded, so we wandered up it.

We emerged on Fairview Road and, to our left, there was a house on fire. This house turned out to be Michael Ryan's house.

We walked up the road and came across a Nissan that had been shot up and inside was a shape covered in a blanket.

We recorded the scene.

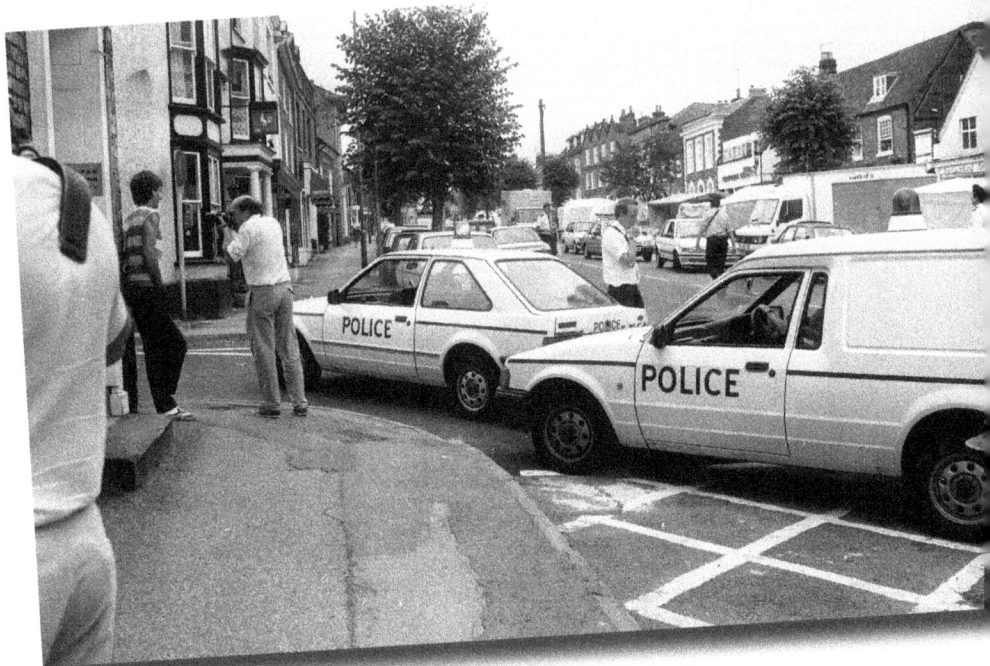

Eventually an off-duty policeman spotted us and rather roughly bundled us into one of the houses. He then told the group of us that the gunman, who was later identified as Michael Ryan, was still active. As it turned out he was holed up in the school at that time, but confusion reigned and we took no chances.

I took this opportunity to try and contact home, but the telephone network had overloaded and was down.

Mobile phones had only just reached that part of the country, and my signal was intermittent to say the least, but I managed to talk, albeit briefly, to Pat and let her know I was in one piece.

Pat, my ever patient wife, knew of my destination as I had informed her while mobile to Hungerford, and I am reliably told that she was rather worried during the time I was there.

On my way to Hungerford, I managed to get a message to Sarah, my other photographer, and dispatched her to the Princess Margaret Hospital. She had been on a day off in Weston, so was about an hour away, but she got there in time to photograph some of the victims arriving there.

Deciding to go with what I had already photographed, I left the house by the back door and down the back alley, emerging on to the High Street. I made my way back to my car, passing the massive press pack that had gathered at the cordon. I think it was the first time I had encountered satellite trucks...

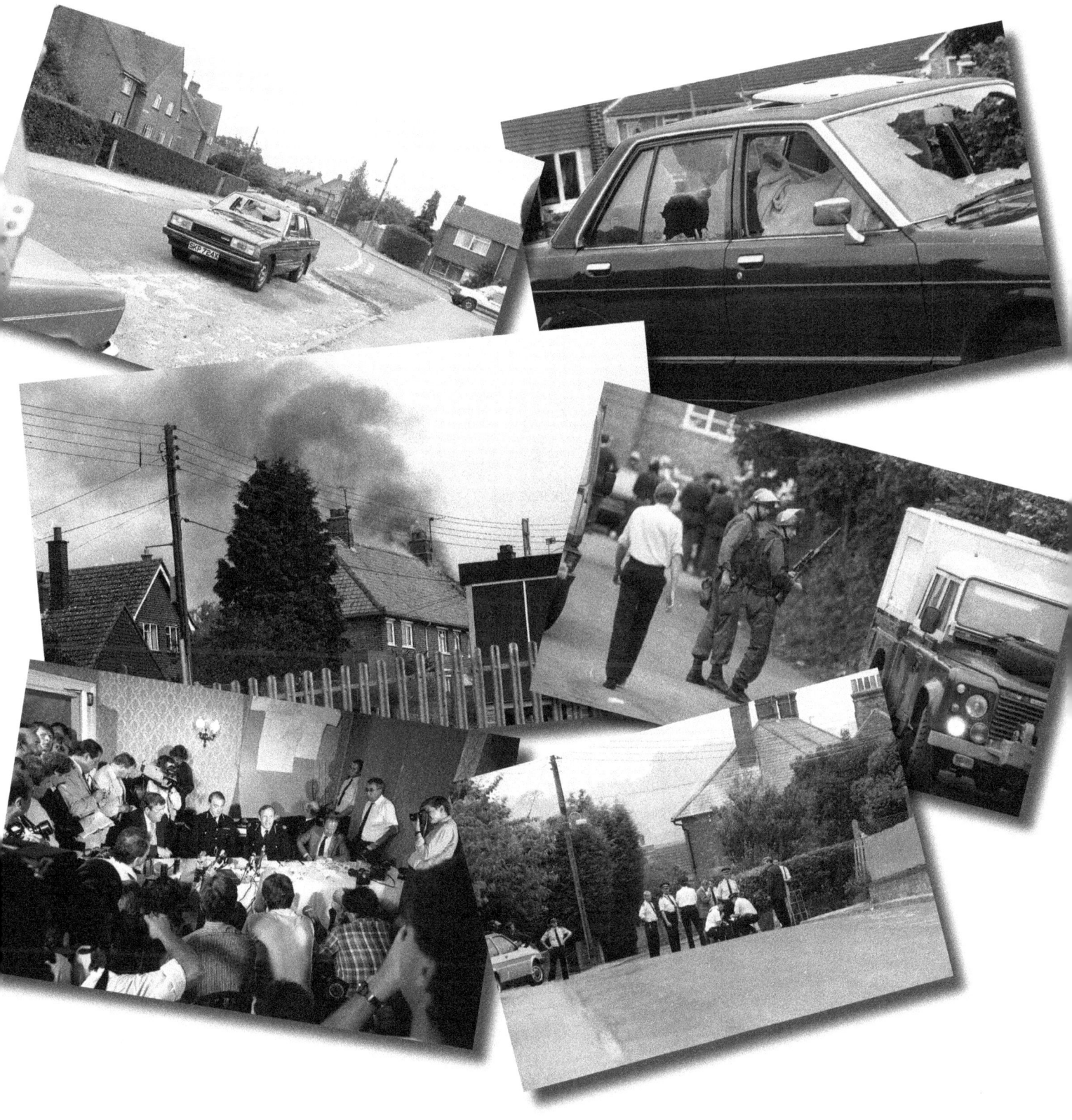

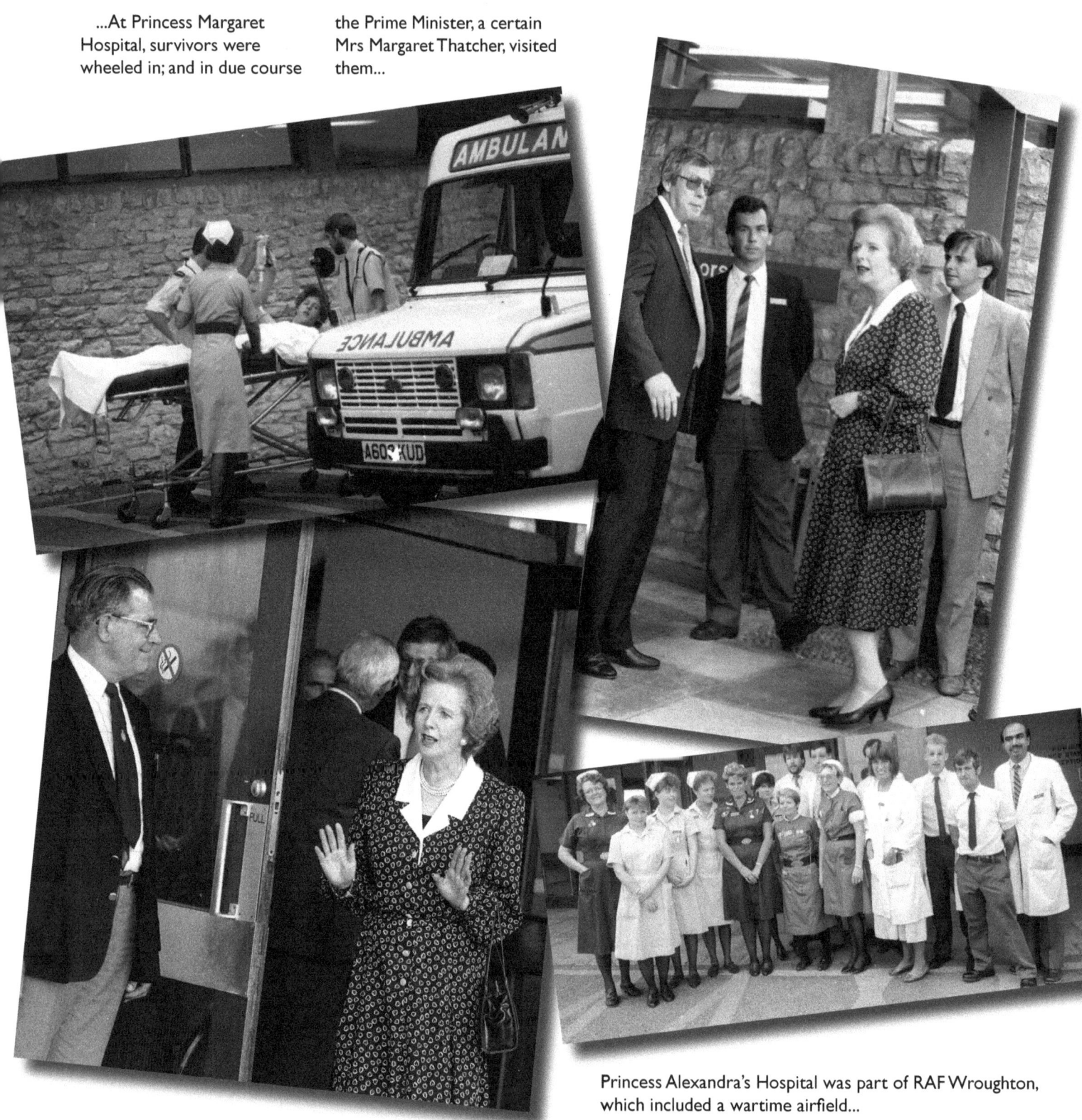

...At Princess Margaret Hospital, survivors were wheeled in; and in due course the Prime Minister, a certain Mrs Margaret Thatcher, visited them...

Princess Alexandra's Hospital was part of RAF Wroughton, which included a wartime airfield...

...I never did get a picture of Michael Ryan.

The only, and famous, image of him was taken by the *Newbury Weekly News* freelance photographer at a photocall with Peter De Savary, when he first moved into Littlecote House.

Ryan was one of the workers in the background of the picture.

I, for some reason, did not go to that photocall; but with the money that was flying around for the image, and what was charged for the rights to use the picture, I could have retired then.

Well, at least I have an archive because of Michael Ryan.

In all the carnage, panic and total confusion there is always a lighter side to the story; I had just received my wire licence, a document that qualified my company to transmit images to London.

At the time there was an 80 mile zone around London where a freelance wire service was banned, so the local newspaper was the only machine allowed; except for mobile Fleet Street machines with their own operators.

I had just managed to negotiate to get a machine, and that wire machine was housed in the home extension where I am writing this. The extension had just been built, but not internally finished.

The dedicated wire lines for one wire machine had been been installed, and the newly-acquired machine was on a stool in the middle of the office floor.

As we were the closest wire point to Hungerford, our services were rapidly called upon and a number of national photographers descended on us to get their films processed and wired to their picture desks in London.

My son and daughter still remember playing cricket on the lawn with the likes of PA's Barry Batchilor and the *Mirror's* late George Phillips, while they waited to send their pictures.

Just to add to the interesting facts file: Vodafone had not put the mast in near Hungerford at that time, so the signal was very patchy. You could tell the Vodafone users, as the only signal available in the High Street was in a few metres square outside the Town Hall, which was where we gathered to make our calls!

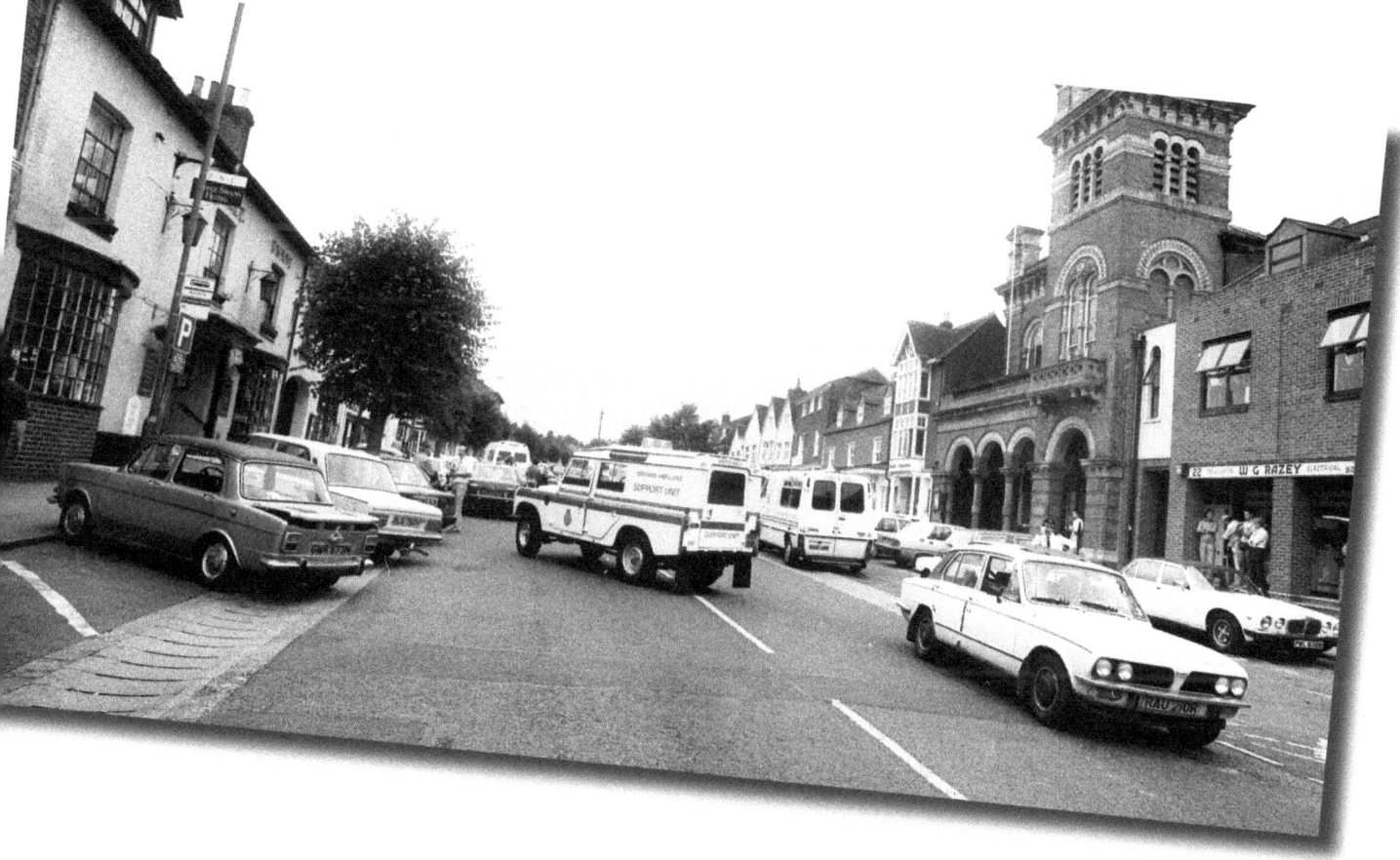

...As part of the job description of a picture agency, one has to look through many documents that fly around in cyberspace.

One such document is the Council's Planning Lists.

On 4th November 2013 I spotted the following:

'Change of use from disused runway/events space at the former Wroughton Airfield to a short term research and development facility for a temporary period from March to November 2014. (Variation of condition 1 regarding a termination date).'

The historic 545-acre airfield at the former RAF Wroughton base is set under the Ridgeway National Trail and overlooking Wroughton, with views of Swindon as a backdrop.

Taken over by the Science Museum in 1972, the airfield is used as a store for the organisation's larger objects and specialist storage of documents, in a modern air-conditioned building which was opened by Prince Edward.

Over the years, I have visited the site for many press days and events including the very popular Wroughton Air Day.

In August of 1992 the Air Day became the Great Warbirds Air Display, and attracted planes from all over the world, including pop star Gary Numan with his WW2 Harvard with Japanese markings.

Numan, a highly regarded pilot, flew in from Duxford for the 2-day show, in which he flew in formation and displayed solo. He was part of a display team that carried out a mock dogfight over the now-disused runways.

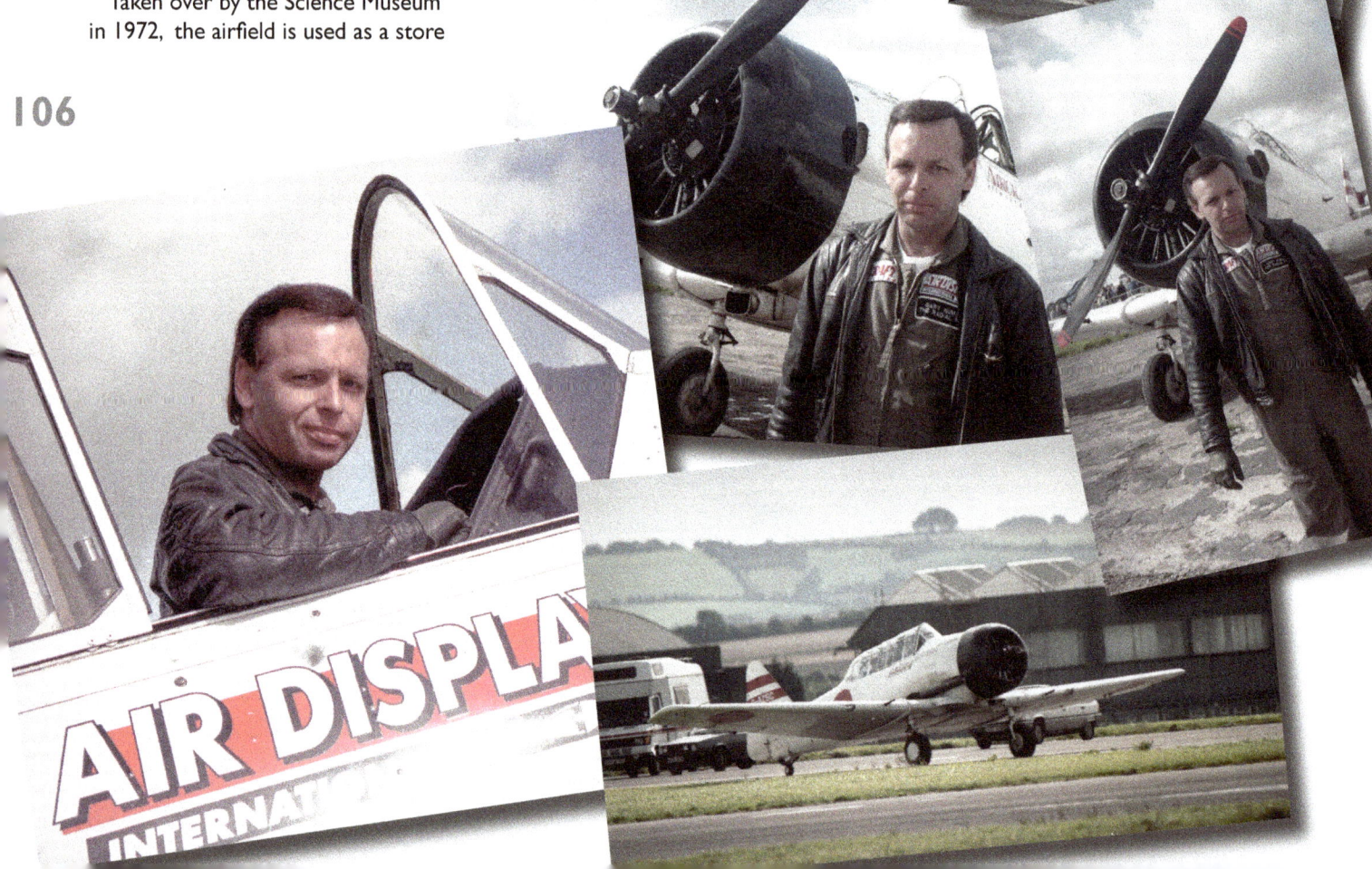

Among the other attractions was the Flying Fortress the 'Sally B,' which was one of the American B17 WW2 bombers that starred in the 1990 film Memphis Belle. Also on the flying list was the Air Atlantique DC3.

At the time, Vic Norman's Wing Walking Circus was a novelty flight, sponsored by Cadbury's brand Crunchie, and three of his Stearman bi-planes, with wing-walking girls, did a display. I must admit that one of the perks of the job was loads of sample Crunchie bars.

No show in those days was complete without the magnificent Vulcan, and this much-loved veteran put in a flypast and short display. Its approach was over the Burmah House as it was then, now Wakefield House on Pipers Way...

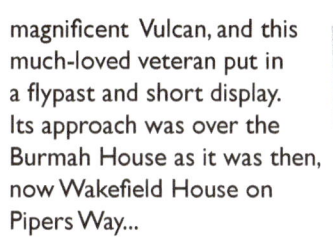

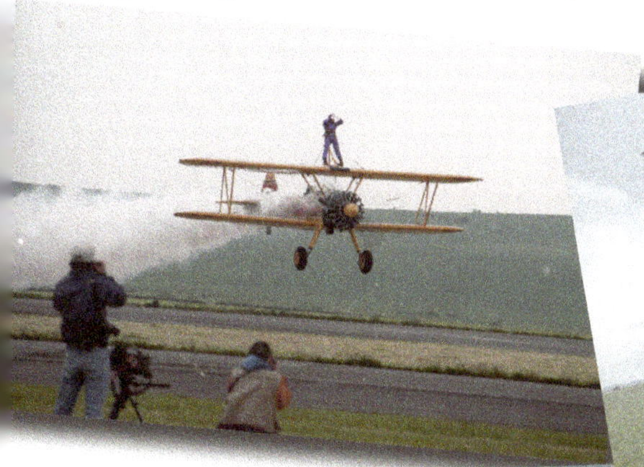

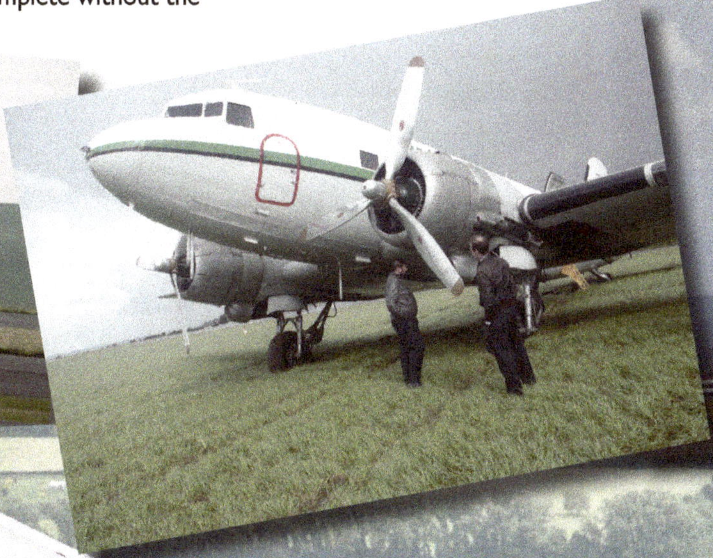

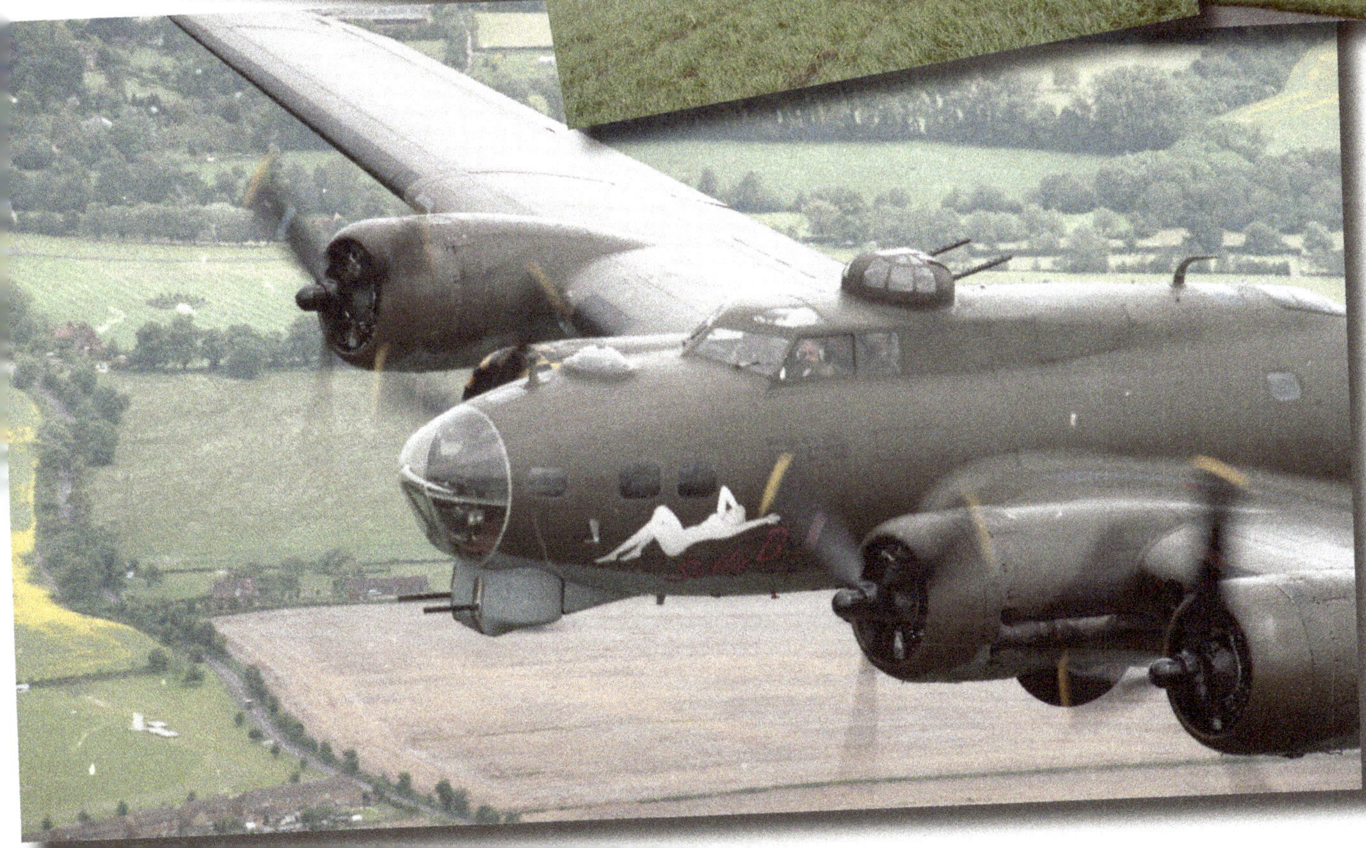

...So, what other aviation gems have I seen at the Wroughton Airfield site?

At the height of the cold war on March 14 1986, when Cruise missiles were stored down the M4 at Greenham Common, a WW2 V2 German rocket caused a stir as it was moved back to London for display. There were some protesters who thought it was its modern day equivalent.

Many aircraft have arrived by various means, flying in or by road, in several pieces or whole.

A de Havilland DH.89 Dragon Rapide with just its wing stubs was brought to the museum through Chisledon and the back gate. With hindsight they should have used the main road, as the plane was too wide for the road and sustained damage as it got stuck just past the Patriot Arms.

The Lockheed Constellation N7777G arrived by road on five lorries, having been dismantled at Dublin Airport by the Aces High Company. The trip to the Science Museum took up most of the main road in Wroughton, and made national pictures to boot.

The plane is famous, as it was used to carry equipment and support staff during a Rolling Stones tour of the Far East and Australia in 1973. Even as it arrived, the Rolling Stones logo could be seen on the side.

Some aircraft flew in using the main runway to its full, such as a retiring RAF De Havilland Dove, in its red, white, and blue colours.

A British Airways Trident Three made its final flight into the Museum, over-flying its sister Trident One for the cameras.

The Trident One was later cut up and transported out of the Wroughton site by road.

An ignominious end to an illustrious career? Not really,.. but do things change?

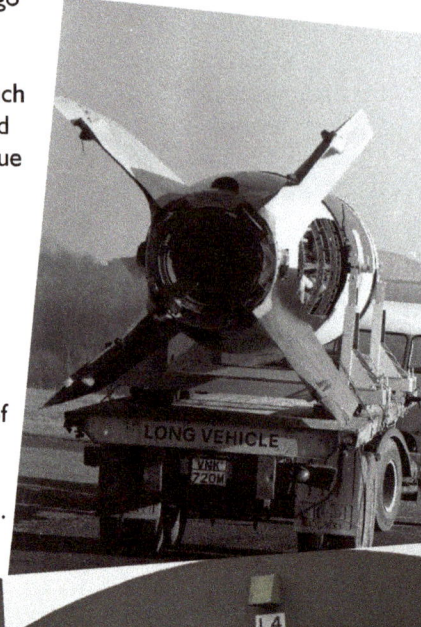

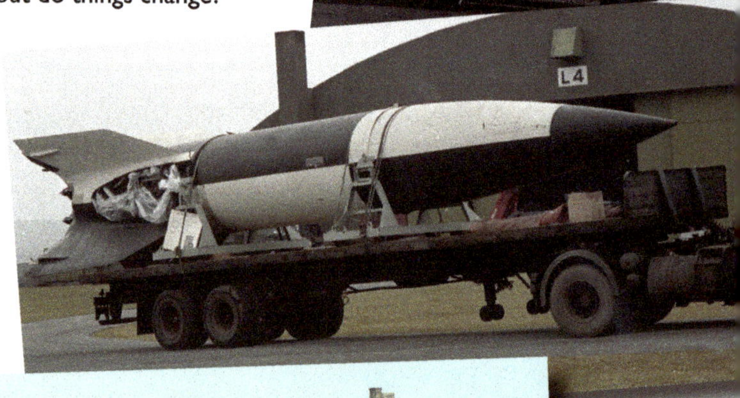

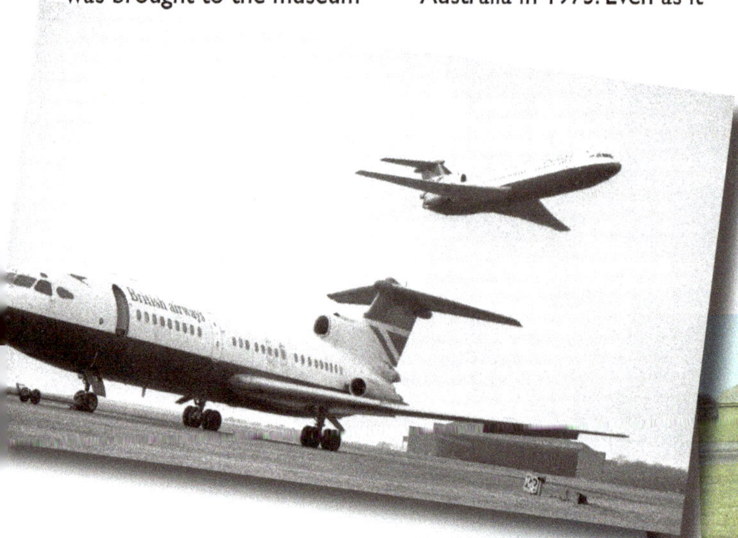

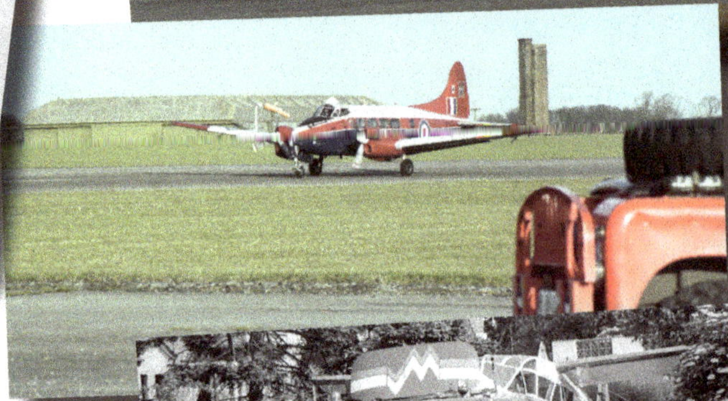

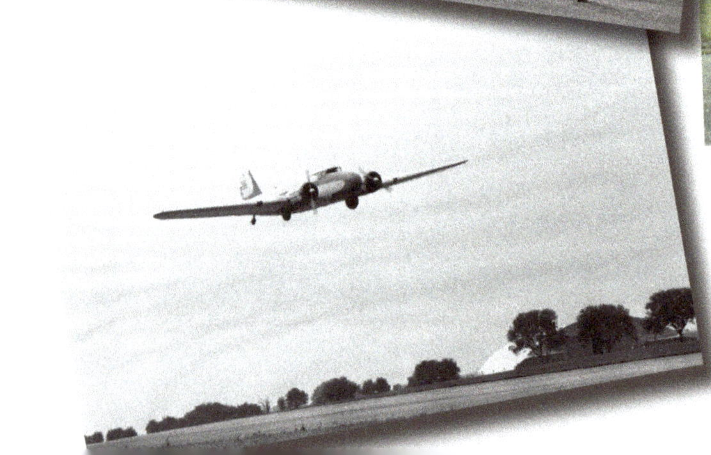

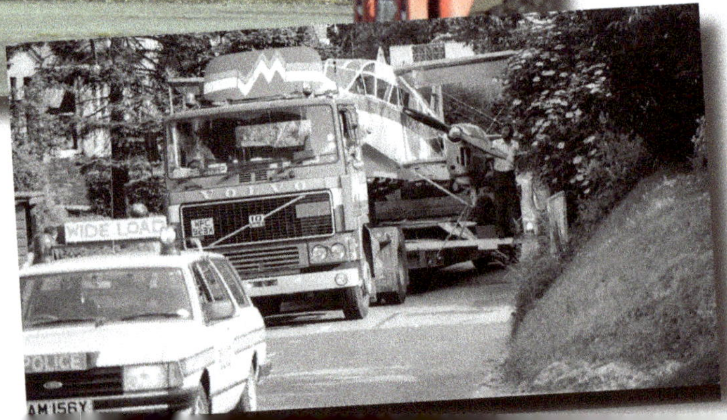

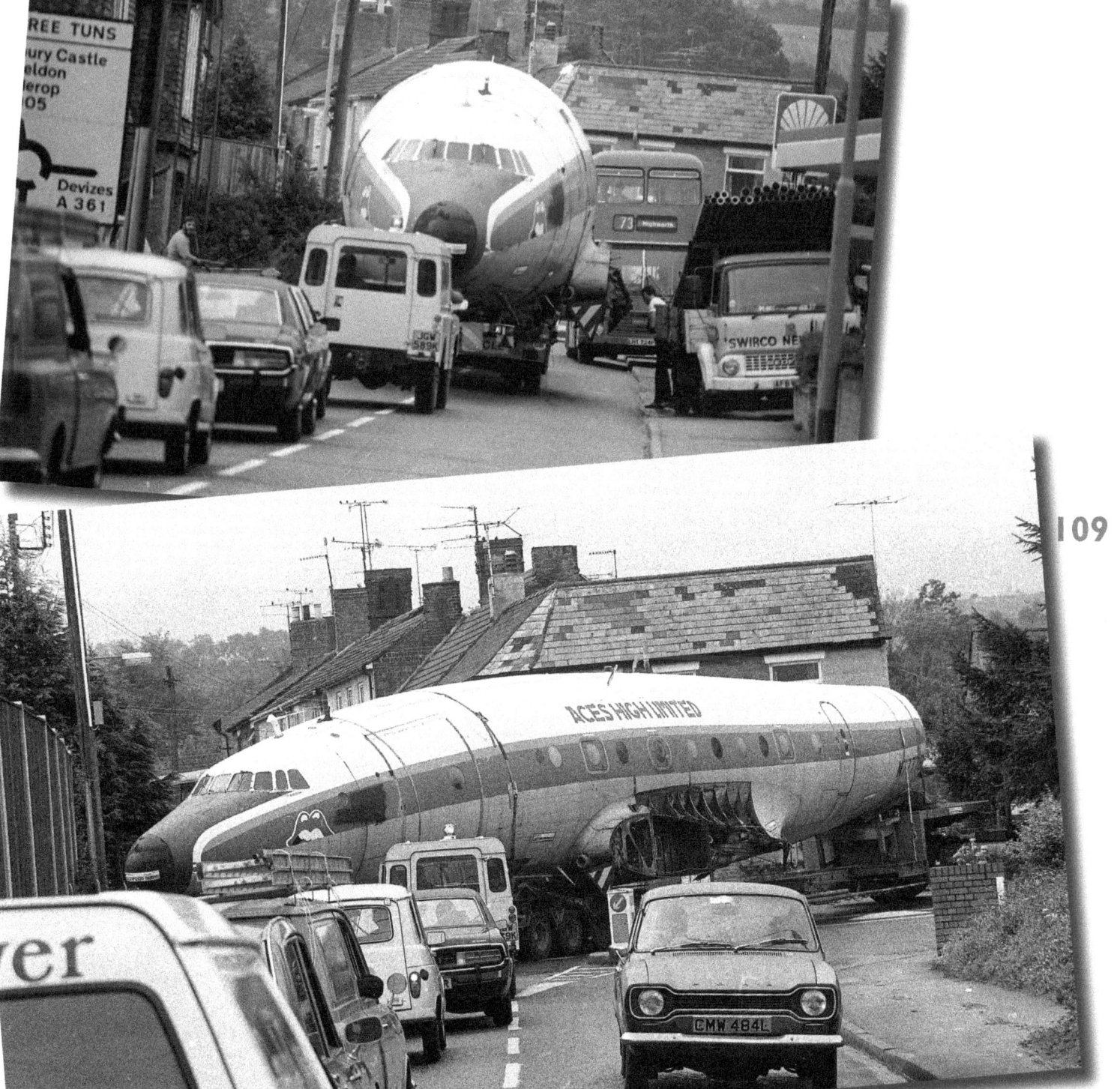

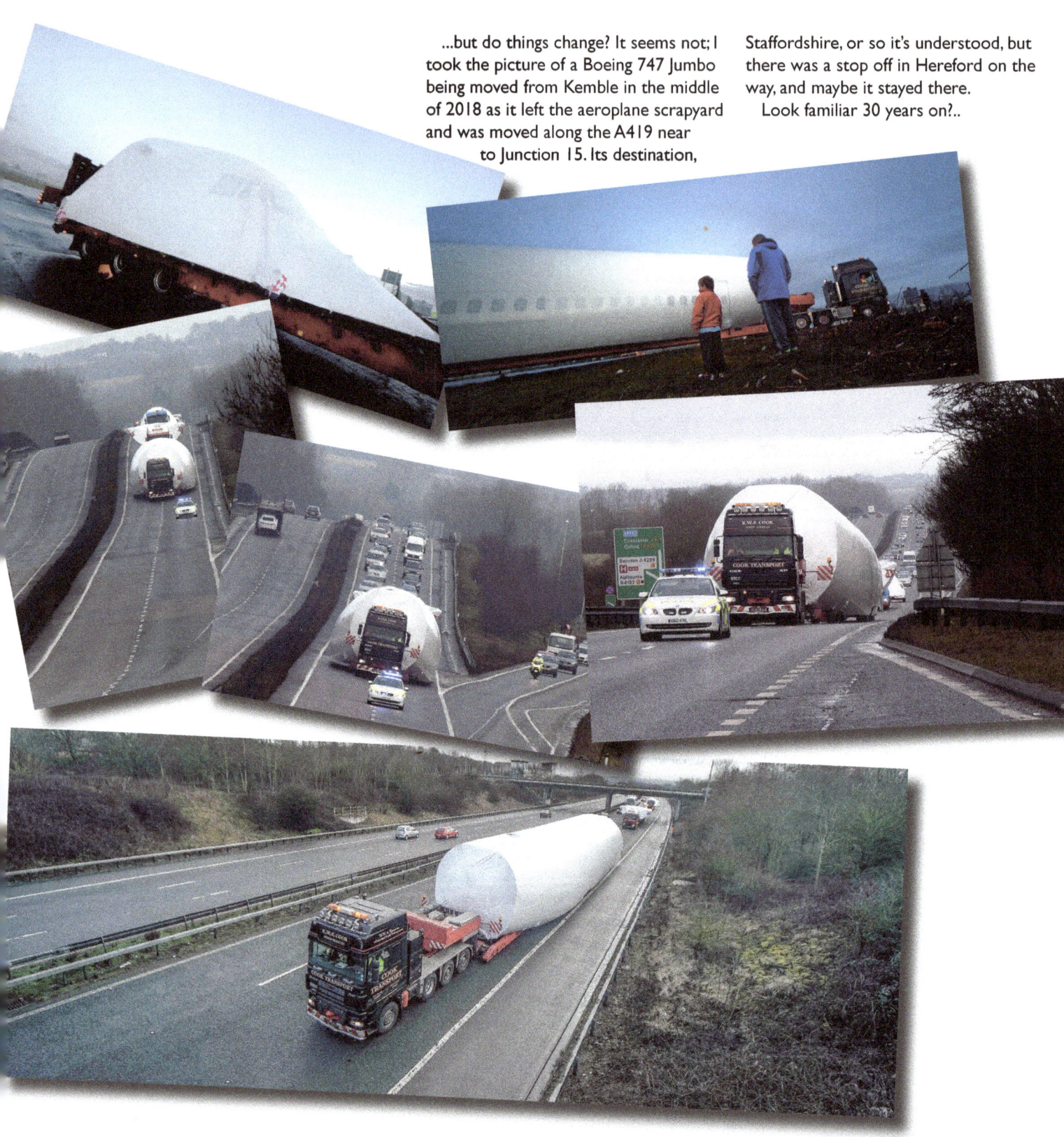

...but do things change? It seems not; I took the picture of a Boeing 747 Jumbo being moved from Kemble in the middle of 2018 as it left the aeroplane scrapyard and was moved along the A419 near to Junction 15. Its destination, Staffordshire, or so it's understood, but there was a stop off in Hereford on the way, and maybe it stayed there.

Look familiar 30 years on?..

...As to the Science Museum site; it is being developed by the Museum into a major tourist attraction, research, and storage site for the antiquities that are not shown now.

The museum opened up their doors for the press and VIPs to inspect the new facility in its early building phase.

The development is massive, and will secure the site's future.

Among the exhibits that drove us around the site was one of the first electric taxis and a Hydrogen-powered next generation vehicle.

Hydrogen power seems to be playing a part in Swindon's economic development at the moment, as we have the hydrogen fuel cell manufacturer, Johnson Matthey at Lydiard Fields, where there is a hydrogen filling station, and Honda has a filling station at the North gate of its plant too. Honda's forklift trucks are hydrogen-powered.

Electricity is obviously a new economic element to life at the Science Museum, as the runway which provided the museum with events and helped deliver some of the exhibits is now covered in solar panels. The 88 acres of photovoltaic (PV) arrays will generate close to 50 GWh of energy each year. This is enough energy to power 15,400 homes.

Swindon's industrial past was steam powered and, during the Second World War, that was augmented by Merlin power, the great engine that powered many of the war's great aircraft including the Swindon-built Spitfire...

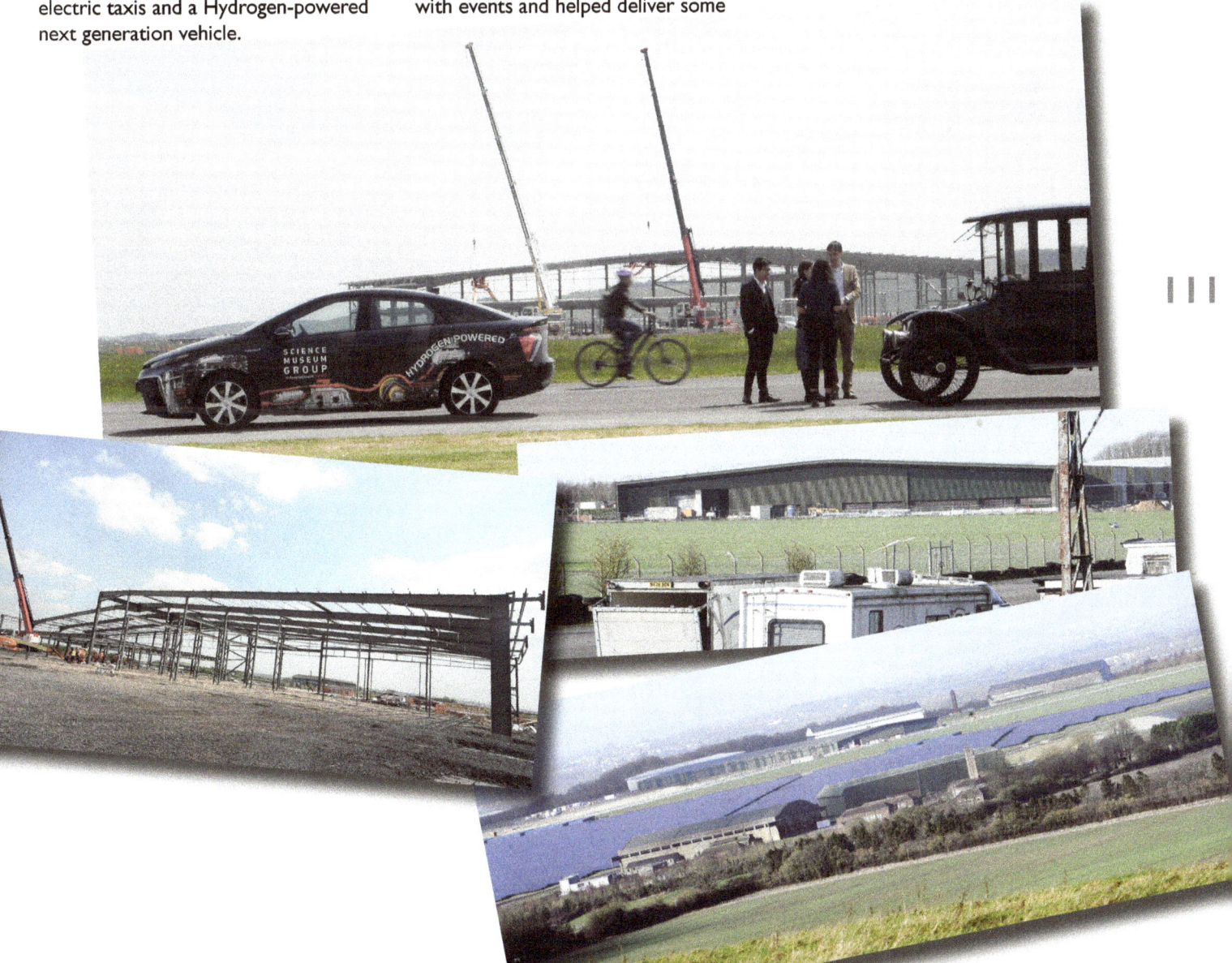

...Spitfires have played a large part in Swindon's industrial heritage, and even as late as 1994 they were making their mark in the town's history.

It's every journalist's dream to sit in a pub and pick up a world exclusive.

It does happen, and it did in January of 1984 when my friendly reporter phoned me to get me to do a picture on the Techno Trading Estate.

He was having a lunchtime cheese, pickle and a pint when he overheard two men talking about building a Spitfire from scratch, in a unit on the Techno Trading Estate.

Further conversations revealed that taxi company owner Clive DuCros had started to build a replica of the prototype spitfire, in one of the industrial units on the estate.

Clive had obtained detailed schematic diagrams of prototype No. K5054 and was in the process of constructing the tail section of the aircraft.

My first series of images was used in many nationals and magazines, having first appeared in the regional *Western Daily Press*.

A year later, I returned to the unit to see that the frame of K5057 had been almost finished, and Clive and woodworker Ron McIlroy were working on something that resembled a Spitfire. Even then it still looked as if there was a long way to go before Clive's dream would be realised.

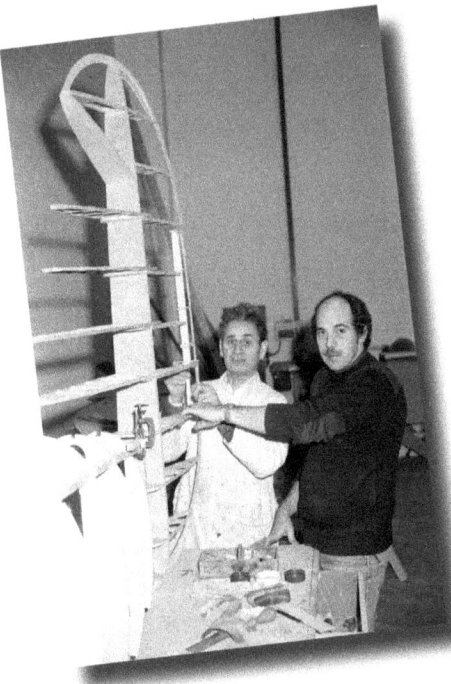

The next major step was on 12 July 1988, when a low-loader took the Spitfire in kit form from Techno to hangars on the Hullavington airfield between Chippenham and Malmesbury, where it was re-assembled and tested.

The plane was pretty well complete, with the Jaguar V12 engine in place and the cockpit cover installed. The only things missing seemed to be the engine cowling and the propeller.

The low-loader moved off, and that was the last we saw of it until the Warbirds show in 1994. It was here, on landing during the press day, the undercarriage gave way and Clive's dream finished nose down in the middle of Wroughton airfield in front of the national media.

Going through the archive following this project, you realise how technology has changed. You can see the quality of the film changing, going from grainy black and white and the large format Ilford XP1 films to colour transparency and high resolution colour negative films that finished the film camera era for press photography.

Cameras changed through that period, too. The first images were taken on a single frame Nikon SLR camera. I used a medium format camera as well so that the grain was lessened. The last shots were on high tech (for those days) Nikon and Canon cameras and high quality lenses.

In 2000 digital imaging took over, and what we can now achieve with events and projects like the Swindon's last Spitfire, we could only have dreamed of then.

It seems amazing that a chance conversation in a Swindon pub could lead to a decade-long project, and I feel proud that this is one piece of Swindon history that I have managed to cover from start to finish.

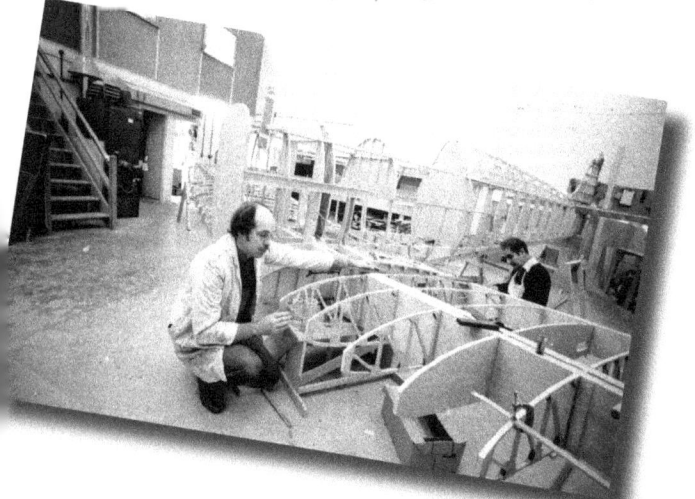

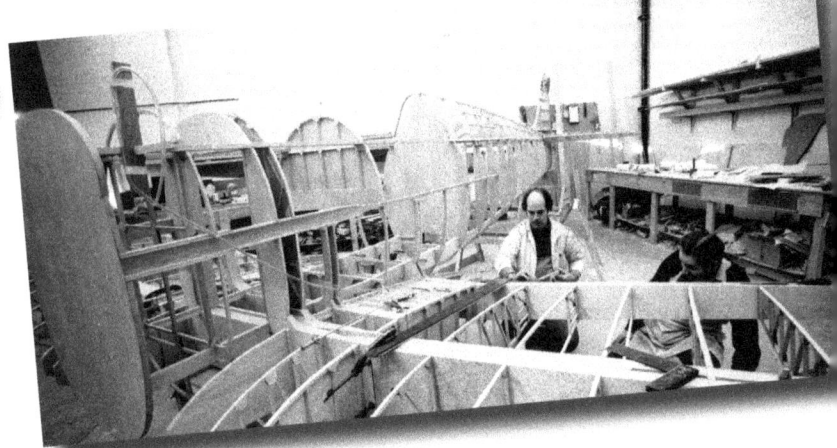

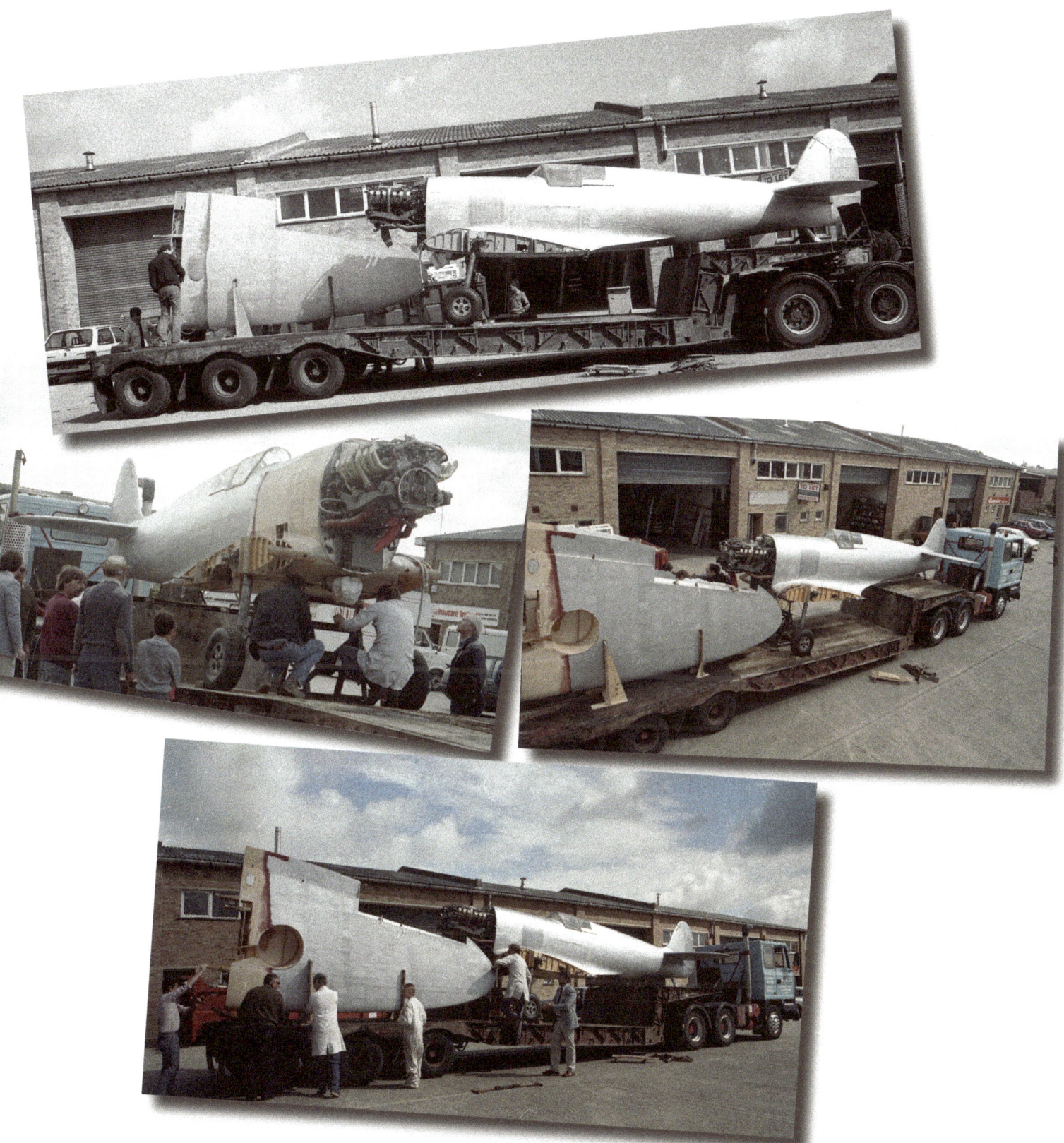

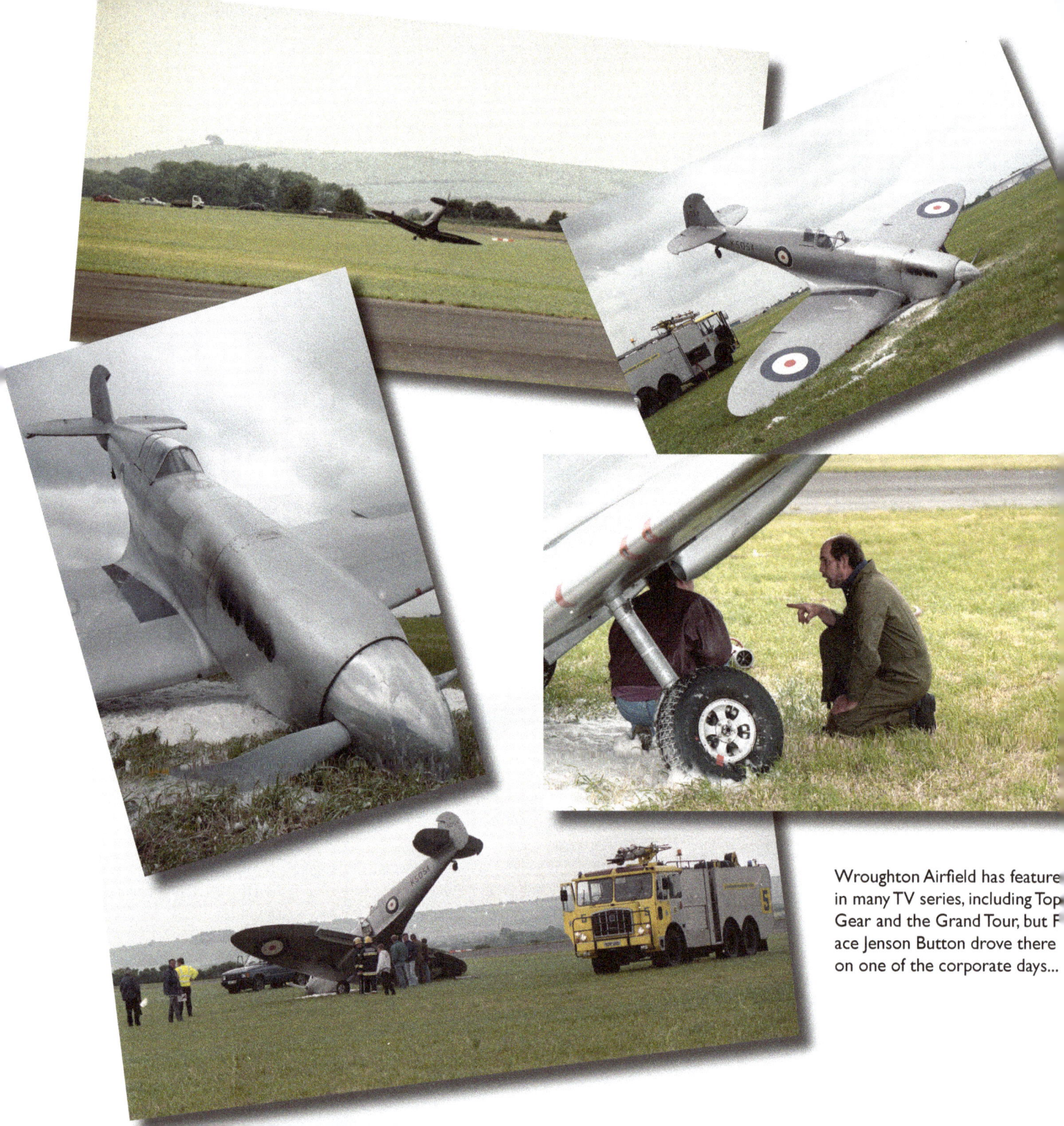

Wroughton Airfield has featured in many TV series, including Top Gear and the Grand Tour, but F ace Jenson Button drove there on one of the corporate days...

...Jenson Button was the British part of the Honda F1 team at the time, and he attended a Honda families day which took over the airfield...

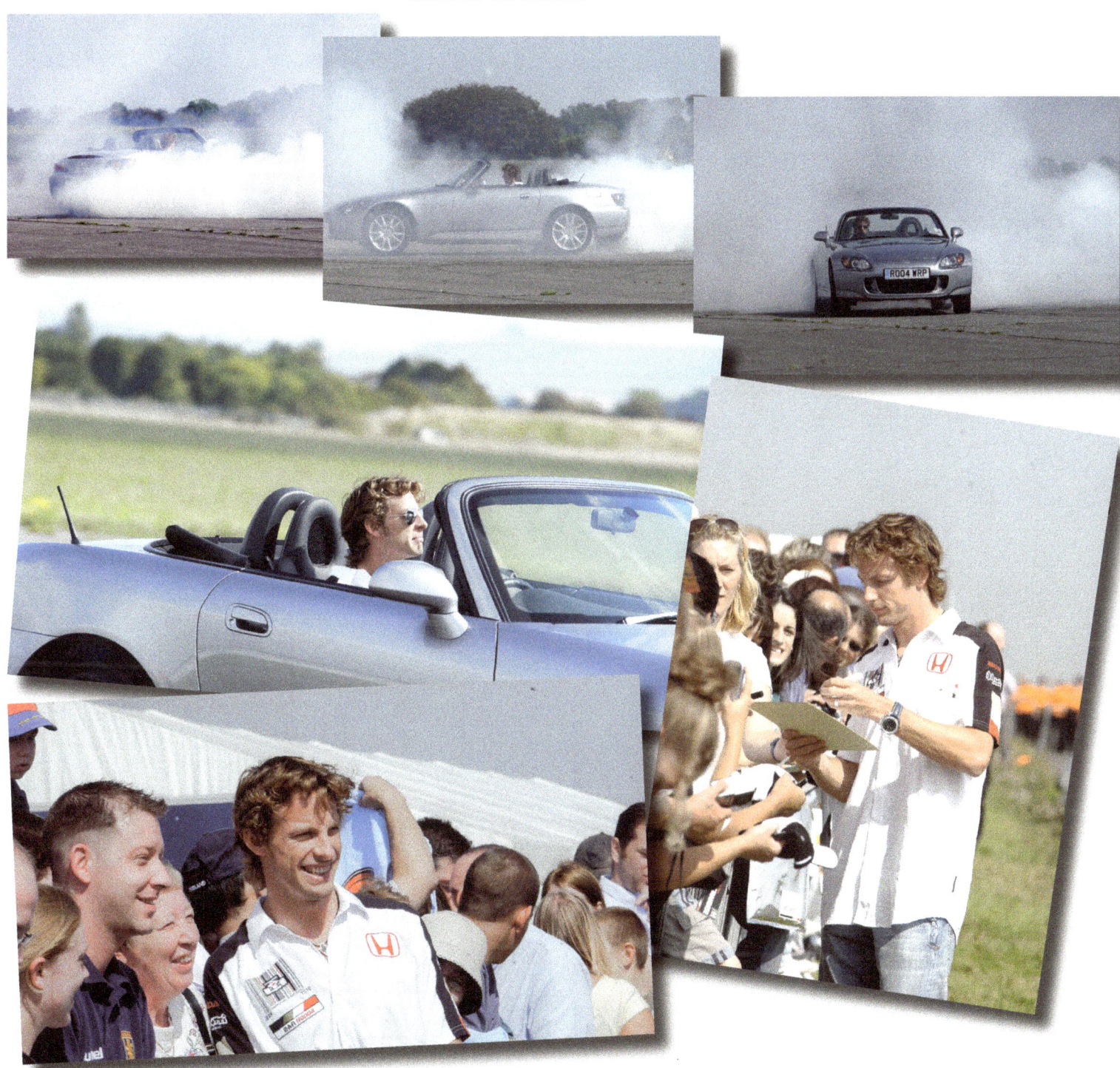

...and so motoring giant Honda acquired an airfield...

...About the same time that the Rail Works was emptied of its last wheels, Honda moved into the town.

The Japanese car giant acquired the South Marston Airfield. It was an active airfield, which had seen Spitfires produced at the factories around the town go wheels-up from its tarmac. Vickers used it as a VIP landing strip, but as they pulled out of the area it was hardly used by them, and only a few local flyers used it.

With the development of Covingham village, the runway was always destined to be decommissioned; so using it as a test track was an ideal alternative.

I was at a business lunch when I heard the news of the Honda acquisition. A friendly business news reporter had received a tip from his sources, and I then went into overdrive to get background pictures.

The first sod-cutting on the Honda site took place on 12 April 1985, and that in itself is a now a piece of Swindon history. The reception, with the smashing of the Sake barrel, took place in the Wiltshire Hotel, which was then managed by the enigmatic Irishman

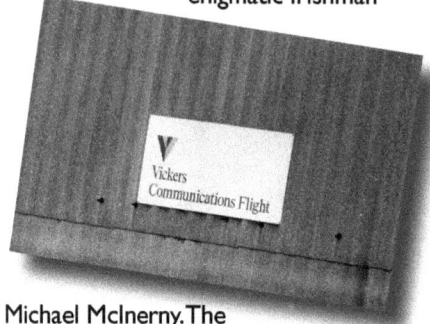

Michael McInerny. The ceremony involved the then Mayor Cllr. Harry Garrett, Honda's Toshio Kume, and Harold Musgrove, the Chairman of Austin Rover.

So, the Honda site was developed into a car plant (at that time an engine production plant), and we photographed the opening of the factory's test track on 30 March 1987 by F1 champion Nigel Mansell and Frank Williams, with the inimitable Murray Walker doing the Master of Ceremonies part. Mansell took his Williams Honda F1 car out on the old runway for a spin; well, many of them actually.

In October of 1989, the fruits of a joint venture with Rover appeared. Honda, according to the book *The Machine That Changed the World*, had taken a 20% stake in the British company, and jointly produced the Concerto/Rover 200 at Longbridge in Birmingham, with panels pressed at the Swindon Rover plant.

We pictured the first batch at Honda's Swindon plant on 9 October 1989, outside the new facility at South Marston.

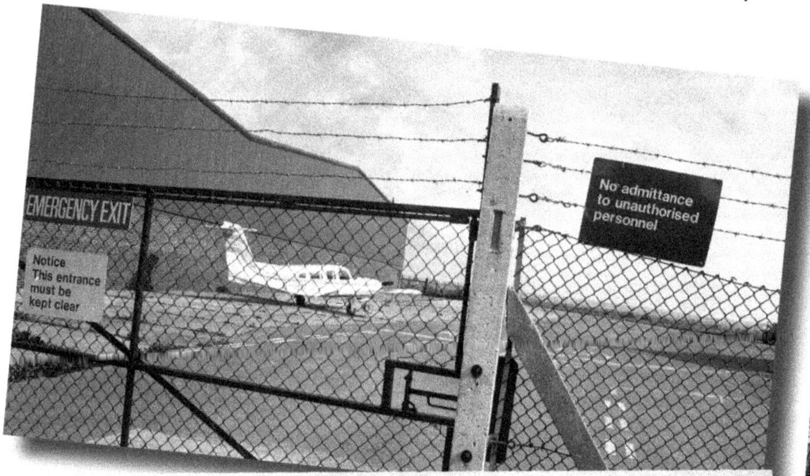

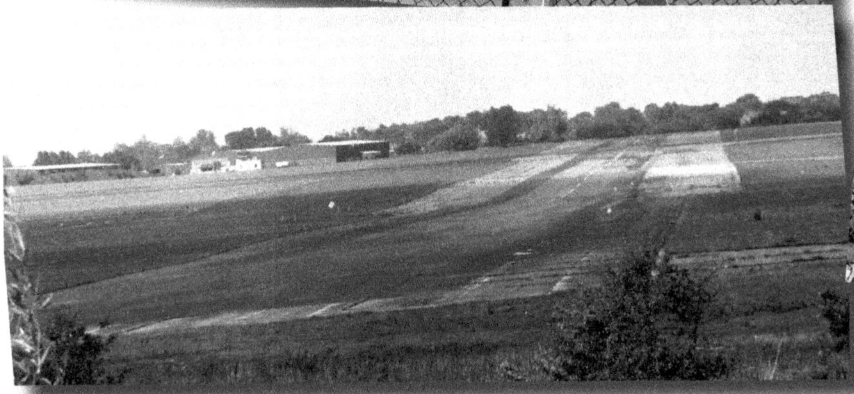

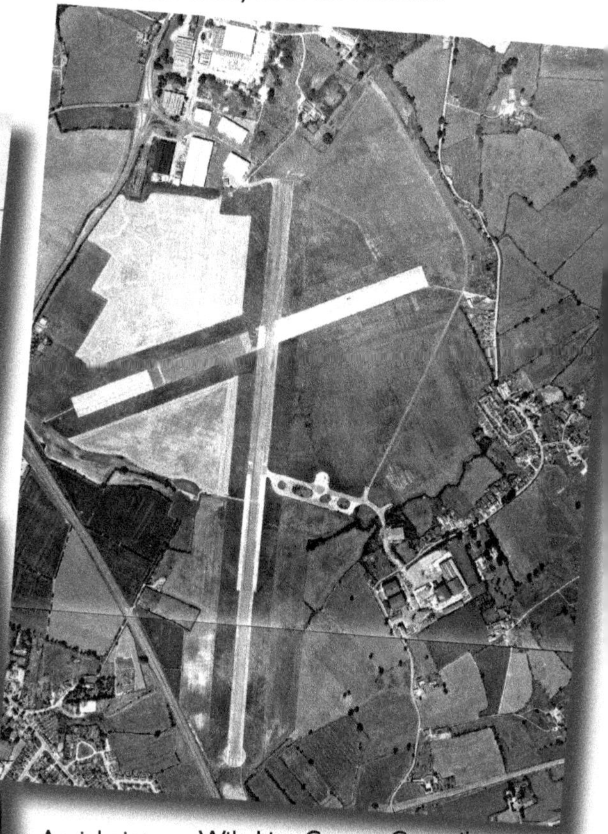

Aerial picture: Wiltshire County Council Press release image.

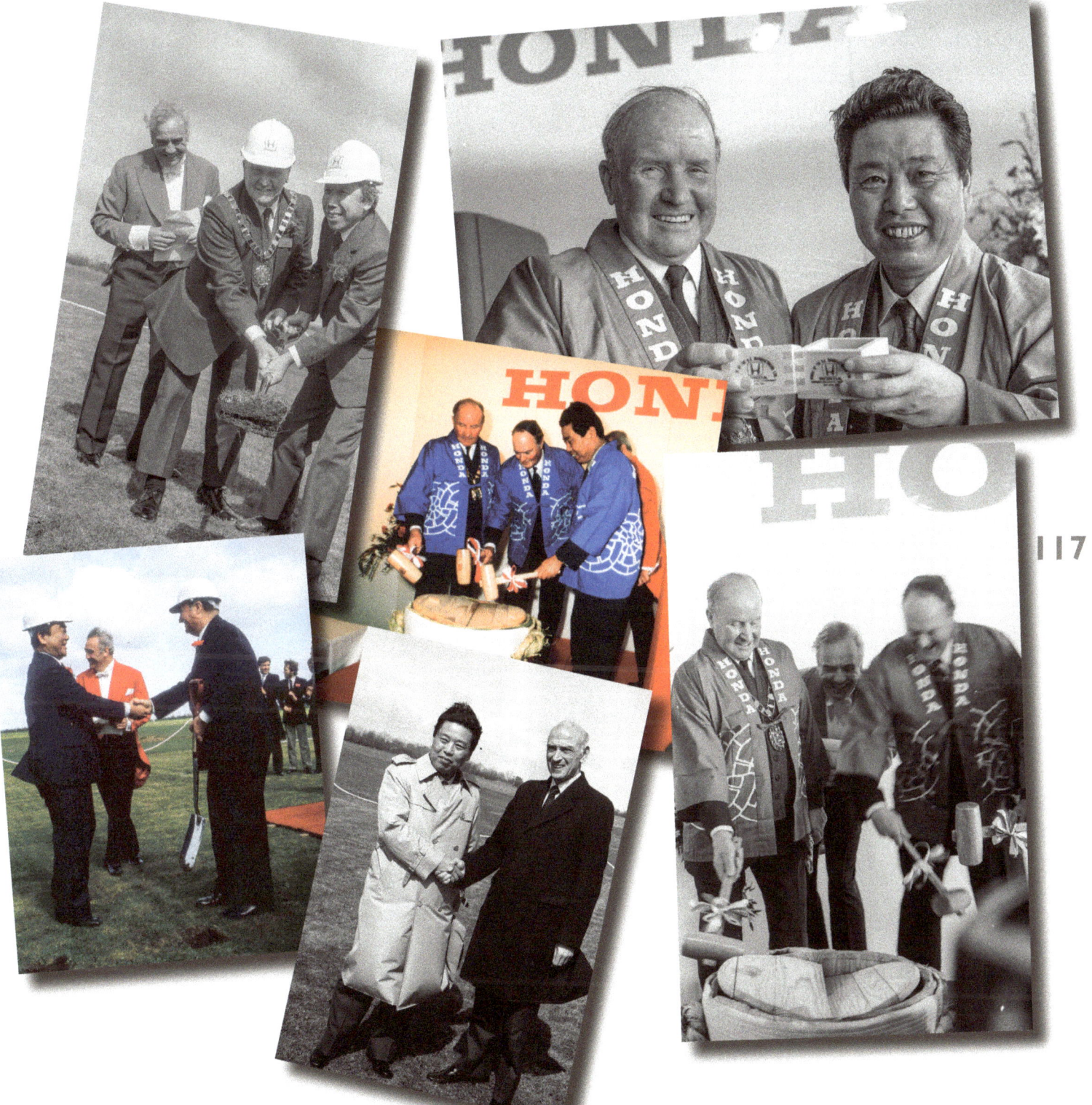

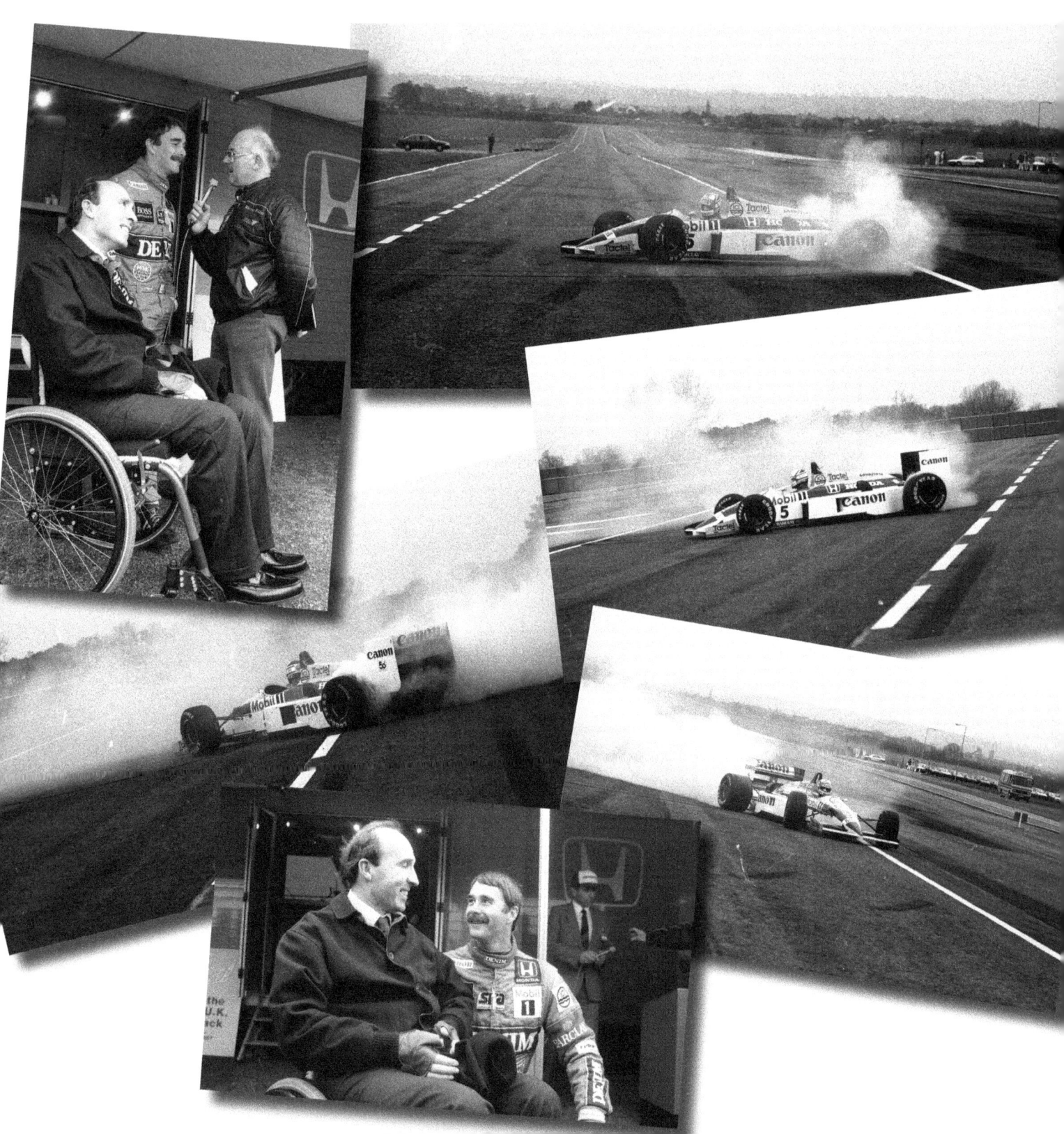

As you may have noticed, there are little stories within the story that make a funny aside. Honda is no exception.

When we started photographing at the plant, we all had to wear Honda baseball caps. There is a downside to photographers, especially stills photographers as we are, wearing caps. The problem is that is you can't work with the cap on normally; you have to reverse it because the peak gets in the way of the flash gun on top of the camera. To overcome this, we reversed the caps which caused a flurry of concern with the management. We were told that reversing the cap was some sort of insult in Japanese culture.

Needless to say, that practice didn't last more than a couple of visits and they abandoned baseball caps.

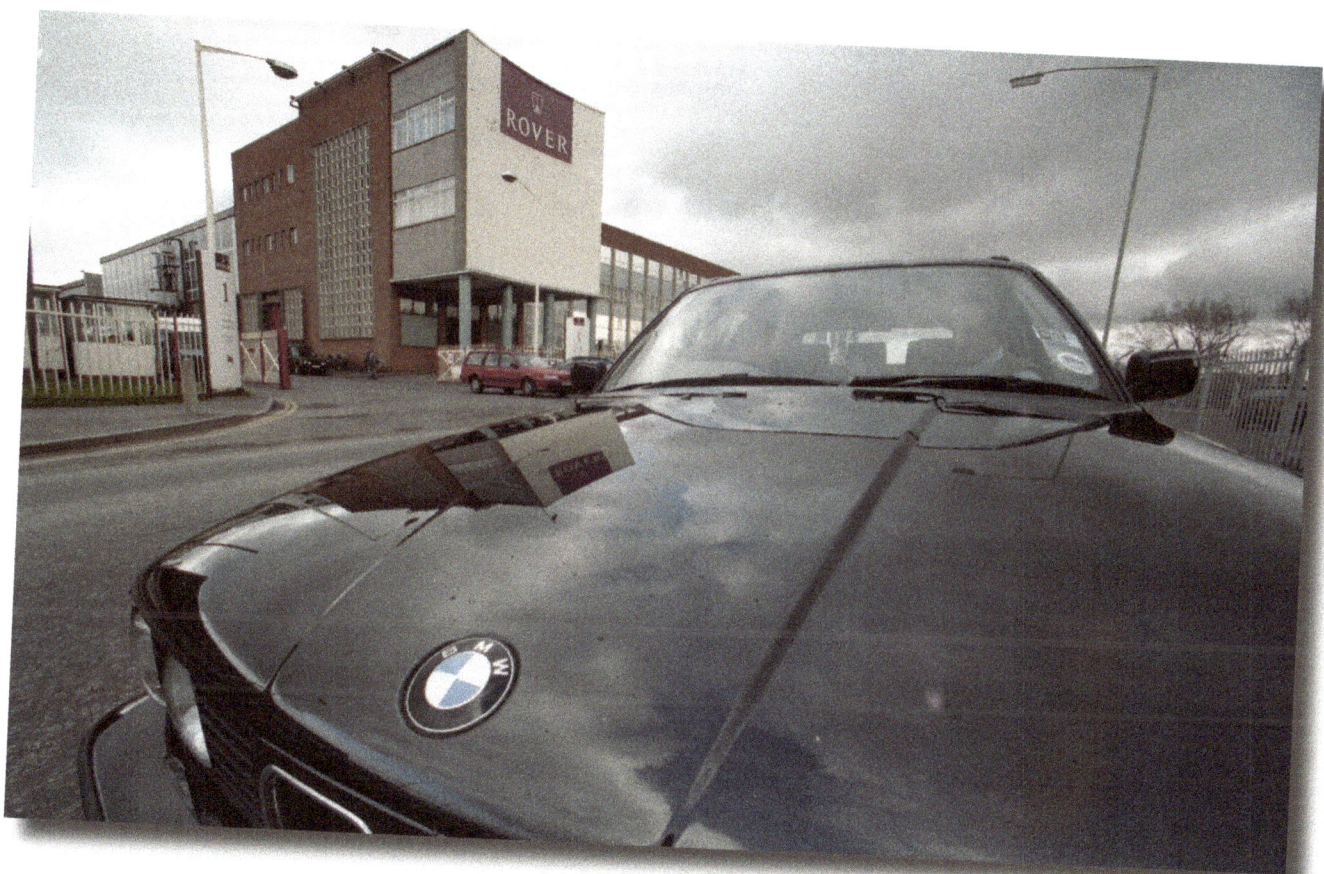

...Honda worked with the Rover plant at Stratton, and they were expected to form a joint company, but things didn't work out; so, at the end of January 1994, when the then owners of Rover BAe (British Aerospace) sold their 80% stake to German car maker BMW, we were tasked by the *Financial Times* to get a picture to illustrate the BMW takeover.

There was a quick call to the BMW dealer, and lo and behold they supplied us with a brand new car to park outside the Rover plant, and the then iconic office block, that has long since been demolished. It's an interesting snapshot in the history of the town, recorded in a few frames of film.

Honda produced Civic, CR-V, Accord, and Jazz models at Honda of the UK Manufacturing Stratton plant, but with political uncertainty surrounding world economics the parent company literally pulled the plug, and announced through the media that they were closing the works on 18 Feb 2019.

The closure decision must have been sudden, as I took pictures of Honda HR staff talking to possible apprentices at the Swindon Jobs Fest four days earlier...

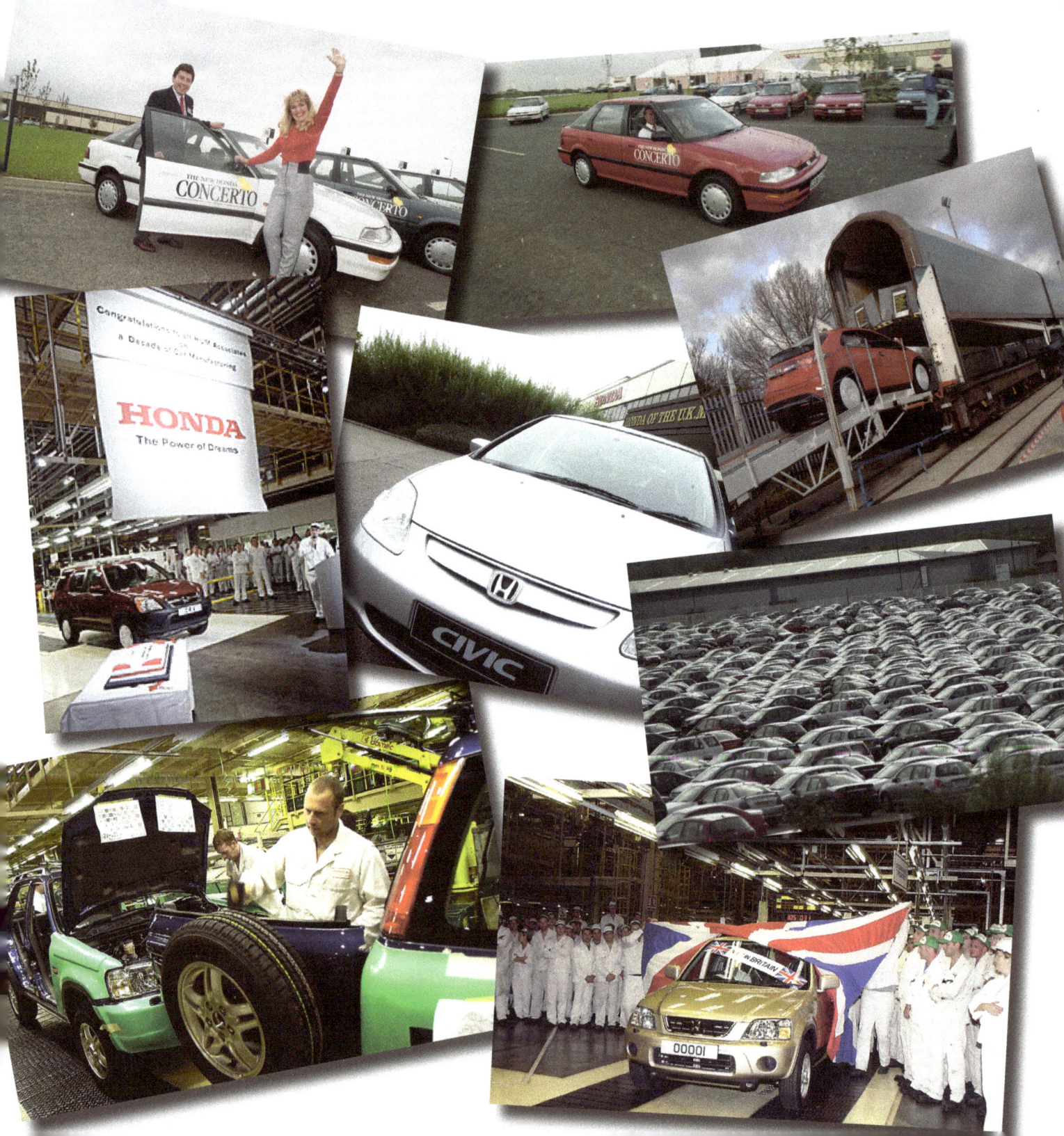

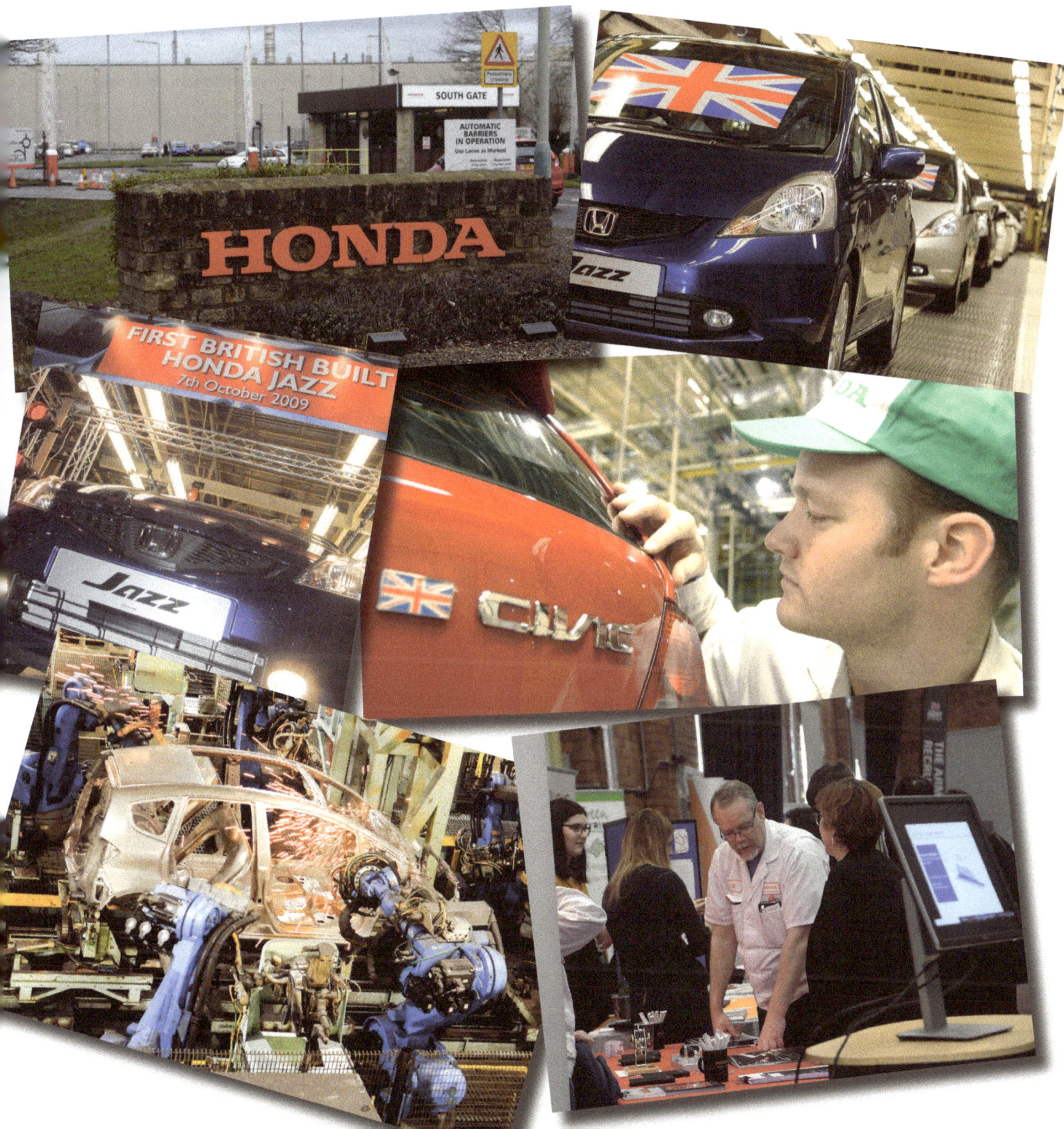

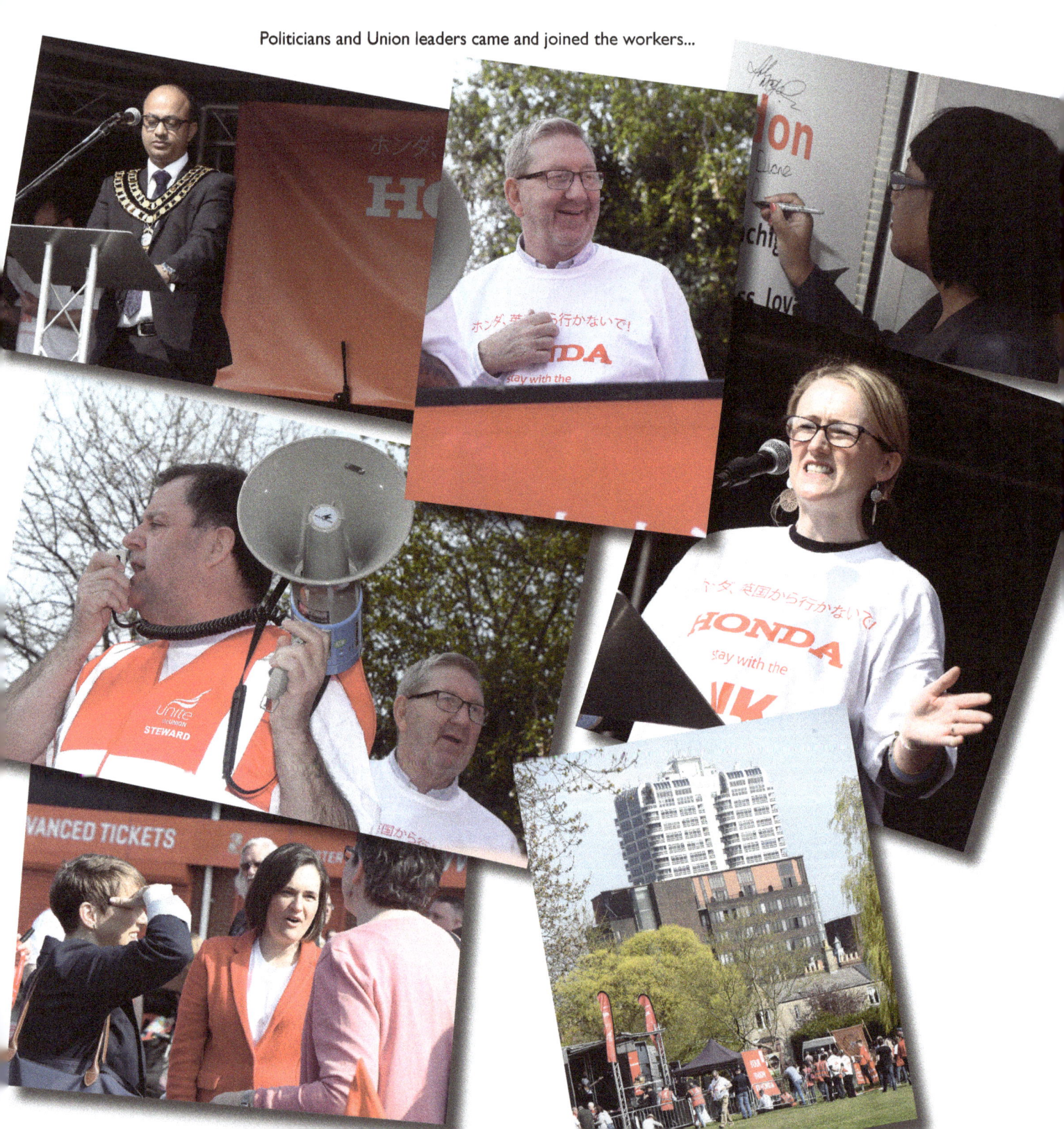

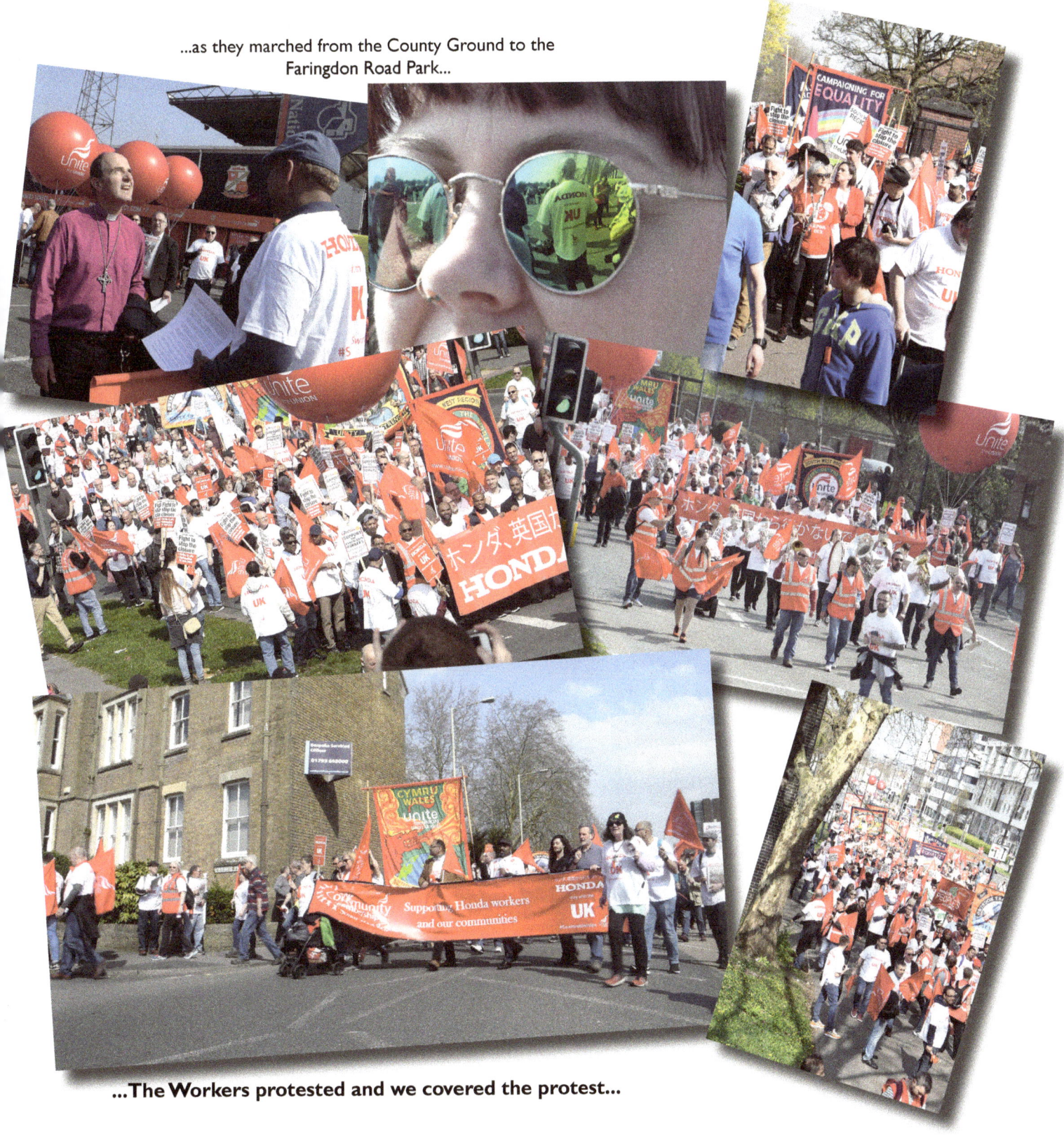

...Sound familiar: You see **A PICTURE IS ONLY THE START OF THE STORY...**

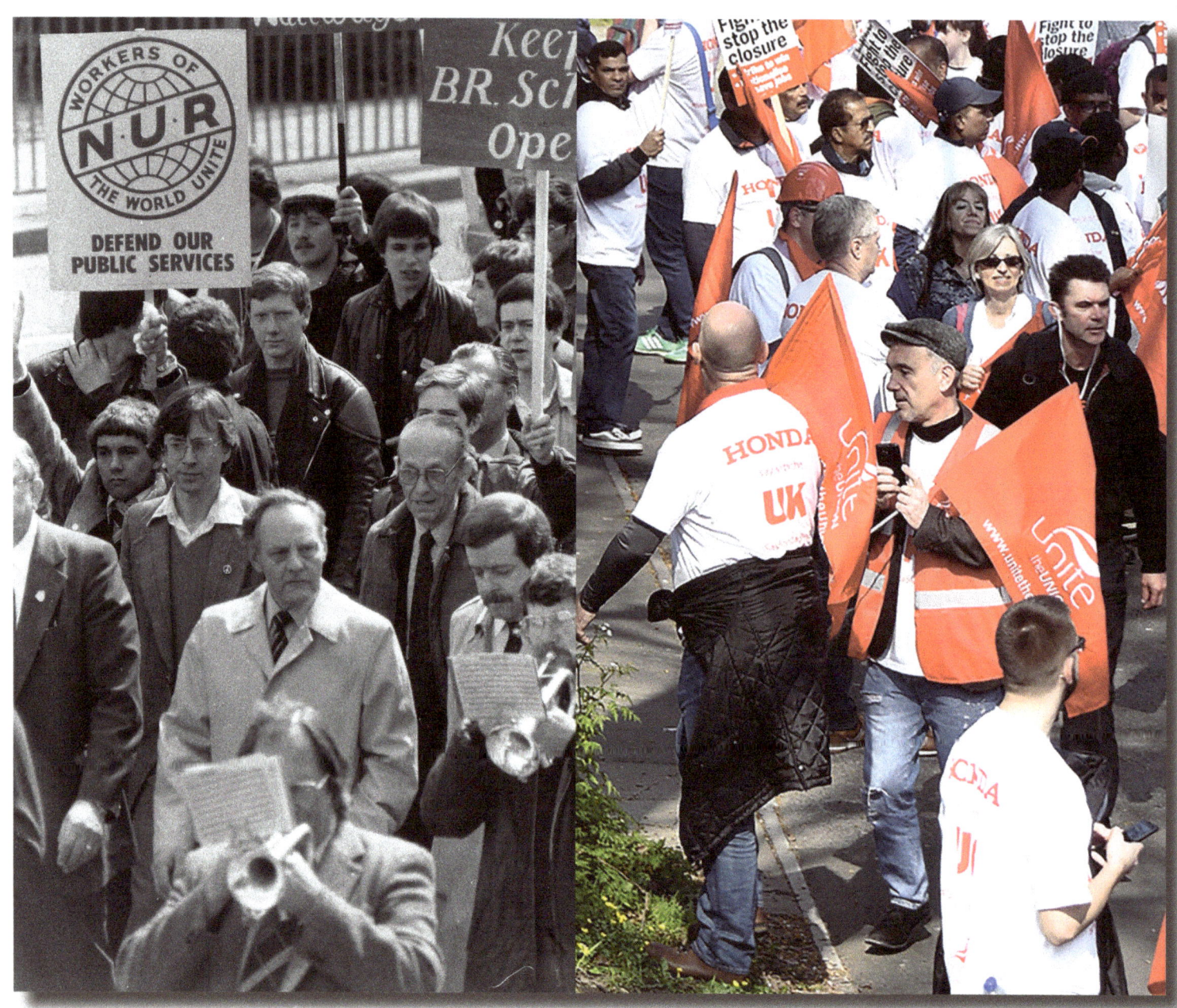

...to be continued...

I must thanks a group of people who have helped me with this meander:

Firstly the photographers:
Richard Wintle
Sarah Johnson
Neil Atkinson
Clint Randall
Vivien Bailey
Mike Otley
Darren Jack
Stuart Harrison
Rachel Davis
Jodie Henderson
Clare Ashley
Blossom Durr
I would like to thank Ian Surtees of Steam Museum and Karen Thompson, PR for Great Kat, for the additional material used.

Those who filed and indexed the material over the years:
Pat Wintle,
Julie Chamberlain,
Sarah Wintle,

The many who helped and advised to put this together:
Graham Carter,
Darryl Moody,
Roger Ogle,
Angela Atkinson,
Ross Wintle,
Rhona Jack,

My publisher:
John Chandler.

My heartfelt thanks go out to my wife, who has proofed this missive, after putting up with me being in my office for hours during the evenings, and repeatedly telling me the scanner in the other office had finished!

Right now let's start on volume 2!!!

www.ingramcontent.com/pod-product-compliance
Lightning Source LLC
Chambersburg PA
CBHW040546220526
45473CB00017B/3039